NO MO

NO MORE LAW!

A bold study in Galatians

Bruce Atkinson

Foreword by Dr R.T. Kendall

Galatians translated from the Greek by Professor James D.G. Dunn

Paternoster:
thinking faith

18 17 16 15 14 13 12   7 6 5 4 3 2 1

This edition first published 2012 by Paternoster
Paternoster is an imprint of Authentic Media Limited
52 Presley Way, Crownhill, Milton Keynes, MK8 0ES
www.authenticmedia.co.uk

British Library Cataloguing in Publication Data

A catalogue record for this book is available from the
British Library

ISBN 978-1-84227-790-4

THE MESSAGE

The translation of the Greek used throughout this book is by James
D.G. Dunn, *The Epistle to the Galatians* (Black's New Testament
Commentary), (Peabody, M.A.: Hendrickson Publishers, 1993)

Cover design by David McNeill at Revocreative
Printed and bound by CPI (Group) UK Ltd., CR0 4YY

To Christopher Cartwright

σίδηρος σίδηρον ὀξύνει ἀνὴρ δὲ
παροξύνει πρόσωπον ἑταίρου

Contents

Acknowledgements

I would like to express my gratitude to Professor James D.G. Dunn for giving me kind permission to use his English translation of Galatians from the Greek. My wife, Nicola, and I have fond memories of being tutored by Professor Dunn at Durham University in the late eighties. His commentary on Galatians has been a great source of help to me, and I recommend it to those who wish to study the epistle further.

I would like to thank the Elim Foursquare Gospel Alliance for giving me an opportunity to express my ministry. The fellowship, support and encouragement that I have received from the Movement over the years are sincerely appreciated.

Finally, I would like to thank Colin and Amanda Dye and all the disciples at Kensington Temple. Without their support this book would not have been possible.

Foreword

The greatest danger in the church at the present time is that the gospel of Jesus Christ is largely passing behind a cloud. The gospel, in many places, has been eclipsed by 'What's in it for me?' prosperity teaching, and an emphasis upon works. When I first came to Westminster Chapel in 1977, I was asked, please, to speak on Galatians. I did this on Friday nights for over four years. It was a life-changing era for many people, including myself. I had just finished my research degree at Oxford, having been immersed in Puritan-type thinking for three years. The Puritans, generally speaking, had become quite legalistic, causing Martin Luther's rediscovery of justification by faith alone virtually to be put to one side. I was so glad that they asked me to teach on Galatians.

Revd Bruce Atkinson, the associate minister at London's Kensington Temple, has done a commendable job in his exposition of Paul's letter to the Galatians. Bruce has given us good, solid teaching in this book. I am thrilled that someone with his background and in his Pentecostal tradition would write so clearly and courageously, when so many in that movement have become works-orientated in their perspective. What Bruce does is to maintain a wonderful balance between the Word and the Spirit, the gospel and the place of the Mosaic Law, freedom from that Law, but with an emphasis upon our responsibility to live godly lives. A Scottish theologian said centuries ago that the person who understands the relationship between the Law and the gospel is a good theologian.

I was especially pleased that Bruce Atkinson has pointed out that we are saved by the faith of Christ – Jesus' own personal faith and obedience. The apostle Paul stressed that we believe 'in' Jesus Christ in order to be justified 'by the faith of' Jesus Christ (Gal. 2:16). The church's general failure to see this important foundation is one of the reasons there has been so much misunderstanding of the place of the Law in the Christian understanding of the gospel. So Paul could say that he lived by faith, namely that 'of the Son of God' (Gal. 2:20). Sadly the Authorized Version is almost alone in being clear on the Greek language that lies behind verses like these. You will do well to read Bruce carefully in this section.

And yet the author of this book puts great stress on the work of the Holy Spirit in the Christian life. He speaks of walking in the Spirit, how this brings freedom and produces godliness. Every new Christian should read this book, and yet there is much in it for the most mature believer.

Colin Dye, the Senior Minister of Kensington Temple, can be justly proud of having Bruce on his staff. Bruce has produced a serious, no-nonsense exposition of the book Martin Luther called his 'Katy Von Bora' (the woman Luther married after he was set free by the doctrine of justification by faith). I pray this book will set you free as well.

Dr R.T. Kendall
Minister of Westminster Chapel (1977–2002)

Preface

What does it mean to be saved? This is the chief question addressed by the book of Galatians. It seems such a simple question, doesn't it? But if we get the answer wrong, the consequences could be awful and eternal. How does one 'get saved'? And once saved, how do we stay saved? Just as in Paul's time, today's church is profoundly confused and sharply divided over the answers to these questions.

The Galatian Gentiles had been saved by Paul's preaching of the gospel – or had they? Now they weren't so sure. Some new teachers had come into their midst with very different answers than Paul to the question of how to be saved. These new teachers had new standards and rules that they claimed would not only save the Galatians, but just as importantly, keep them saved. Obedience to these commands would not only show the Galatians but everyone that they were truly part of God's saved people. These new teachers had introduced the Galatians to the Law of Moses!

This teaching about Christians living by the Law of Moses was new to the Galatians. It had played no part in their daily Christian living so far. Paul had never told them that they needed it and they weren't schooled in it. So when a group of Jewish Christian missionaries came to Galatia who disagreed with Paul's view of the gospel, they became confused.

The Jewish missionaries taught that clear boundaries must be put into place in order to separate the new believers from the world around them. These boundaries were external and outward for all to see: circumcision, obedience to food laws, indeed the whole Jewish Law itself. These 'Judaizers' taught that if the Galatians really were saved, then they had to demonstrate it by obedience to God's commands. They were now told that they had been saved in order to live by God's Law. Paul, on the other hand, believed that far from being saved to follow God's Law, they were actually saved from it! To him the Law was no longer needed because life was now led by the Spirit. The Spirit-filled life had replaced obedience to the Law. The book of Galatians draws us into the first-century church's battle over the nature of the gospel. It was a nasty conflict full of factions, strong personalities, politics, and pressure groups.

Paul had blazed an evangelistic trail across the Gentile world and thousands were coming to Christ. But hot on Paul's heals followed others who preached a gospel radically different to his. This battle for the gospel reached its climax in Galatia where opponents of Paul actively sought to turn his converts against both him and his gospel.

We will also find that Galatians is a powerful record of personal encounters with the living God. Pentecostal by experience, Paul understood there was a dynamic dialogue between scholarly theology and a personal experience of the Spirit of God. Scripture is the final authority regarding all matters of faith, but Paul does not only turn to Scripture to present his case for the true gospel, he also utilizes his own personal experience of the Holy Spirit, and also that of the Galatian Christians themselves, to prove the validity of the gospel that he preached.

Bible truth, after all, is not just to be understood intellectually, but can also be experienced through personal and supernatural encounters. It is the truth that actually sets us free. Paul argues in Galatians that what really separates us from the world is not obedience to rules, but our present ongoing experience of the Holy Spirit. The experience of the Spirit and his accompanying manifestations were to become one of Paul's main arguments to persuade the Galatians to remain steadfast in gospel grace.

What about you? Before you take a journey through Galatians, where do you stand on such issues? Do the Ten Commandments play a role in your Christian life? Do you believe that you can lose your salvation? Do you live by rules or by the Spirit, and do you even know the difference between the two? Are you really and truly living the Spirit-filled life? Do you know what it really means to be free?

The letter to Galatians addresses all these issues and more. I pray that the message of the Spirit that was spoken 2,000 years ago to the Galatian church will resonate in your spirit as clearly today. I pray that you might hear the voice of the Spirit crying, *no more law!*

Martin Bruce Atkinson
Kensington Temple,
Notting Hill Gate
London

Introduction

The letter to the Galatians: who, when, what, how and why?

Letters, emails and texts are fascinating forms of communication. No matter how long or short a message may be, there is always so much to learn – not only from the words used in the message itself, but from the circumstances that caused the communication in the first place. Similarly, Galatians was written as a letter by a specific person to a specific group of people for a specific reason and at a specific time. We should recognize this from the outset if we are truly going to be able to understand the message it contains.

To appreciate what God is saying to us through this portion of Scripture, it is imperative to find out as much about its background as possible. I have read books and listened to sermons that have treated verses of Galatians as if they were generated by an impersonal computer in heaven and then downloaded to earth. When people treat Scripture in this way they usually misunderstand it somewhere down the line. When we read specific books in the Bible we should always ask the questions, *who, when, what, how, why?* We shall ask these questions about the letter to Galatians because the answers are key to understanding the epistle itself.

Who was Paul?

Who wrote Galatians, and to whom was it addressed? No one doubts that the author of the letter to the Galatians was the apostle Paul. In fact, if you want to know what kind of man this apostle to the Gentiles was (Gentiles simply refers to all nations and peoples apart from Israel), then this is an excellent letter to read.

I love reading biographies of great men and women. Even better are autobiographies, where people write personally about their lives. If you want to know what it takes to be a great general, businessman, sportsperson or poet, you need to read books about their lives and especially books where you get it 'straight from the horse's mouth' – from the men or women themselves. Galatians is a very personal letter because Paul reveals so much about his life's struggles, passions, defeats and victories. To find out what a real 'breakthrough' ministry is like, we should read this letter.

Paul the Pharisee

The apostle Paul, before he came to follow Christ, was known as Saul. He was schooled in one of the strictest forms of Judaism, similar to the Orthodox Jews of today. He describes his religious pedigree in Philippians 3:5–6

> I was circumcised when I was eight days old. I am a pure-blooded citizen of Israel and a member of the tribe of Benjamin – a real Hebrew if there ever was one! I was a member of the Pharisees who demand the strictest obedience to the Jewish law. I was so zealous that I harshly persecuted the church. And as for righteousness, I obeyed the law without fault. (NLT)

The Pharisees had been a powerful, purifying movement in Judaism in the 150 years before Christ. They were the spiritual descendants of the early Hasidim (meaning the 'pious') formed around 170 BC. The Hasidim resisted the attempts of their Greek rulers to force all Jews to adopt Greek culture and renounce their own. The Pharisees (meaning 'separate ones') modelled and taught a strict observance of the Jewish Law as the only means to remain a faithful part of God's covenant people. Their teachers were known as rabbis and they had a whole series of traditions and rules (not found in Scripture) that they believed went back to the time of Moses. The Pharisees believed these traditions had been handed down from generation to generation. Known as the Oral Law, Jesus would confront many of these non-biblical traditions during his ministry on earth.

There were many different sects within Judaism during Paul's time, and numerous views on what it really meant to be a true covenant Jew. Not only were Jews distinguished from Gentiles by circumcision, but also by such things as food laws, which governed not only what they ate but also who they ate with. All this was essential to the Jewish sense of identity. The term 'sinner' was a well-used one in first-century Judaism – the different Jewish sects tended to call anyone (including one another) who did not live according to their particular form of tradition, a sinner! No wonder we see such importance placed upon the use of the term 'sinner' throughout the Gospel accounts.

Paul had been an outstanding Pharisee. He had studied in the school of the famous Rabbi Gamaliel. In today's terms it would be like having a PhD in Old Testament studies from Oxford or Cambridge University.

This background is extremely important for any reader of Galatians. At this time, many Jewish Christians were concerned that the identity of the church should also be expressed by certain traditions such as circumcision and food laws. They were fearful of being contaminated by the Gentile world, of living like sinners and losing their special relationship with God as Jews. The huge numbers of Gentiles becoming Christians further concerned many Jewish believers that their heritage could soon disappear for good. They felt that they had to keep their Jewishness at all costs.

Apostle to the Gentiles

Paul had forcefully persecuted the church in its earliest days, imprisoning and even sentencing believers to death. He saw 'the Way' (as Christianity was first known) as a great threat to the authentic community of God, and he thought that as a Pharisee he was the best representative of Judaism that could be found. The book of Acts tells us that Paul even held the coats of the men who stoned Stephen. Jesus died in 30 AD and Paul had his famous encounter with Christ on the road to Damascus between 31 and 33 AD (see Paul's own account in Acts 26:12–18). It was at that point that his life was turned completely around and he received his divine calling to take the gospel to the Gentiles. Paul then spent three years in Arabia. In about 35 AD, he visited Jerusalem and stayed with Peter, meeting James whilst he was there. Paul then began evangelizing the Gentiles, basing himself in the city of Antioch.

The Council of Jerusalem

After fourteen years of powerful evangelism, Paul returned to what would be the Council of Jerusalem mentioned in Acts chapter 15 (meeting around 49 AD). This was a very significant assembly and Paul refers to it in Galatians. At the Council it was confirmed that Paul would preach the gospel to Gentiles, who were recognized as full members of the church of Christ without needing to be circumcised. Despite some opposition, the gospel's freedom from the Law seemed to have triumphed. It was established that Paul had been called to bring the gospel to the Gentile world without calling on them to be circumcised.

The fallout with Peter in Antioch

Antioch had become the major missionary sending centre to the Gentile world. It was the base for Paul's ministry. The Antioch church consisted of a majority of Gentiles, but also contained a large number of Jewish believers. The influence of the Judaizers began to spread. The Judaizers were actively following in the steps of Paul to convert *his* converts to their false gospel, which included the necessity of keeping the Jewish Law. The Council of Jerusalem had been clear in regard to its position on circumcision, but not so clear on the issue of food or table fellowship. The Judaizers in Antioch began to insist that Jewish Christians no longer have food fellowship with Gentile Christians.

We shall discover that Peter and even Paul's close associate, Barnabas, were won over by the Judaizers' arguments. Peter decided to no longer table fellowship with the Gentile believers of Antioch. This was a major step backwards for the gospel, especially when we remember that it was also during table fellowship that the bread and wine of Holy Communion was celebrated. Paul stood his ground, but lost the argument. From that point on Paul moved from Antioch, making bases at Corinth and then Ephesus. Paul had lost the battle at Antioch, but was determined not to lose the war over the truth of the gospel of grace.

Who were the Galatians?

Galatia was not a city, but a Roman province. It is found in the highlands of Anatolia in modern-day Turkey. Ankara, the present Turkish capital, was also the capital of ancient Galatia. The area was named Galatia after the migration of the Gauls (or Celts) into the area in the early third century BC. The assemblies that Paul would have pioneered in Galatia would have been predominantly Gentile. There is a great discussion in academic circles about whether the letter to the Galatians was directed only to South Galatia or whether it included North Galatia also. If Paul had also managed to reach North Galatia it means that the letter may have been written a few years later than if it addressed only the initial evangelization of the South. Really, it doesn't matter – the most important thing to remember is that the Council of Jerusalem took place *before* Galatians was written. The epistle to the Galatians could have been written any time from the early fifties AD.

The Judaizing missionaries plagued the footsteps of Paul. It is amazing how even today, wherever the gospel gains ground, cults and false teachers are not far behind it, like wolves trying to devour the sheep. Paul was astonished and annoyed that the young church in Galatia had succumbed so quickly to a false gospel. Was this going to be Antioch all over again? Not if Paul had anything to do with it! The power, force and emotional intensity of the letter to the Galatians show Paul battling once and for all to destroy the false gospel of salvation by works.

The message of Galatians

Because Paul's letter reacts to a departure from the true gospel by the Galatians, it also means that Paul will need to give a crystal-clear account of what the gospel really is. Galatians is extremely important because, more than any other book in the Bible, except perhaps Romans, the gospel is explained in the clearest way possible.

If you approach the Scriptures to discover the answer to the question, *what does it mean to be saved?* it is important where you start. Always start where the doctrine is most plainly and specifically taught. Some preachers base their doctrine of salvation not primarily on Galatians or Romans, but selected verses of the synoptic gospels (Matthew, Mark and Luke) and the epistle of James. If you wish to understand the doctrine of salvation, start with the three books that specifically address the topic of how to be saved: Galatians, Romans and the Gospel of John. These three books are the foundation upon which the doctrine of salvation should be built.

The theologian F.F. Bruce summarizes the primitive message of the gospel found in Galatians like this

> Jesus our Lord, the Son of God, was sent into the world by his Father when the due time came. He was born into the family of Abraham and lived under the Jewish Law. He was crucified by his enemies, but in death he gave himself for his people's sins. God raised him from the dead, to be the saviour of all who believe in him; he has sent this Spirit into their hearts, enabling them to call God 'father' as Jesus did, to exhibit his love in their lives and to look forward confidently to the realisation of their hope.[1]

By the time Paul wrote Romans, he had effectively conquered the threat of the Judaizers to the church – so much so that he could even graciously call on Christians to be patient with the weaker brethren who still followed aspects of the Jewish Law (Rom. 14). The letter to the Galatians was to play a huge part in this victory over the false gospel.

1.

The Supernatural Gospel

(Gal. 1:1–5)

Greetings from Paul (1:1–5)

(1) Paul, apostle – not from human beings nor through a human being, but through Jesus Christ and God the Father, who raised him from the dead – (2) and all the brothers with me, to the churches of Galatia. (3) Grace to you and peace from God our Father and the Lord Jesus Christ, (4) who gave himself for our sins, in order that he might rescue us from the present evil age, in accordance with the will of our God and Father; (5) to whom be glory forever and ever, amen.

All of Paul's New Testament letters, apart from Galatians, start in a relaxed, polite manner, yet show a touch of formality. He often begins by commending or complimenting the people or person that he is writing to. Often he will tell them how much he appreciates them by giving thanks for them. He also frequently reminds them that they are in his thoughts and prayers. If you take just a couple of minutes you can flick through the beginnings of Paul's letters in the New Testament and you will see not only a common pattern, but how different Galatians is from that pattern – not only in the content of the greeting, but also its tone.

Paul is very emotional at the beginning of this letter. He deals with many serious issues in other letters, but nothing affected him more than his concern for the truth of the gospel. Paul wants to get the greeting to the Galatians over with as soon as possible and get straight down to business. But even in the greeting he is making powerful points. Have you ever replied immediately to an email in anger? Have you ever pressed the send button and then thought, 'What have I done?' (and 'recall' never seems to work). Emails written in haste and with angry emotions usually don't achieve their aims. Why is Paul so fiery in Galatians, right from the start?

There is a time for holy anger or zeal. Jesus demonstrated it a number of times in his dealings with the Pharisees, and most famously in cleansing the Temple. Remember, Galatians is not only the letter of a man named Paul, but it is also the 100 per cent infallible Word of God. It is so wonderful to read the Bible and see all the characteristics and personalities of the human authors displayed. But it is also amazing to know that the Holy Spirit carried them along, superintending their thoughts, yet without violating them, so that they would also write exactly what he desired.

The Bible's authors' whole lives and personalities, their failings as well as their strengths, were used by God to produce his perfect Word. Paul's anger, impatience and bluntness are not just expressions of his personality, but also an indication of how God himself wanted this letter to be written. God required this portion of Scripture to be passionate, serious and aggressive. Because the gospel is the only power that can save, it must be defended at all costs.

Paul introduces himself as 'apostle': 'Paul, apostle – not from human beings nor through a human being, but through Jesus Christ and God the Father, who raised him from the dead.' Pow! Paul comes out of the corner in the first round, and connects with a left hook in the first sentence.

I have entitled the first fifteen verses of Galatians 'the supernatural gospel' because from the start this is the main theme of the section. By 'supernatural' I mean in the sense of divine power. The word 'apostle' means 'one who is sent' and can be therefore be understood both in the sense of a messenger and also a commissioned ambassador. That Paul had to defend his divine calling from the start shows how much his authority had been questioned and undermined by the Judaizers. Paul was not only an apostle in the Ephesians 4:11 sense of the word – he was also one of the foundational eyewitnesses of the risen Lord, and specifically called to be the apostle to the Gentiles.

Supernatural calling

Paul breaks off his greeting in an unexpected way by defining the origin of his call as divine. Paul's authority came from God. It was not an authority of human origin. His authority was not political or denominational. Neither was it derived from popular support. It was an authority and commissioning that came from a divine source. He was appointed by the Lord.

Even in today's church many take the title 'minister' but don't have the supernatural anointing to back it up. This normally causes them to turn to human means of authentication and advancement. The Judaizers were such ministers. As Paul will explain later in the letter, it is always flesh that persecutes the Spirit, the 'Ishmaels' who persecute the 'Isaacs'. Paul's confidence was in his supernatural calling, and he was not afraid to refer to it.

Resurrection authority

Paul explains that his supernatural calling is based on the most important miraculous event in history: the resurrection of Jesus Christ from the dead. Christianity stands on the fact that Jesus rose from the dead. The basis of all faith and thus of all Christian ministry is the truth of the resurrection. If Christ was not raised from the dead all is in vain, but if he was raised then absolutely all things are possible for those who believe. It was the risen Christ who confronted Paul on the road to Damascus and called him to apostleship. This is the only time Paul mentions Jesus' resurrection in this letter, and it is interesting that he does so in relation to defending his ministry.

Paul tells the Galatians that his ministry is not one to be judged from a human standpoint because it is rooted in the supernatural calling of God. All true ministers will likewise have their own personal story of a supernatural calling, although each experience will, of course, be unique to each person. Paul in chapter 3 will appeal to a common supernatural experience that all the Galatian Christians have encountered through consciously receiving the Spirit. But here he is focusing on his divine calling as a minister of the gospel.

I recall as a non-believer kneeling in Durham Cathedral at the age of 18 before my interview to become a theology student. I muttered a 'good luck' prayer: 'God, if I become a student at Durham, I will give my life to you and your service.' To be honest, I didn't even know what I was saying. Suddenly a stillness and a powerful blanket-like presence fell upon me. For twenty minutes I knelt in this strange presence. Then, as an 'unbeliever', I got up and went to my interview. I was dazed but divinely called. Others may doubt my calling, but I know it came through a personal experience with the Lord. I was ordained before I was even saved, and I like that. People get so caught up with the issue of Paul's conversion, but Paul never saw himself so much as 'converted' by God but rather called. Maybe we should no longer speak of converts but of those that are called, for to be called is also to be commissioned to a supernatural, divine plan.

> (2) and all the brothers with me, to the churches of Galatia. (3) Grace to you and peace from God our Father and the Lord Jesus Christ, (4) who gave himself for our sins, in order that he might rescue us from the present evil age, in accordance with the will of our God and Father; (5) to whom be glory forever and ever, amen.

It is remarkable that in the first five verses of Galatians we have already had the core of the message of the gospel. We have the divinity of Jesus as Lord, we have his death on the cross for our sins, his resurrection and our deliverance from the power of sin and evil, and also we receive God as our Father.

Grace and peace

All we need – indeed, all the human condition longs for – is grace and peace. Martin Luther said that grace and peace are the two friends that deal with the twin torments of our lives: sin and a guilty conscience. Luther says in his commentary on Galatians, 'These two words grace and peace contain in them the whole sum of Christianity. Grace contains the forgiveness of sins; peace a quiet and joyful conscience.'[1]

Conscience is the broken mirror in the heart of every individual that dimly reflects the reality of who we are at the core of our being. We are sinful, guilty, shameful human beings. We can ignore and recoil from this painful image, but its reality will never change until grace and peace enter our hearts through the gospel. Grace simply means 'total undeserved favour' and it usually refers to God's unconditional love for us. Peace means a life in harmony with the Holy Spirit. A healed, freed and assured life springs from a healthy heart filled with the Holy Spirit. As Paul says here, this grace and peace comes from only one source. You can't get it from any religion or from meditation, from a political party, worldly success, or even any other human being. It comes directly and only from God the Father through his Son and by the precious Holy Spirit. Nothing but faith in the gospel can bring us into an experience of what we so desperately need.

A rescue mission

Humankind needs a mighty deliverance. The death of Christ was not only to deliver us from the penalty of our sin; it also has delivering power to rescue us from the fallen and demonically ruled age that we live in. James Dunn, in his commentary on Galatians, puts it this way

> Paul certainly had no doubts that the present age was marked by corruptibility, superficiality, folly and blindness, or that humankind as heirs of Adam were caught under the reign of sin and death. In earliest Christian understanding, Christ's death was the key to deliverance from the seductive and corrupting introversion of this age's self-delusion, since by his death he broke both the power of sin and the power of death. For those who identified with this Jesus as Lord the spell was broken . . .[2]

The world we live in is fallen. The fall of Adam in the Garden of Eden was a real, historic event of the most catastrophic kind. Often atheists point to the brokenness and suffering of the world as an argument that if God created the world that we live in, then he must be a very cruel being indeed. Many also point to the existence of suffering as proof that there is no God. After all, if we had been God we would have created such a better, kinder and more just world, wouldn't we?

As Paul introduces the gospel in these first few verses, he acknowledges that the age we live in is evil. Far from being an expression of God's character, it is actually at enmity with his nature and purpose. God is so concerned with the present state of human affairs that he sent his Son to die in order to deliver us from it. This is not to say that the world doesn't still show faint reflections of the Creator's goodness, nature and power. We have seen his signature written all over creation. In fact, the beauty we see can be overwhelming, and if we can still spy out such beauty in an evil and fallen world, what must it have been like to dwell on the earth when God called it good? Imagine how it will be when God creates a new heaven and a new earth at the end of the age.

The evil of the world is primarily spiritual, moral and supernatural in nature. We are under its 'spell'. It blinds and deceives us from the truth around us and within us. It holds us in bondage to demonic addiction. Paul tells us that 'the god of this world, has blinded the minds of those who don't believe' (2 Cor. 4:4, NLT).

In Galatians 3, Paul will ask who has bewitched or put the Galatians under a spell. The gospel delivers us from sin, Satan and the chains of evil. Of course, as pilgrims in a foreign land we still live in and experience the evils of the world around us. But by faith in the power of Christ's death we can experience deliverance from the spiritual deception and domination of this present evil age. By the power of the Holy Spirit we can live as flaming lights in the midst of darkness.

I can't emphasize enough the fact that the gospel actually delivers us out of one spiritual realm into another. Regeneration (being born again) translates us from the kingdom of darkness into the realm of the kingdom of God. The moment we become Christians we are completely dead to the reign of sin and evil; we leave its territory altogether. In his exposition of Romans 6, Dr Martyn Lloyd-Jones puts it like this

> How can I say that I am delivered from the rule and the realm of the devil and of sin, when I still fall into temptation? Look at it in

this way. Think of two fields with a road between them. The field on the left represents the dominion, the kingdom, the territory, the empire of sin and Satan. That is where we all were by our natural birth. But as a result of the work of the Holy Spirit, we have been taken hold of and transferred to the field on the right of the road – 'Delivered from the power of darkness and translated into the kingdom of his dear son.' I was on the left; I am now here on the right. Yes, but I spent many a long year in the first field and the devil is still there with all his powers and his forces. This is a picture of what often happens. As a Christian I am here in the new field and Satan cannot touch me, as we are told in 1 John 5:18, 'that wicked one toucheth him not.' He cannot touch us because we are no longer in his kingdom. He cannot touch us; but he can shout across the road at us. Every Christian who falls into sin is a fool. The devil cannot touch us, why then do we listen to him? Why do we allow him to frighten us? Why do we pay any attention to him? When he speaks to us we listen to him and fall under his spell. We should resist him.[3]

We shall see later in the epistle of Galatians that this translation from the kingdom of darkness is at the heart of our living in holy freedom.

Finally, in this opening to the letter we see that gospel deliverance is the very will of God the Father. The sovereign will of the Father is self-evident in Paul's teachings. His calling, the message of the gospel, the gift of the Spirit, all are part of the Father's plan. Paul would have said a hearty amen to the apostle John's statement

> But as many as received Him, to them He gave the right to become children of God, to those who believe in His name: who were born, not of blood, nor of the will of the flesh, nor of the will of man, but of God. (John 1:12,13, NKJV)

It is not surprising that with all this powerful teaching in the first four verses of Galatians, Paul bursts into a doxology (a short expression or hymn of praise to God). But this doxology is very important, completing this initial presentation of the details of the gospel. Paul ascribes to God our Father 'glory forever and ever, amen'.

Glory means the splendour, majesty, authority and power of a person made known and demonstrated. Glory has a great deal to do with the reputation, renown and fame of the individual concerned. The gospel, even more importantly than being the means of salvation for human beings, is the unveiling of the very glory, splendour and character of God.

As the Westminster Shorter Catechism says, 'Man's chief end is to glorify God, and to enjoy him forever.' History is not human-focused, but God-centred. The death and resurrection of Jesus Christ was primarily to *glorify the Father* through the salvation of humankind from sin.

2.

Shocked to Cursing

(Gal. 1:6–13)

(6) I am astonished that you are so quickly turning away from the one who called you in the grace (of Christ) to another gospel, (7) which is not another, except that there are some who are disturbing you and wanting to turn the gospel of the Christ into something else. (8) But even if we or an angel from heaven preach to you a gospel contrary to what we preached to you, let him be accursed! (9) As we said before, I now also say again: if anyone preaches to you something contrary to what you received, let him be accursed! (10) For am I now trying to persuade men, or God? Or am I seeking to please men? If I were still trying to please men, I would not be the slave of Christ. (11) For I want you to know, brothers, that the gospel preached by me is not of human origin. (12) For it was not from a human being that I received it, neither was I taught it, but through a revelation of Jesus Christ.

Paul couldn't wait to get through his greeting and deal with the issues of the gospel. The Galatians would be expecting Paul to give some sort of thanksgiving for their lives at this point, but Paul had absolutely nothing to thank God about in regard to their present condition. When he uttered his 'astonishment' at their turning away, it was the exact same word used in the New Testament for when people were 'amazed' at Christ's miracles. Paul was as amazed at their backsliding from the gospel as if he'd just seen an astonishing miracle – except that this present astonishment was one of incredulity.

Turning from the grace of Jesus

Paul was hard on the church of Galatia because he knew that they were really turning from their *calling in grace* – a theme Paul has already introduced in his brief greeting. They were turning away from a free, underserved, unconditional, unmerited gift of grace – eternal life. They were also turning from the one who called them; they were turning away from Christ himself. Some translations talk about 'deserting Him who called you' (v. 6, NASB). The 'desertion' from Jesus was that the Galatians no longer believed in the simplicity of the gospel. They now believed they had to prove themselves acceptable to God through obedience to the Law.

Gospel or not?

The word 'gospel' simply means good news, glad tidings or a joyful message. In the book of Isaiah we see the term gospel or good news used in a way that both Jesus and the early church would have been very much aware of. In Isaiah 40 – 66 we have a series of announcements of good news that herald restoration, salvation, freedom and the favour of God to Israel. Jesus, in Luke 4:18–21, explains the good news in his manifesto for ministry which he proclaimed in Nazareth

> THE SPIRIT OF THE LORD IS UPON ME,
> BECAUSE HE ANOINTED ME TO PREACH THE GOSPEL
>   TO THE POOR.
> HE HAS SENT ME TO PROCLAIM RELEASE TO THE
>   CAPTIVES,
> AND RECOVERY OF SIGHT TO THE BLIND,
> TO SET FREE THOSE WHO ARE OPPRESSED,
> TO PROCLAIM THE FAVORABLE YEAR OF THE LORD.
>   (vv. 18,19, NASB)

In his explanation to John the Baptist in Matthew 11:4–6, Jesus again defines his gospel in audio-visual terms

> Go and report to John what you hear and see; the BLIND
> RECEIVE SIGHT and the lame walk, the lepers are cleansed and
> the deaf hear, the dead are raised up, and THE POOR HAVE THE
> GOSPEL PREACHED TO THEM. (NASB)

Like Jesus, Paul believes the gospel is preached not only in terms
of forgiveness of sins, but that it should also be accompanied by
supernatural, miraculous signs (Gal. 3:5). Paul talks about the
gospel of the Judaizers. The Galatians have turned to 'another
gospel, which is not another'. In our English translations we only
have one word for 'another', but in the New Testament Greek
Paul uses two different words. The first of these is *heteros* which
means another of a *totally different kind*. For example, you may see
two animals in a field; one is a cow and another is a sheep. They
are completely different kinds of animal, and the Greek word you
would use here would be *heteros*. So Paul was saying, 'You have
turned away to another gospel of a totally different kind.' In fact,
today we use the theological word 'heterodoxy' to describe a
belief that is not in line with biblical truth.

Paul then uses a different word for 'another' in verse 7, *allos*,
which means 'another of the same kind'. If you saw two animals
in a field, a pig and another pig, you would use the word *allos*
meaning another of exactly the same type. Paul is making
absolutely sure that the Galatians know that there is only one true
gospel and that there aren't any alternatives to it. He is saying
that the Galatians have turned to 'another gospel (*heteros*) of a
totally different kind, which is not another (*allos*) of the same kind
at all.'

Perverters of the gospel

Have you ever met people who disturb your peace? You are having a pleasant day and then some person just disturbs your tran-
quillity, shakes your spirit and leaves you in a state of agitation.
We have already seen that grace and the peace of the gospel is the
answer to the human condition. But there are those who wish to
disturb our peace with God, interfere with it and cause us to
doubt our status as children of the Father.

(7) which is not another, except that there are some who are disturbing you and wanting to turn the gospel of the Christ into
something else.

Paul confronts these troublemakers. They are perverters of the
gospel, taking that which produces life and twisting it to produce
death, turning freedom into bondage and hope into fear. The
Greek word for 'disturb' is likened to the calm sea being stirred
up by a storm. The word was also used to describe a political confrontation such as rioting. Changing the gospel into something
else isn't a soft adjustment or a slight difference in opinion. It
brings incredible spiritual turbulence and destruction.

Angelic authority

The Judaizers were no angels, but the Galatians believed their
false teaching. Paul had even been treated himself as an angelic
messenger when he evangelized in Galatia, and perhaps this is in
the back of his mind when he brings up the subject. It was in
Lystra, Galatia, after Paul had healed a man crippled from birth
that the crowd thought Paul and Barnabas were gods in human
form. They thought Barnabas was Zeus (king of the Greek gods)
and Paul, Hermes (Zeus's messenger) (Acts 14:8–20). The church
of Galatia would know this story, so it would have made a
special impact when Paul said that even if he or an angel from
heaven preached a different message to the one they had
received, they should reject it. The point Paul was making is that
the authority of the gospel preached to them was not bound to
the one who preached it. It is the message even more than the
messenger that counts.

Paul is also alluding to a theme that he will pick up later in the
letter. The Law that the Galatians were turning to had actually been
delivered to Moses by God through the agency of angels, whereas
the gospel was given directly to us by God the Son himself. The
Galatians were turning to a second-hand angelic revelation when
they accepted the Law. They were putting angelic revelation above
that delivered by Christ. An angel would never preach another
gospel after the Lord had personally delivered it himself.

Interestingly enough, the idea of angelic revelation being authoritative is still very prevalent in Pentecostal and charismatic circles today. I have read books where people have claimed to be taken on visits to heaven and hell by angels, yet the knowledge they receive about salvation can sometimes be contrary to that contained in the New Testament. When I have tried to explain this to some people, they find it hard to understand that I could criticize such angelic revelation because, 'After all, Bruce, you haven't been to heaven or hell or met an angel like this author did!' Paul insists we must accept the gospel on its own supernatural authority, no matter what the status of any person who seeks to change it – even if it be an angelic being.

Cursed is the messenger of the false gospel

Paul was so serious about the purity of the gospel that he says twice that anyone who preaches a gospel different from the one he preached to the Galatians is accursed. The word Paul specifically uses is *anathema*. In the ancient Greek version of the Old Testament, the Septuagint (LXX), this Greek word is used to refer to things that are under the divine ban, or *herem* in Hebrew. *Herem* literally means 'to close, to narrow, to shut and to stop'. When something in the Old Testament was put under God's ban, no one was able to keep it. The object or individual was set aside for destruction before God, and it was not allowed to remain within the covenant community of Israel. The best example of this is found in Joshua 7, where the spoils taken from Jericho that were meant to be under the ban of God were kept back by Achan. So when Paul calls the false gospel preachers 'accursed', he means that their teaching is so abhorrent that they deserve to be set aside for destruction by God. He wants them closed down and stopped. Paul's desire is for them to be removed from the life of the community of God so that they trouble it no more.

Not a spin-doctor!

One of the accusations against Paul was that he had changed the Jewish gospel to please his Gentile audience. The Judaizers believed that Paul 'spun' the gospel message to gain a popular response – that he was a human-pleaser. Paul was accused of preaching cheap grace, a gospel without standards. His enemies claimed that Paul had removed the need for circumcision and food laws out of expediency, not gospel conviction. Instead of calling the people to holiness expressed through the Law, and specifically circumcision and food laws, Paul was simply saying, 'Only believe in the good news of Jesus and you are acceptable to the Father.' His news sounded too good to be true in the Judaizers' minds – an offer of a free eternal pardon from God with no visible change required. You can imagine the Judaizers' conversation going something like this: 'No wonder Paul is so popular. He just tells them what they want to hear – no outline of repentance by good works to prove they are serious! We could all have large churches if we preached that soft soap. Paul is just looking for converts, but we are searching for serious disciples who love the Lord enough to be circumcised and obey his Law, proving they have been soundly converted.'

Even later, when Paul wrote the letter to the Romans, he still had to defend himself against such charges. He was accused of preaching a gospel that promoted a license to sin – that the more you sin the more the grace of God is revealed, therefore you should go ahead and keep sinning. But Paul never taught this. On the contrary, Paul couldn't understand how anyone who had been delivered from this present evil age would ever want to partake of it again. The whole point is that sin is the very enemy from which we have been delivered. The gospel delivers us *from* sin, not *to* sin.

> What shall we say then? Are we to continue in sin so that grace may increase? May it never be! How shall we who died to sin still live in it? (Rom. 6:1,2, NASB)

We must remember, though, that it was the gospel of grace through faith alone that provoked this false charge, chiefly because Paul refused to add any type of human effort to the grace of God's saving work.

Paul emphatically denies the charge of being a human-pleaser. Rather, he is a God-pleaser. Paul calls himself the 'slave of Christ'

(v. 10). This is the title he uses to introduce himself in the letter to the Romans. A slave exists to please his master and, where necessary, represent him. Paul could be so confident in his call as the apostle to the Gentiles because he was so humble in relationship to Christ who called him. Paul was the apostle to the world and the complete slave of Christ. This very powerful combination of titles reveal how Paul regarded himself and what produced his boldness before people, yet his meekness before God.

Revelation knowledge

> (11) For I want you to know, brothers, that the gospel preached by me is not of human origin. (12) For it was not from a human being that I received it, neither was I taught it, but through a revelation of Jesus Christ.

We are coming to the end of the first section of Galatians 1:1–12 which I entitled the supernatural gospel. Here Paul speaks about the origin of the gospel. He has already introduced us to its basic contents. John R.W. Stott, in his book *The Message of Galatians*, writes concerning this opening section of the letter: 'How can we recognise the true gospel? Its marks are given us here. They concern its substance [what it is] and its source [where it comes from].'[1]

Paul has explained that his calling as an apostle is from God, not human beings. Now he follows this up by saying that the gospel that he preached was also not from human beings. His call and his message did not come from human sources.

What were the young Galatian Christians to do? Competing gospels were demanding their allegiance. Which one was from God? The Judaizers must have made the Galatians doubt Paul's authority and his message. Paul says that he did not receive the contents of the gospel by tradition, or from any human teacher, and neither did he invent it. Paul tells them that he received the gospel from Jesus Christ himself in a personal encounter. This encounter was when Christ appeared to him on the Damascus road. The gospel is not just about what Christ did for us; the 'good news' is actually Jesus himself. The knowledge of the gospel was received by an impartation of divine revelation. The Galatians either had to accept what Paul was saying or reject it; there was no halfway house. He had been taught directly by Jesus. No wonder he could ridicule the idea of even an angel coming with another gospel, for he had received it from the Lord himself.

3

Paul's Testimony

(Gal. 1:13–24)

(13) For you have heard of my way of life previously in Judaism, that in excessive measure I persecuted the church of God and tried to destroy it; (14) and that I progressed in Judaism beyond many of my contemporaries among my people, being exceedingly zealous for my ancestral traditions. (15) But when it pleased the one who set me apart from my mother's womb, and called me through his grace, (16) to reveal his son in me, in order that I might preach him among the Gentiles, I did not consult immediately with flesh and blood, (17) nor did I go up to Jerusalem to those who were apostles before me, but went away into Arabia and returned again to Damascus. (18) Then, after three years, I did go up to Jerusalem to get to know Cephas, and I stayed with him fifteen days. (19) Other of the apostles I did not see, but only James, the Lord's brother. (20) What I write to you, please note, before God, I am not lying. (21) Then I went off into the territories of Syria and of Cilicia. (22) I continued to be unknown by sight to the churches of Judea which are in Christ. (23) The only thing they kept hearing was that 'Our former persecutor now preaches the faith which he once tried to destroy'. (24) And they used to glorify God because of me.

One distinct aspect of my Pentecostal heritage is the emphasis on personal testimony. We believe that every Christian's experience of salvation is a supernatural story that can be told. Each Christian has a unique salvation testimony to tell. Often in our evangelistic services we will include an individual's testimony about their life before and then after their faith encounter with

Christ. Paul's autobiographical section takes up nearly one fifth of the whole letter. It is enthralling to hear him talk about his pre-Christian life, and then how he progressed in his ministry and calling. It is fascinating to hear his testimony.

Paul claimed that he was divinely called, and also that he received the gospel from the Lord Jesus himself. He now backs up his claims by telling the tale of his calling and ministry. The Judaizers must have been trying very hard to destroy not only Paul's message but also his reputation for him to feel the need to share his story like this. We know that in the ministry if you lose credibility in the eyes of people they will stop listening to you, even if your message is true. Paul has to tell his side of the story and set the record straight.

The premier league Jew (1:13,14)

(13) For you have heard of my way of life previously in Judaism, that in excessive measure I persecuted the church of God and tried to destroy it; (14) and that I progressed in Judaism beyond many of my contemporaries among my people, being exceedingly zealous for my ancestral traditions.

It was ironic that the Judaizers saw themselves as defenders of the Law against Paul. If anyone knew and had lived zealously for the Law, it was Paul. I can imagine him thinking, 'Who are these people? Who do they think they are dealing with? I was an elite minister and disciple of the Law, the crème de la crème, top of the premier league!' Paul had been a fanatical zealot for the Jewish Law

If anyone else has a mind to put confidence in the flesh, I far more: circumcised the eighth day, of the nation of Israel, of the tribe of Benjamin, a Hebrew of Hebrews; as to the Law, a Pharisee; as to zeal, a persecutor of the church; as to the righteousness which is in the Law, found blameless. (Phil. 3:4–6, NASB)

Paul was blameless in his former pursuit of the Law. He wasn't claiming to be perfect, but under the provisions in the Law for sacrifice for sin, he really could claim to be impeccable in his conduct before people. He wasn't afraid of living by the Law – he had done it 24/7 all his life until his conversion. When he was accused of having no respect or regard for the Law, he reminded the Galatians that he had been matchless when it came to both understanding it and practicing it.

Interestingly, the word 'Judaism' isn't found anywhere else in the New Testament except here in verse 14. Judaism was a word describing a movement that focused very much on maintaining its identity in the face of increasing Gentile influences, especially through the outward acts of the Law, such as food laws and circumcision. Paul still regarded himself as a Jew, but he saw himself as having discarded one Jewish movement, Judaism, for the new and authentic Jewish movement that was Christianity.

Paul the destroyer

Paul had been an enemy of the fledgling church. He did all that he could to destroy it. Christians heard Paul's name, 'Saul of Tarsus', and feared for their lives. He was like a leader of the secret religious police, rooting out men, women and children who followed Christ. When he found Christians, he imprisoned them; some he helped sentence to be executed. He even held the coats of the men who stoned Stephen to death.

Paul shows what he was like before he believed the gospel. He is telling the Galatians that if they were so impressed by these Law-preaching Judaizers, they should recall that he had been light years ahead of them in his former life as a Pharisee.

'Come and follow me'(1:15–17)

(15) But when it pleased the one who set me apart from my mother's womb, and called me through his grace, (16) to reveal his son in me, in order that I might preach him among the Gentiles, I did not consult immediately with flesh and blood, (17) nor did I go up to Jerusalem to those who were apostles before me, but went away into Arabia and returned again to Damascus.

Paul may have been the last foundational apostle of the church to be called, but he certainly didn't feel a sense of inferiority. On the road to Damascus, Jesus appeared to him and made effective the call that had been on his life since birth. 'Come and follow me, Paul,' Jesus said. Paul understood that his personal call by Jesus Christ had been determined even before he was born. Paul must have had the prophet Jeremiah's call to the nations in mind when he mentions being set apart in his mother's womb

> Before I formed you in the womb I knew you, And before you were born I consecrated you; I have appointed you a prophet to the nations. (Jer. 1:5, NASB)

John Calvin commenting on verse 15 said this

> This setting apart was the purpose of God, by which Paul was appointed to the apostolic office, before he knew that he was born. The calling followed afterwards at the proper time, when the Lord made known his will concerning him, and commanded him to proceed to the work. God had, no doubt, decreed, before the foundation of the world, what he would do with regard to every one of us, and had assigned to everyone, by his secret counsel, his respective place. But the sacred writers frequently introduce those three steps: the eternal predestination of God, the destination from the womb, and the calling, which is the effect and accomplishment of both.[1]

Called not converted

Paul saw his experience with the risen Lord more a calling than a conversion. He encountered Christ for a purpose beyond his own personal redemption. Like Paul, every Christian has been called by God even before they were born. When we receive Christ into our lives we aren't just new converts, we have been called up for active service for Jesus. It is important that a new believer learns right from the start that they have been called to fulfil a God-ordained destiny.

Arabian Bible school

Having explained his divine calling as the apostle to the nations, Paul also wants to establish that the contents of the gospel that he received were given directly to him from the Lord. It is interesting to think that the original twelve disciples spent three years following and learning from Jesus. Paul also had his three years in discipleship school in Arabia, following Christ and being taught by the Holy Spirit. All this happened before he even spoke to any of the Jerusalem leaders. He was totally independent from the leaders of the church of Jerusalem, both in his calling and his Christian education during these three years – he got it all directly from the Lord.

Peter's guest room (1:18–24)

(18) Then, after three years, I did go up to Jerusalem to get to know Cephas, and I stayed with him fifteen days. (19) Other of the apostles I did not see, but only James, the Lord's brother. (20) What I write to you, please note, before God, I am not lying. (21) Then I went off into the territories of Syria and of Cilicia. (22) I continued to be unknown by sight to the churches of Judea which are in Christ. (23) The only thing they kept hearing was that 'Our former persecutor now preaches the faith which he once tried to destroy'. (24) And they used to glorify God because of me.

What an amazing story so far. Paul was persecutor of the church, then, blinded by the light of Christ, he received his call from the Lord on the road to Damascus. He received a personal revelation and tutoring of the gospel from Jesus himself, three years of training for ministry, and now made a visit to 'the Rock', Cephas (Peter), as his honoured house guest. Surely the Galatians should see that Paul was the real thing. His experience was real, his calling was real and, most importantly, his gospel was real.

Character assassins

The Judaizers were claiming that they had the true Jerusalem gospel, and that Paul was a rogue who had perverted the gospel that the other apostles preached. Rumours, slanders and twisted truths were all being used to bring Paul down – that's why he had to give such an account of his life to defend himself to the Galatian Christians. Once they had received him and his gospel with joy, but now they treated both him and his message with suspicion. Paul felt so assaulted by these character slurs that he even exclaimed in exasperation, 'I am not lying!' Only those of us that have been on the end of venomous lies designed to destroy us can possibly know the frustration of having to exclaim that we are not what we have been portrayed to be.

Sharing and partnering in ministry

Paul went up to Jerusalem specifically to get to know Cephas. He stayed with Peter for two weeks. The Greek word used here for 'getting to know' Peter is *historesai*, which can also be used in the sense of interviewing someone. Paul not only wanted to get to know Peter, but also wanted to learn about his experiences with Jesus. The fact that Paul didn't spend time with anyone else but Peter (and, briefly James, the Lord's brother) shows that this was relationship building for the future.

Peter did not teach Paul the gospel; Paul had received that already. The Judaizers probably wanted to make it look as if Paul had gone to Peter as a novice pupil to learn the gospel, so that they could deny his apostolic claims. They could also then claim that when the two of them fell out in Antioch, that it was Peter's disciple, Paul, who was in rebellion. But Paul had come as an equal to meet Peter, and spent much of his two weeks preaching in Jerusalem. Paul was called to take the gospel to the Gentile world, and Peter to the Jews. They were very different men with very different backgrounds, educations and callings, but both esteemed the other's ministry. They shared in fellowship as well as in ministry and they became friends. This friendship would be tested to breaking point.

Paul set off to preach in regions outside of Judea. He became renowned as a preacher of the Christian faith. People rejoiced in his ministry. Fourteen years later, when his missionary endeavours were bearing incredible fruit, he would need to confront the Judaizers at the famous Council of Jerusalem.

4.

The Council of Jerusalem

(Gal. 2:1–10)

(1) Then after fourteen years I travelled up once again to Jerusalem with Barnabas, taking Titus also with me. (2) I travelled up in accordance with a revelation. And I laid before them the gospel which I proclaim among the Gentiles, but privately to those held in repute, lest somehow I was running or had run in vain. (3) But not even Titus who was with me, though a Greek, was compelled to be circumcised. (4) But because of the false brothers smuggled in, who sneaked in to spy on our freedom which we have in Christ Jesus, in order that they might enslave us, (5) to them not even for an hour did we yield submission, in order that the truth of the gospel might remain for you. (6) But from those reputed to be something – what they once were makes no difference to me, God shows no partiality – for to me those of repute added nothing. (7) But on the contrary, when they saw that I had been entrusted with the gospel for the uncircumcision, as Peter with the gospel for the circumcision, (8) for he who worked with Peter for the apostleship of the circumcision worked also with me for the Gentiles, (9) and recognised the grace given to me, James, Cephas and John, those reputed to be pillars, gave to me and Barnabas the right hand of fellowship, in order that we should be for the Gentiles, and they for the circumcision; (10) with the one qualification that we should remember the poor, the very thing which I have eagerly done.

Paul's next major visit to Jerusalem was fourteen years later. There is an important difference of opinion over what visit to

Jerusalem Paul is referring to in this passage. Some believe that Paul is talking here about the time of a famine relief trip to Judea, and that it was during this trip that he met the apostles in Galatians 2. This occasion took place in Acts 11:30. Agabus had prophesied that a great worldwide famine was approaching, and the church in Antioch took up an offering for the relief of poor Christians in Judea.

> And in the proportion that any of the disciples had means, each of them determined to send a contribution for the relief of the brethren living in Judea. And this they did, sending it in charge of Barnabas and Saul to the elders. (Acts 11:29,30, NASB)

However, there is no reference to Paul meeting any apostles, let alone Peter and James. Neither does it mention that he actually went to the city of Jerusalem, simply to Judea, so he may or may not have gone to the great city on this occasion. He met a body of elders, perhaps those linked to the feeding programmes we know of in the early church of Acts. Apostles, of course, can also be elders, but it would be strange to omit the term as Luke differentiated between the two later in Acts 15:6.

Some have argued that this must have been the meeting that Paul was talking about in Galatians 2, because it was the second time he talked about going to Jerusalem, and the later Council was the third occasion. But Paul does not specifically state that the meeting in Galatians 2 with James and Peter was the second time he travelled to Jerusalem after his conversion. He simply says he went up 'again'. The Greek word for 'again' is *palin* which simply means, 'again, a renewal or repetition of an action'. It could easily mean 'again for the third time' as much as it could mean 'again for the second time'.

It is believed by some that because Paul said that he met 'privately' (Gal. 2:2) it must have taken place during a secret meeting during the relief mission, and that Luke didn't feel he was at liberty to talk about it in Acts. But all of this is arguing from silence. The Council of Jerusalem was also a closed, private leadership session consisting of only the apostles and elders. And if this was such a secret meeting, why would Paul now reveal it publicly? If we want an example of a meeting that wasn't private we can see one very soon, when Paul publicly rebukes Peter in front of the whole church for being a hypocrite.

If Paul is talking about some secret meeting during a famine relief trip, this would mean that both Peter and James were going to welch on their agreement with him later in Antioch – because men from James, Peter and indeed Barnabas opposed him in the second half of Galatians 2. If the Council of Jerusalem was partly to sort out this mess in Antioch, then the three aforementioned men changed their opinion twice, because by Acts 15 all of them would be reunited alongside Paul.

Why would they even need a Council of Jerusalem if the men of repute had already dealt with this issue in Acts 11? And why would they have kept the meeting a secret? For what purpose? Indeed, Paul had been given the public right hand of fellowship at this meeting (Gal. 2:9); this was open support for all to see. I believe that Paul is referring in Galatians 2 to the Council of Jerusalem in order to remind his readers of the support he had been given by the very men he would have to later confront.

Circumcision?

The question of whether the Gentile converts should be circumcised or not took a while to surface as a major issue in the book of Acts. Until Acts 13 there is very little evidence of any major ongoing outreach to the Gentiles. Acts 11:19–21 tells us that the gospel spread, but limits its impact to Jews and Greek Jews only

> Now those who were scattered after the persecution that arose over Stephen traveled as far as Phoenicia, Cyprus, and Antioch, preaching the word to no one but the Jews only. But some of them were men from Cyprus and Cyrene, who, when they had come to Antioch, spoke to the Hellenists, preaching the Lord Jesus. And the hand of the Lord was with them, and a great number believed and turned to the Lord. (NKJV)

Paul was only teaching in Antioch for one year before the famine relief trip, and on his return both he and Barnabas were commissioned to start their first missionary journey. Up to this point there was no major move of salvation among the Gentiles, although Peter had reaped the first fruits earlier on in a one-off, Spirit-led outreach (Acts 10:44). When Paul and Barnabas set off on their inaugural mission, it took them a while to find their feet. It seems they focused on preaching the gospel to the Jews in synagogues. Even the encounter with the proconsul at Paphos was in the context of dealing with a false Jewish prophet named Bar Jesus. It was only after preaching again to the Jews in Pisidian Antioch, and being rejected, that they began preaching to the Gentiles (Acts 13:46). When they returned to Antioch they gave them the amazing news that God, 'had opened the door of faith to the Gentiles' (Acts 14:27, NKJV). At the Council of Jerusalem the apostles and elders would hear about the Gentile mission for the first time from Paul and Barnabas.

Before this historical point, at the end of Acts 14, there was no need to discuss circumcision because there had been no effective Gentile mission. It just wasn't a big enough issue to debate. But now, almost immediately on Paul's return, the sparks begin to fly. The church in Antioch starts full-scale Gentile evangelism and, in response, some Jewish Christians insist that the new converts be circumcised. The argument that took place between Peter and Paul couldn't have occurred during this short period, because Peter was already in Jerusalem during Acts 15, and also at this point Barnabas was still in full support of Paul (Acts 15:2). If this had been the time when men from James, Peter and Barnabas argued with Paul, then they very quickly changed their tune in Jerusalem. If they were arguing with Paul before the Council, why were they arguing about table fellowship when the clear, central issue was circumcision? It just isn't plausible. They weren't that double-minded.

Paul, in Acts 15:2, determined to go up to Jerusalem to sort this out. In Galatians 2:2 he says that it was a revelation from God to go up to Jerusalem and deal with this backlash against the success of the gospel to the Gentiles – to nip it in the bud.

You may think it doesn't really matter which meeting Paul is referring to in Galatians 2 – the relief trip or the later Council of Jerusalem. But it does matter, big time! The question of which trip Paul is referring to changes the whole context and feel of the letter to the Galatians. I wrote earlier that it is important to understand the circumstances that any letter is written, therefore:

If Paul is referring in Galatians 2 to the relief trip of Acts 11:29

- Then Galatians was written *before* the Council of Jerusalem.
- Paul's argument with Peter over table fellowship would therefore have taken place *before* the Council at Jerusalem.
- The Council was called to sort out everything, including the whole Galatian problem.

If Paul is referring in Galatians 2 to the Council of Jerusalem in Acts 15

- Then Galatians was written *after* the Council at Jerusalem.
- His argument with Peter over table fellowship took place *after* the Council of Jerusalem.

I am convinced that Paul is referring to the Council of Jerusalem in Galatians 2, where only the issue of circumcision was properly dealt with, not table fellowship. The Judaizers would bring up table fellowship as an issue after the Council with Peter in Antioch.

Acts 15 and the Council of Jerusalem

Before we go any further we should read Acts 15:1–21

> Some men came down from Judea and *began* teaching the brethren, 'Unless you are circumcised according to the custom of Moses, you cannot be saved.' And when Paul and Barnabas had great dissension and debate with them, *the brethren* determined that Paul and Barnabas and some others of them should go up to Jerusalem to the apostles and elders concerning this issue. Therefore, being sent on their way by the church, they were passing through both Phoenicia and Samaria, describing in detail the conversion of the Gentiles, and were bringing great joy to all the brethren. When they arrived at Jerusalem, they were received by the church and the apostles and the elders, and they reported all that God had done with them. But some of the sect of the Pharisees who had believed stood up, saying, 'It is

necessary to circumcise them and to direct them to observe the Law of Moses.'

The apostles and the elders came together to look into this matter. After there had been much debate, Peter stood up and said to them, 'Brethren, you know that in the early days God made a choice among you, that by my mouth the Gentiles would hear the word of the gospel and believe. And God, who knows the heart, testified to them giving them the Holy Spirit, just as He also did to us; and He made no distinction between us and them, cleansing their hearts by faith. Now therefore why do you put God to the test by placing upon the neck of the disciples a yoke which neither our fathers nor we have been able to bear? But we believe that we are saved through the grace of the Lord Jesus, in the same way as they also are.' All the people kept silent, and they were listening to Barnabas and Paul as they were relating what signs and wonders God had done through them among the Gentiles.

After they had stopped speaking, James answered, saying, 'Brethren, listen to me. Simeon has related how God first concerned Himself about taking from among the Gentiles a people for His name. With this the words of the Prophets agree, just as it is written,

"AFTER THESE THINGS I will return,
AND I WILL REBUILD THE TABERNACLE OF DAVID WHICH HAS FALLEN,
AND I WILL REBUILD ITS RUINS,
AND I WILL RESTORE IT,
SO THAT THE REST OF MANKIND MAY SEEK THE LORD,
AND ALL THE GENTILES WHO ARE CALLED BY MY NAME,"
SAYS THE LORD, WHO MAKES THESE THINGS KNOWN FROM LONG AGO.

Therefore it is my judgment that we do not trouble those who are turning to God from among the Gentiles, but that we write to them that they abstain from things contaminated by idols and from fornication and from what is strangled and from blood. For Moses from ancient generations has in every city those who preach him, since he is read in the synagogues every Sabbath.' (NASB)

Taking it to the enemy

Paul and Barnabas returned to Antioch triumphant after their
amazing first missionary journey, but the joy didn't last long.
False teachers came from Judea saying that in order to be saved
you had to be circumcised. Paul and Barnabas confronted them
in heated exchanges. Paul decided to fight this out, not in
Antioch, but to take the battle to the very nest of these vipers –
Judea. He knew he needed to stamp this out at its source.

When our ministries and churches are being attacked by false
religions and teachings, it is not enough just to defend ourselves
and our converts apologetically (apologetics is defending the
truths of the gospel) – we need a restoration of the lost art of
polemics (attacking false teaching) in the European church. Many
of Paul's letters have strong, unflinching polemics in them.
Apologetics and polemics are the twin guardians of the gospel –
we have to make sure we use them both. Paul didn't just defend
the gospel, he attacked falsehood vigorously and hacked at its
root.

Led by revelation

Paul wanted the Galatians to know that it was by the initiative of
the Holy Spirit that he went to Jerusalem. He was not *summoned*
to Jerusalem, he went because he was *led by the Spirit* to go there.
He took Barnabas, his close associate, but even more intriguingly
he took Titus, a Gentile Christian. Titus was the perfect test case:
a radically saved, uncircumcised Gentile. Imagine the Judaizers'
faces when they saw this young, tongue-speaking man on fire for
the Lord, realizing that they would have to convince everyone
that he would be unsaved if he refused to be circumcised.

Paul was greeted by the church in Jerusalem, and he then
spoke to the apostles and elders regarding the gospel that he was
preaching and the problem with the Judaizers. As he did this, the
leaders of the Judaizing party, who had been Pharisees like him
before conversion, stood up and made themselves known.

Imagine the scene: surrounded by the apostles and elders of
the whole Jerusalem church and its Judean satellites in a closed

meeting, Paul is explaining the gospel given personally to him by Jesus Christ. The leading Judaizers are listening to a man they knew over fourteen years ago as their old partner in Pharisaism. They are remembering his zeal for the Law, his elite status in the movement and, whilst listening to his words, they fasten their eyes on Titus, an uncircumcised Greek Gentile! Paul is proclaiming the gospel of grace by faith alone and without circumcision, and they can stand it no longer. They stand up, shouting Paul down, proclaiming circumcision and adherence to the Law for salvation. Paul raises his voice louder and rebukes them. Paul has flushed out the enemy.

Peter agrees with Paul

The apostles and elders realize that this issue has been brought to a place where it needs to be dealt with decisively. The hardliners proclaiming mandatory circumcision for all believers were making a concerted effort to carry the day. Time is made for a debate, and across the floor the opponents quote Scripture at one another. The debate goes on and on, for the future of the fledgling church is at stake. It was obvious that Paul would accept nothing but the total freedom of the gospel. Acts 15:7 tells us that Peter finally stood up and spoke. The content of his speech has remarkable similarities to Paul's defence of the gospel in Galatians

- the Gentiles will hear the gospel and believe
- God, who knows their hearts, has testified to them by giving them the gift of the Spirit
- he has made no distinction between Jew and Gentile, cleansing their hearts by faith
- they should not test God by putting the yoke of circumcision and the Law on them, which not even the Jews can bear – it is not necessary
- Jews are saved through the grace of the Lord Jesus in the same way Gentiles are

Some modern scholars have accused Paul of developing his own Pauline gospel, distinct from other apostles, but we can see that the main points of Paul's gospel are found in this summary of Peter's speech. After Peter finishes, Paul and Barnabas testify to the miracles, signs and wonders that God did through them among the Gentiles. As we will see in Galatians 3, supernatural experience of the gifts of the Spirit is an argument for the authenticity of the gospel of grace. Paul had presented the same gospel to the apostles that Peter preached.

Paul didn't doubt his gospel when he presented it to the apostles. He wanted to know that he wasn't running in vain, that the work he was doing would not be undermined or disowned by the Judean churches. There was a grave danger in Paul's mind that there could be a church split. We can see in Galatians 2:6–10 that although Paul coveted highly the unity of the faith and the support of the apostles, especially that of James, Cephas and John, if they decided against him he would not accept their judgement, and the fellowship between Jerusalem and Antioch would be broken. Thankfully, they were right behind him and there was unity and continuity in the gospel between Jerusalem and the Antioch mission to the Gentiles led by Paul – at least for the present.

Titus left Jerusalem with Paul and Barnabas – a very relieved young man in more ways than one!

5.

Food Fight in Antioch

(Gal. 2:11–14)

(11) But when Cephas came to Antioch I opposed him to his face, because he stood condemned. (12) For before certain individuals came from James, he used to eat with the Gentiles. But when they came, he gradually drew back and separated himself, because he feared those of the circumcision. (13) And the rest of the Jews also joined with him in playing the hypocrite, so that even Barnabas was carried away with their hypocrisy. (14) But when I saw that they were not walking straight towards the truth of the gospel, I said to Cephas in front of everyone: 'If you, a Jew, "live like a Gentile and not like a Jew", how is it that you compel the Gentiles to Judaise?'

It is disturbing that so many Christian commentators try to play down the 'food fight' in Antioch. Some of the early church Fathers were so embarrassed about this apostolic bust-up that they said that the Cephas mentioned couldn't possibly have been the apostle Peter, but must have been another Cephas altogether! We should not try to whitewash what Scripture presents, even if it is distasteful or embarrassing.

Anyone who knows about controversies in church history and church politics will be aware that the godliest of people can be found fighting the nastiest of battles against each other. The trouble with high level Christian leadership controversies is that the fierceness is often accentuated by the fact that the different parties are both convinced that they have God on their side. This was no small disagreement in Antioch; it was a nasty spiritual punch-up.

It is not necessary for us to sanitize this episode; they were human beings just like us and, apart from the Scripture they were inspired to write, all the apostles were as fallible as you and I.

Paul was an ambassador of the Antioch church – he had used it as his base for reaching out to the Gentiles with the gospel. The Council of Jerusalem had clearly backed Paul, and the Gentiles were not expected to be circumcised.

Remember, the Council's conclusion was simply a decision by church leaders; it did not carry scriptural authority, even though it was recorded in the book of Acts. Maybe even calling it a 'council' is misleading – it was really more of a consultation. The Judaizing party may have felt that they had lost the battle for the time being, but not the entire war. Even with the Council's conclusions it was still unclear as to what extent the Gentile Christians were expected to obey the Jewish food laws. The Jerusalem meeting had asked the Gentiles to avoid food sacrificed to idols, food from animals slaughtered by strangling, and blood. Was this simply a request to help unite two very distinct communities coming together in one faith? Or was this a compromise that would allow the Judaizers an opportunity to fight back and get the circumcision issue back on the early church agenda through the auspices of food laws?

What does it mean to be a Christian?

It was in Antioch that followers of Jesus were first called Christians, and the argument between Peter and Paul is about what it means to be 'a Christian'. Both in Jerusalem and in Antioch the arguments were not just over religious laws or practices. Many of us in the modern world might wonder what all the fuss was about. We might also think that the discussion over circumcision and food laws has no application to our lives today. If that's what we think, then we are very mistaken.

The fundamental issue at stake in the food fight at Antioch is what it means to be a Christian. How do you define who is a Christian and who isn't? If I asked you to write ten things that would show you that someone was a Christian, what would you write? That they go to church each week? That they don't smoke?

That they read their Bible each day? That they don't swear? That they dress modestly? That they refrain from adultery and fornication?

Paul was convinced that food laws did not have anything to do with being a Christian, and after describing his argument with Peter he will expand on what it *really* means to be a Christian.

What does it mean to be a Jew?

The question 'What does it mean to be a Jew?' had been a big issue for centuries, ever since the Greek and then Roman empires had begun to try to Hellenize the Jews (force the Jews to adopt Greek culture and civilization). Circumcision, food laws and table fellowship were all at the heart of demonstrating one's Jewishness. Think today of Islam and how it attempts through dress, food and prayer times to define itself outwardly – it is a very similar scenario. There was a great fear amongst the Jews that if they weren't careful, in a few generations they would lose not only their heritage, but also their identity. They feared that Jews might soon become extinct as a unique people.

The food and table fellowship laws were not just about identity, though, they were also about purity and holiness. Observance to the food and table fellowship laws helped keep one sanctified in terms of the Mosaic Law. The laws were an act of worship, obedience and devotion to God. These laws had brought God right into the homes of Jewish folk, right into their family dining rooms, and had done so for untold generations. It must have been very hard to even think about discarding such holy, family and community traditions. These traditions helped maintain a cohesive identity for a dispersed nation.

The same old Peter?

This episode reminds me about the strengths and weaknesses of Peter's character. He was either walking on the water with Jesus, or denying him in front of a maid. He was capable of great acts of holy boldness, but was also susceptible at times to cowardice, fear, intimidation and peer pressure. He had become good friends with Paul, having hosted him for two weeks in the past, and he had stood shoulder to shoulder with him in defence of the gospel in Jerusalem. He wasn't a scholar, he was a fisherman, but he was also a powerful apostle of faith. He had dealt with the Judaizers before over the Cornelius incident of Acts 10. Peter had seen a vision on a house-top

> He fell into a trance; and he saw the sky opened up, and an object like a great sheet coming down, lowered by four corners to the ground, and there were in it all kinds of four-footed animals and crawling creatures of the earth and birds of the air. A voice came to him, 'Get up, Peter, kill and eat!' But Peter said, 'By no means, Lord, for I have never eaten anything unholy and unclean.' Again a voice came to him a second time, 'What God has cleansed, no longer consider unholy.' (Acts 10:10–15, NASB)

So, the Lord himself had previously dealt with him over the issue of unclean food, and in Acts 11:2 and 3 he faced criticism for eating with Gentiles

> And when Peter came up to Jerusalem, those who were circumcised took issue with him, saying 'You went to uncircumcised men and ate with them.' (NASB)

Peter was acknowledged as the apostle to the circumcised at the Council of Jerusalem, yet he had also been the first to preach to the Gentiles. He had a revelation that all foods were clean, and table fellowshipped with Gentile believers. On arrival in Antioch, he enjoyed table fellowship with both Jews and Gentiles indiscriminately. He would eat whatever his Gentile hosts gave him, perhaps even enjoy a nice bacon sandwich! He was free in his Christian liberty.

Legalistic Christians

Paul tells us that when certain individuals from James arrived, Peter gradually drew back and separated himself from fellowship with the Gentiles. Peter knew James and his followers well. James had become the most prominent leader in Jerusalem over the years. Peter had received a revelation of the freedom of the gospel of grace by faith alone, and witnessed the Spirit at work in Gentiles, but it appears that James hadn't received such a deep understanding. James had met Titus and accepted that circumcision was not necessary for Gentile believers to become Christians, but nevertheless, being part of the Jerusalem church meant that he and his followers lived in a Jewish environment that didn't really have much to do with Gentile Christians on a day-to-day basis.

James had not developed himself or his followers in the truth and liberty of the gospel, and that is to his discredit. The men from James carried his spirit and his bias towards Jewish tradition. Peter knew this. In the past it had been relatively easy for him to be very Jewish when he was in James's church, and then very Gentile when he was with Gentiles. But now the two spheres of influence had drawn together in Antioch, and he had to make a choice.

I know Christians who act like Peter. They know what Christian liberty is, and enjoy it and recognize it among others. But as soon as they are with legalistic believers, they revert to rules and regulations that they would never follow by conscience. I remember one church that had a tradition of historical abstinence from alcohol, and even though in current times the majority did responsibly partake of alcohol, they felt constrained about being open about their freedom. (Even today, many legalistic Christians believe that if you partake of alcohol you are at best unsanctified, and at worst unsaved). On one occasion they hired a venue with accommodation for a convention, but insisted that even the self-contained bars be shut. Within a couple of hours of opening, however, the conference grocery shop had sold out of alcohol! The management of the venue could not understand why this group would buy alcohol and yet, at the same time, ban it. Didn't they trust their people to be mature enough to handle alcohol responsibly? Maybe they felt some would abuse it? Maybe they felt they should accommodate the minority of legalists? The minute you protect someone from abusing their liberty, you have robbed them of it, even if you think you are just trying to help. But rules and regulations, indeed the Law itself, was for 'immature children' and not for heirs and sons of God.

I recall a good friend of mine, someone who I would never have thought would have struggled with legalism. One day I was preaching on Christian liberty, and at the end he came and confided in me that all his Christian life he had felt that pork was unclean. He even felt ill when he saw pork in the supermarket. He now felt liberated, and understood that the kingdom of God was not about food or drink. I immediately treated him to a Bacon Double Cheeseburger at Burger King, and guess what? He enjoyed it!

> for the kingdom of God is not eating and drinking, but righteousness and peace and joy in the Holy Spirit. (Rom. 14:17, NKJV)

This verse in Romans echoes the sentiments of Galatians 2. It also prepares us for our later study on the fruit of the Spirit, for it is fruit of the Spirit, not rules, that are the hallmark of authentic Christianity. But unfortunately, many in church today don't know the difference between compliance to rules and regulations and the fruit of the Holy Spirit.

Reverse gear

Did Peter withdraw from table fellowship with Gentiles out of his concern for the principle of not causing his weaker brothers from Jerusalem to stumble? After all, there are genuine believers whose weakness in conscience or past history should be taken into account in the practice of our liberty. This type of Christian is weak in gospel faith (see Rom. 14); they are God's strugglers whose tender consciences need gentle care until they mature. The men from James were not weaker brothers, though – and they weren't asking for personal sensitivity because they couldn't yet, out of conscience, eat with Gentiles. On the contrary, they were demanding that everyone else conform to their view. This is the true spirit of legalism, being more concerned with other people's actions than our own, and expecting everyone to conform to our image of what a Christian is and isn't, and what a Christian should and shouldn't do.

Legalistic Christians are the ugliest people in the world. They are unforgiving, judgemental and mean. A legalistic person will only forgive you on condition that you acknowledge their position as correct; they believe you have to deserve their forgiveness. They turn their illegitimate offence into a pretence for righteous anger.

Peter was intimidated not only by their attitude, but also by their clever Judaizing arguments. Obviously, to these men food and table fellowship laws were part of Jewish Christianity, and they were concerned that Peter had thrown his Jewish heritage away. The Gentiles may not need to be circumcised, but they had to take the food laws into consideration. The problem is, of course, that you can't pick and choose from the Law. It's like the story of the camel getting into a tent. As soon as you let his nose in, all of him enters! It is the same with the Law. Paul taught that you either follow the whole of the Law or none of it. The Law cannot be divided into parts. These men from James were clever and persuasive – they spoke in terms of holiness, purity and obedience. Was it too much to ask that Jewish heritage be acknowledged by Jewish believers? I really believe they were trying to bring the Law in through a side door, and then the discussion on circumcision would definitely begin all over again.

Peter would have been told that if he didn't comply with the Judaizers' demands it would cause a split with James and his church. Who would want to split from the Lord's own brother? Paul says fear was Peter's prime motivation for withdrawing from the Gentiles, and it must have been the same with Barnabas and the rest. This fear stemmed from the clever arguments and threats of the Judaizers. Wasn't Peter the apostle to the circumcised? Yet the men from James thought that his living like a Gentile would alienate the very people he was called to reach. They felt that if Peter continued to eat with Gentiles he would be reneging on his call to be an apostle to the Jews. The very unbelieving Jews that he was meant to reach would consider him unclean and reject him before he could ever preach the gospel to them. They insisted that Jewish believers should remain pure in their food and table fellowship. Maybe they even gave him an ultimatum: 'It's us or them – choose who you will eat with, Jew or Gentile!'

Peter, in trying to please the men from James, was actually putting the gospel into reverse gear. He was compelling the Gentiles

to live like Jews by sending them the message that unless they
became circumcised (for that was the reason they could not food-
fellowship with them), they would be socially cut off. In trying to
be diplomatic, he was allowing the Law to get its nose into the
church of Antioch.

The Lord's Supper

This attack by the Judaizers also struck at the heart of Christian fellowship – the Lord's Supper, breaking bread, Holy Communion.
This act of worship took place during fellowship meals in the
homes of believers. You can see what the end result would be of
bringing this ordinance under Jewish food and table fellowship
laws. It immediately excluded all those who were not circumcised.
Table fellowship was not just important for Jews; throughout the
Gentile world and in all ancient cultures the practice of hospitality
was the principal characteristic of a healthy community. Who you
ate with and who you didn't eat with was a tremendous statement.
One day Gentiles were breaking bread with Peter himself, the next
day they weren't allowed in the same room as him. I am sure that
many of the Gentiles, loving their leaders, would have seriously
considered circumcision to keep unity. But Paul would have none
of it, for he knew that the very gospel he had received from Christ
was being challenged.

Face to face with another gospel

Paul was left alone. Even Barnabas sided against him. But what
was the point of unity if the gospel itself was sacrificed? He knew
that Peter and Barnabas believed in the gospel by grace alone
with no 'add-ons', but they had been outmanoeuvred by the
Judaizers and had capitulated to the party of circumcision. When
he had left the Council of Jerusalem, Paul thought that the defeat
of circumcision was also the end of the Law in the church. He
hadn't been concerned by the request for Gentiles in Antioch not
to eat blood, strangled meat or food dedicated to idols. The
Gentiles were free from circumcision and thus the Law, so these

were to him only requests and nothing more. However, those of the circumcision party interpreted the food requests as an opportunity to put circumcision back on the agenda. If only the Council of Jerusalem had exhibited the boldness to pronounce all foods clean, instead of fudging the issue.

Paul publicly rebuked Peter because it was important that the Gentiles see that Peter and Barnabas's public withdrawal was dealt with openly. Paul called them hypocrites. The Greek word for 'hypocrite' means 'to play a part', and the phrase was used in regard to pretence. The act of withdrawing by Peter and Barnabas was totally inconsistent. They were deceived by the Judaizers into seeing the Law as a sanctifying force. To be saved in the beginning through faith and then to persevere through the Law was a contradiction in terms. But Peter, at this moment in time, couldn't see that and now neither could the Galatians who found themselves in a similar situation.

Peter, of course, was already circumcised; he didn't need to do that again, but his actions over table fellowship (and I don't believe Peter understood the consequences of his actions at the time) actually confirmed the requirement of circumcision – the very thing he had argued against at Jerusalem. Legalism usually sneaks into our lives through a side door without us noticing.

Paul was facing a church split. It must have been extremely disappointing and painful to have Barnabas oppose him. He saw that they were not walking straight towards the truth of the gospel. The picture is that their walk in the gospel had become one of limping in the wrong direction. We often think about people who backslide as those who are living in obvious, sinful practices, but to return to the Law or to become a legalist is equally to backslide from Christ. Peter and Barnabas were backslidden. Paul had to straighten out Peter as he had to straighten out the Galatians in regard to the gospel, the Law, and how to live in Christian freedom.

Paul loses at Antioch

I used to assume that Paul won the argument in Antioch, but actually there is no evidence here in Galatians to suggest that he did. We already know that the rest of the Jews joined Barnabas and Peter in their hypocrisy. If, during this incident, Peter had accepted Paul's rebuke and returned to table fellowship with Gentiles, Paul would certainly have mentioned it in this letter to the Galatians.

It seems that Paul's words fell on deaf ears; the Judaizers had won a victory in Antioch. It is interesting that from that time onwards, Antioch was no longer Paul's base for missions. He moved further away to Corinth and Ephesus. This Judaizing could have been truly crushed at Antioch, had Peter and Barnabas not compromised. But from now on, wherever Paul went, the Judaizers followed giving accounts of the food fight in Antioch, undermining his work and apostolic authority. This is what they had done in Galatia, and this is why Paul had to give his own version of past events to counter that of his enemies.

We know that by the time Paul wrote Romans, he felt so confident that he had won the battle over the gospel that he could be gracious and ask people to beware of stumbling, weaker brethren who were still struggling with aspects of legalism. Also, the absence of concern regarding Judaizers and circumcision in Paul's later letters shows us that the epistle to Galatians was successful in dealing with the arguments and opposition of the Judaizers.

The lessons to be learnt from the Antioch food fight are significant. When it comes to the truth of the real gospel there is absolutely no room for compromise, no matter how angry or offended people get. If you add anything to the gospel of grace, no matter how small, you have opened a door that will transform the good news of grace into a doctrine of salvation by works.

Antioch had fallen into theological error. Don't ever underestimate how hard it is to keep walking straight towards the truth of the gospel, for our fleshly nature is biased towards gaining security in religion, external laws and codes. We need to remember that the gospel is spiritual – it cannot be grasped by the carnal mind. Only the Holy Spirit can keep us in the true liberty of the gospel.

6.

Trusting in the Faith of Christ

(Gal. 2:15–21)

(15) We are Jews by nature and not 'Gentile sinners', (16) knowing that no human being is justified by works of the law but only through faith in Jesus Christ, and we have believed in Christ Jesus, in order that we might be justified by faith in Christ and not by the works of the law, because by works of the law shall no flesh be justified. (17) But if in seeking to be justified in Christ we find that we too are 'sinners', is then Christ a servant of sin? Impossible! (18) For if I build again the very things which I demolished, I demonstrate that I myself am a wrongdoer. (19) For I through the law died to the law, in order that I might live for God. I have been crucified with Christ; (20) and it is no longer I that lives, but Christ lives in me. And the life I now live in the flesh, I live by faith which is in the Son of God who loved me and gave himself for me. (21) I do not nullify the grace of God; for if righteousness is through the law, then Christ has died to no purpose.

This portion of Galatians is a continuation of Paul's remembrance of the Antioch food fight, and this is the actual argument that he put to Peter there. When he says, 'We are Jews . . .' he is recalling speaking to Peter, Barnabas and the Jewish Christians of Antioch.

Paul knows the significance that the Judaizers gave to the fact they were in a covenant relationship by the virtue of being Jews by birth. In verse 15 he quotes their own arguments back to them. The Gentiles were presumed sinners, because they did not hold to the covenant commandments, especially circumcision and food laws. Verse 16 is a powerful summary of Paul's whole teaching on justification and the word he uses for 'knowing' is *eidotes* – a word used to describe a well-known fact that is not open to debate. Paul says we know that no one is justified by the Law. He knows that Peter and Barnabas should never have questioned this established fact.

Justified

Justification means 'to be declared right', to be vindicated, to be put in the right. It is a legal term meaning that we are pronounced 'not guilty' by the judge. It isn't just about declaring someone not guilty of charges against them, however. It goes further than this, putting us in a positive position – like when someone goes to court and comes out both vindicated and compensated. Justified means 'Just-as-if-I'd never sinned'. We could go further by saying, 'It's just-as-if-I'd never sinned, aren't sinning or never will sin' because to be justified by faith is an act that deals with all past, present and future sin.

The words 'justified' and 'righteous' come from the same word in the Greek New Testament, *dikaio*. Paul is talking about how to be justified before God. How does a sinful human stand justified before a holy and righteous God? Certainly not through the Law. The Law of Moses was never given as a means of salvation, it was the guardian and tutor of Israel until Christ came (Gal. 3:24). So works of the Law could never put someone in right relationship with God. Even the sacrificial system included in the Law for the forgiveness of sins was only a temporary measure and a type of the sacrifice of Christ to come – it could not atone for sins in and of itself.

Sometimes, the Jewish understanding of the Law during this period has been unfairly portrayed by scholars. The argument has often been made that the Jews were striving for a perfect life that would qualify them to be accepted by God, and that through good works alone they believed that they could gain justification before him.

The majority of Jews knew they could not get the perfect 'A' grade required by following the Law. For most Jews, it was not about achieving a 100 per cent score in the Law to qualify them for heaven. They knew that it was by grace that they had been born a Jew, and they put their trust in God's election, faithfulness, mercy, and the atoning work of animal sacrifice to make up for their sins. The real concern to the Jew was not whether one lived perfectly or not, but that one kept inside the basic religious boundaries that identified a person as Jewish.

It may well be that the Judaizing Christians believed that Christ's death on the cross replaced the animal sacrifice part of the Law, but left the rest of the Law intact. They may have preached that a person was saved by faith in the blood of Christ's atonement in order to live according to the Law, and that his sacrifice covered mistakes and sins in a way that the former animal sacrifice foreshadowed. If this was the case, the expectation would be that all Christians must be circumcised and obey the Law to be a part of God's covenant. But Paul will soon make it clear that through the death of Christ we have actually died to the Law. Christ did not die to equip us to live under it.

The fundamental question of what made someone a Jew was also the question that would determine whether a person was part of God's saving covenant. If you didn't live within the fundamental covenant boundaries, you were therefore outside the promises of God, and lost. Now, to the Judaizers, there was nothing more fundamental in defining oneself as a Jew than circumcision, food and table fellowship laws. This is what the whole argument in Jerusalem, Antioch and now Galatia was all about.

Christ's faith saves

Someone once said, 'a little Greek is a dangerous thing' meaning that people who only know a few New Testament Greek words are liable to make errors. But it is also true to say that ignorance of Greek may be a dangerous thing, for without some knowledge of Greek we are totally dependent on the translators to interpret the correct meaning of New Testament Greek grammar. Always remember, whatever English version of the Bible you read has been translated by people who made a series of decisions regarding how to interpret certain words and phrases. The way that they translate particular passages can often be influenced by their own personal prejudice.

It was whilst listening to recordings of Dr R.T. Kendall's first ever Friday night teaching series at Westminster Chapel, London (1977), that the translation of this passage rendering 'faith *of* Christ' rather than 'faith *in* Christ' really made an impression on me. Indeed, this is how the King James Version actually translates the phrase in Galatians 2:16,20. R.T. Kendall believes that we should translate the passage like this: '. . . knowing that no human being is justified by works of the Law but only through *the faith of Jesus Christ*, and we have believed in Christ Jesus, in order that we might be justified *by the faith of Christ* and not by the works of the law, because by works of the law shall no flesh be justified.'

The italicized phrases in the above passage are genitive that is 'of Christ', not 'in Christ'. Although scholars have tried to make the case that the genitive in its context is objective (through faith in Jesus), Paul used this tense on purpose because he was trying to explain something about how the faith of Christ saves us.

Many evangelical Christians, when they refer to justification by faith, focus on the role played by *their own* faith in Christ and their own act of believing. This is important, but there is a deeper truth that makes our own act of faith rock solid. We are saved 'by the faith of Christ', and it is *his* faith and *his* faithfulness that is the foundation of our whole Christian life.

Faith as a work in contemporary Christianity

In contemporary Christianity, our own faith takes the pre-eminent role in most people's understanding of salvation. Your faith, or lack of it, becomes the crucial point concerning whether you are going to heaven or not. You may have faith in Christ today, but what if you don't tomorrow? How do you even know your present faith is genuine? What is your assurance that you have genuine faith?

The Puritans of the sixteenth and seventeenth century were obsessed by the question of how to know that their faith was authentic. They claimed to believe in justification by faith in Christ alone, but actually taught that you could only know the genuineness of your saving faith by the subsequent good works produced in your life. Misunderstanding the letter of James, they felt that they had to prove they had genuine saving faith by living a life of obedience to the moral Law. But the faith James talks about in his epistle is not referring to how to be saved from our sins. James is concerned that Christians put their faith to work in dealing with the trials of life and meeting such specific practical needs as hunger and nakedness. If Christians don't put their faith to work it is useless in this respect.

Have you ever wondered whether you are saved are not? Have you ever felt spiritually low and concerned that you may have lost your faith and salvation? Have you ever heard preachers tell you that if you don't live according to a certain standard of holiness, you risk losing your salvation? I heard one preacher say that you are only saved by the holiness that you display in your life today and that tomorrow, if you were to backslide into sin, you would lose your salvation.

What level of holy living must you attain in order to be sure that your faith is real and that you are truly saved? How many boxes do you need to tick in the list of righteous works to make the grade with God? Is saving faith only valid if it is accompanied by works? The Judaizers claimed that one was saved by faith in Christ, but then what? How did you demonstrate to those around you, and indeed yourself, that your faith was genuine? Surely by being circumcised and following the Law of Moses, they said.

Faith in his faith

Being justified by the faith of Christ simply means that we accept that our salvation was accomplished by his life, death and resurrection. Jesus' perfect faith in his Father and faultless obedience as his Son are credited to our account before God. We are saved by all that Jesus did in his life and ministry, culminating in his death, resurrection and ascension. Everything Jesus did was on our behalf. We are saved by his own life of faith and faithfulness to the Father.

The obedient life of Jesus and all his perfect works of faith were credited to us as if we had done them ourselves. That he was obedient on our behalf means that we don't need to trust our own obedience for salvation.

Imagine having a spiritual bank account. Before you came to Christ you were not just in debt to God through sin, you were declared completely and utterly spiritually bankrupt. But Christ redeemed you – and he did not just wipe out your eternal debt, reducing it to zero, he also deposited into your account all that he had accomplished. Everything he was, is and ever will be was accredited to your account before God. You have a positive righteousness before God that can never go into overdraft. You are a zillionaire in the Bank of Righteousness! Your salvation, your faith all rests on simple trust in what Jesus has done for you. His faith in God and his faithfulness to his Father has been credited to your account.

Who's holding who?

I remember a story of an air balloon disaster. The balloon was anchored to the ground by numerous ropes during a fair. Suddenly, a strong gust of wind broke the anchors and the balloon rapidly began to ascend. The immediate reaction of some men close by was to grab the nearest ropes and try to pull the balloon down. But another gust of wind jerked the balloon up with the men still holding on to the ropes and in an instant they found themselves too high to let go. They were soaring higher and higher, their arms beginning to ache with tiredness. A horrified crowd watched as first one and then another lost the strength to hold on and plummeted to their deaths. However, one man remained, his strength seemingly unconquerable. As he became but a dot in the sky, the crowd marvelled at his apparent superhuman strength.

Hours later, the balloon found its way back to earth with the man still attached and alive. An ambulance rushed to the scene, expecting to find the man in an extreme state of exhaustion. But when the man touched the ground he simply walked away in full vigour and strength. The paramedic wanted to examine him and couldn't understand how he had hung on to the rope for so long and yet was not fatigued. 'It was easy,' said the man. 'When I found myself in the air I tied the loose rope below me around my waist. I stopped holding onto the rope and let the rope hold onto me.'

Are you holding on to Christianity by the strength of your faith? Forget it. You can't work your faith well enough to hold on. At best you will become a legalist, trying to measure whether your faith is real by a process of constant self-examination. At worst you may faint and give up, exhausted from the burden of trying to prove your salvation, and then find yourself falling back into the paths of discouragement, sin and bondage. We are saved by the faith of Christ. He holds onto us (like the rope around the man's waist) so that we can never, ever fall from saving grace. All we need to do is accept and recognize this fact in our hearts, and we can celebrate our new life of liberty and assurance. The most profound question we can ask ourselves is not 'Do I have faith?' but 'Do I have Christ?'.

The famous theologian Karl Barth was so convinced that Jesus did everything for humanity's salvation that he went too far in his teaching. He said that we don't even need to believe at all, because Christ believed for us. In other words, *all* humanity is saved because Jesus did it all. Barth was right that Jesus believed God on our behalf, but we see in Galatians 2:16 that although the faith of Christ is mentioned twice, so *our faith* in him is also mentioned.

Christ did it all, but we must ratify his work in our hearts by faith. Like the man in the illustration, we have to put the rope around us to hold us. In other words, we must believe in him and his complete saving work. When the eyes of our hearts are supernaturally opened so that we can really 'see' what he did on our behalf, we have saving faith. Our imperfect faith now rests on his perfect and indestructible faith. Romans 1:16,17 speaks about us trusting in Christ's faith that justifies us

> For I am not ashamed of the gospel, for it is the power of God for salvation to everyone who believes, to the Jew first and also to the Greek. For in it the righteousness of God is revealed from faith to faith; as it is written, 'BUT THE RIGHTEOUS man SHALL LIVE BY FAITH.' (NASB)

These verses are talking about the righteousness of God being revealed by the faith of Christ – what he did in his life, death, resurrection and ascension on our behalf. We believe because it has been revealed from his faith to our faith. The faith of Christ has been imparted into our hearts.

The two men

The first Adam's original sin was unbelief, as he succumbed to the lies of the serpent. By comparison, Jesus, the second Adam, had perfect faith in God and lived an unblemished obedient life of faith on earth. Adam failed his satanic temptation, but Jesus passed his. We were damned by Adam's act of unbelief, but we are saved by Christ's obedient life of faith

> For if by the transgression of the one, death reigned through the one, much more those who receive the abundance of grace and of the gift of righteousness will reign in life through the One, Jesus Christ. So then as through one transgression there resulted condemnation to all men, even so through one act of righteousness there resulted justification of life to all men. For as through the one man's disobedience the many were made sinners, even so through the obedience of the One the many will be made righteous. (Rom. 5:17–19, NASB)

Can you see that just as one man ruined us by his unbelief, one man saved us by his obedient faith? Christ did at all! There is nothing for us to do to get to heaven but to look to him. It is his obedience, not ours, that justifies.

The just shall live by faith

Paul quotes Habakkuk 2:4 in Romans 1:17 and Galatians 3:11. It is also referred to in Hebrews 10:38.

> Behold, as for the proud one, His soul is not right within him; But the righteous will live by his faith. (Hab. 2:4, NASB)

The phrase 'the just (or righteous) shall live by faith' was the cornerstone verse of Luther's Reformation in the sixteenth century.

In this passage, the prophet Habakkuk has been waiting on the Lord for his word. The answer comes that he is to write on a tablet for the appointed time. Two types of people are then described. The first type of person is not just; he is proud, self-sufficient, lifted up. This man will not wait for the vision; he will do it his way. The second type of person is righteous; he will wait for the promise because he has faith in the reliability and faithfulness of the Promise Giver to deliver.

You can translate verse 4 as 'the just will live by his faith' or just as easily, 'the just will live by his faith/faithfulness' – that is, the faith/faithfulness of God. The Jewish Qumran community in their commentary on this verse translated it 'the just will live by God's faithfulness' and this was also the way that the Jews traditionally understood this verse. This trusting in the faithfulness of the Promise Giver is exactly what Paul means in Romans 1:17 when he says that 'the righteousness of God is revealed from faith to faith' (NASB), and he quotes Habakkuk 2:4 to explain this. The righteousness of God is revealed from Christ's faith to our faith. Christ's faith and our faith are connected. Our faith is founded on his faithfulness.

When this verse is quoted in Hebrews for the third time in the New Testament, it is from the perspective of not casting away our confidence, but remaining patient in order to receive what is promised. Again, it is trusting and resting on the reliability of the Promise Giver to do what he has promised – it is having faith in his faithfulness. The object of our faith is the faithfulness of God to his promises. *Living by faith is all about a personal trust in the reliability of God.*

So, when it comes to being saved and justified before God, there is nothing for us to do but simply believe that Jesus did it all for us. From Christ's birth to his ascension, his whole life was substitutionary. As far as being justified is concerned there are no salvation caveats, no arbitrary church moral codes, no Law, no works of faith to confirm salvation, no acts of personal obedience, nothing, absolutely nothing, but simply trusting in him.

This is the gospel of Jesus Christ.

Preaching Christ as a minister of sin?

There may be some readers who are a little perplexed by what I
have been saying. Am I saying that you can be justified by faith
and yet remain in sin? That we have a license to sin because our
standing before God is dependent on faith in Christ alone? Am I
preaching a Christ who says that it doesn't matter how you live?
Have I made Christ a minister of sin?

This was exactly the accusation made against Paul's teaching –
that his message of free grace was a license and encouragement
to sin. But the accusation is mistaken. The gospel of grace is actually a license to be *free* from sin! Such false allegations forget that
the very purpose of the gospel is to deliver us from the realm and
power of sin. Nevertheless, it is possible to be justified by faith
and yet remain in sin and abuse the grace of God and this, as we
shall see later in Galatians 5, is a very serious, sorrowful and self-
destructive situation to be in.

The very nature of grace requires that it must always remain
open to abuse. Paul in verse 17 and also in Romans had a habit of
anticipating people's reaction to his gospel message. It was as if
he was saying, 'I know what you're thinking, and these are the
questions that some of you knee-jerkers will be asking.' Here are
some examples of Paul anticipating his reader's objections

> But if, while seeking to be justified in Christ, we ourselves have
> also been found sinners, is Christ then a minister of sin? May it
> never be! (v. 17, NASB)

> What shall we say then? Are we to continue in sin so that grace
> may increase? May it never be! How shall we who died to sin still
> live in it? (Rom. 6:1,2, NASB)

> For sin shall not be master over you, for you are not under law but
> under grace. What then? Shall we sin because we are not under
> law but under grace? May it never be! (Rom. 6:14,15, NASB)

Have you noticed how Paul often uses the same phrase, 'May it
never be!'? Paul points out that such reactions to his gospel are
not just slight misunderstandings of what he is teaching; these

responses are mischievous and to be rejected outright. The three questions asked above are subversive and hostile to his teaching, not just simple honest queries. They were levelled at him by the Judaizers, who spread vicious rumours that Paul was a libertine. But if we find that we ourselves have sympathy with their accusations, it is because we don't yet understand what Paul is really saying.

My question to all ministers of the gospel is this: have you ever been misinterpreted in the same way Paul was? If not, I guarantee you aren't preaching the New Testament gospel.

The three passages from Romans I quoted are important because they all deal with the same kind of accusation that Paul dealt with in Galatians 2:17. Paul has bypassed the Law by talking about seeking justification in Christ while we are still sinners. The incredible thing is that Christ justifies the ungodly whilst they are in that sinful state. Only faith in Christ is required. This in turn leads to the false charge that because justification is all of grace, it is like being given a license to sin – that Christ is a minister of sin because he makes sin permissible. The allegation is that Paul was claiming that the more we sin, the more we will be forgiven and thus the more the grace of Christ will be demonstrated; that because the Law has no power over us we can now sin all we like. Paul's answer is, 'May it never be!'

Dead to sin

We will look at the ethics and moral principles of the gospel in Galatians 5 and 6, but a brief allusion to Paul's answer to these accusations should also be made here.

Those who believed that Paul's gospel promoted and excused sin couldn't be more deluded. The gospel's primary purpose is to deliver us from the realm and authority of sin, which is the very opposite to a life of fleshly, sinful indulgence. Dr Martyn Lloyd-Jones put it like this in his book on Romans 6

What is the business of grace? Is it to allow us to continue in sin? It is to deliver us from the bondage and the reign of sin, and to put us under the reign of grace. So when a man asks, 'Shall we

continue in sin that grace may abound?' he is merely showing that
he has failed to understand either the tyranny of the reign of sin,
or the whole object and purpose of grace and its marvellous reign
over those who are saved . . . A man who is justified, and who is
under the reign of grace, cannot think like that, still less act like
that.[1]

The answer to all these accusations is found in one word, *death*.
Romans 6:1 declares that we won't continue in sin because 'How
shall we who died to sin still live in it?' (NASB) Throughout the
rest of Romans 6 Paul explains how we have been severed from
our enemy, sin, through death

> Or do you not know that all of us who have been baptized into
> Christ Jesus have been baptized into His death? Therefore we have
> been buried with Him through baptism into death. (vv. 3,4, NASB)

> For if we have become united with Him in the likeness of His
> death . . . (v. 5, NASB)

> knowing . . . that our old self was crucified with Him, in order that
> our body of sin might be done away with, so that we would no
> longer be slaves to sin; for he who has died is freed from sin. (vv.
> 6,7, NASB)

> Even so consider yourself dead to sin, but alive to God in Christ
> Jesus. (v. 11, NASB)

This theme of death to sin as an answer to the charge of licentiousness is also made by Paul in Galatians 2 to answer the claim
that he had made Christ a minister of sin

> (19) For I through the law died to the law, in order that I might live
> for God. I have been crucified with Christ; (20) and it is no longer
> I that lives, but Christ lives in me . . .

When we are born again (regenerated) we receive life – it is a
new, miraculous birth within us. We are raised spiritually from

the dead. Regeneration (being born again) translates us from the realm of sin into the realm of grace; it translates us from being 'in Adam' to being 'in Christ'. When we are born again, we are not just made *alive* in Christ, we also *die* to sin and its power! When Christ fulfilled the Law and died for our sins, we also died to the Law. Because of our union with Christ, we can say that in him we have fulfilled the Law. We have died to it, so we are free to live unto God without fulfilling any rules or regulations. We have complete access to the Father's love by faith.

The wall of the Law that separated humanity from God by exposing human sin has been demolished by Christ's death. Paul couldn't understand why we would want to build up the Law's wall of separation again and put ourselves once more under judgement for sin. And this is what the Judaizers were doing in Galatia. Brick by brick they were rebuilding the very wall that Christ had demolished.

Christ united!

We often hear the phrase about us being 'in Christ', but what does that mean? The unregenerate person is counted as being 'in Adam', meaning that everything that happened to Adam at his fall also happened to his offspring. The judgement that Adam received, we all also received. His curse became our curse, and the sin and death that reigned in fallen Adam also reigned in us. All that the fallen Adam became we also became. All the judgement he received through sin we also suffered, for we were united with Adam (Rom. 5:12–21).

But when we were regenerated we were severed from Adam and our 'old man' (everything we were in Adam) died (Rom. 6:3–6). Now we find ourselves in Christ, and everything Jesus became through his obedience we too become, because we have been united to him. His righteousness before the Father now becomes ours. His obedience to God becomes our obedience to God. His life is our life, his death is our death, his burial our burial, his resurrection our resurrection. His reign on high is our reign on high, for we are even seated with him in heavenly places (Eph. 2:6).

When Jesus died, 'He died to sin once for all; but the life that He lives, He lives to God' (Rom. 6:10). When Christ died he was separated from the realm and sphere in which sin operated, and because we are united in his death, so we also have died once and for all to the realm of sin. His crucifixion was, in reality, also our crucifixion. His burial was indeed our burial.

When someone physically dies, they depart this life and this world. Once dead, we can't communicate with this world any longer and we can't walk or talk in it any more. We have been translated into a new realm, either heaven or hell, and there is no return. In the same way, through faith in Christ, we have been crucified with Christ, we have died to sin, and we have died to the Law. We can no longer function in the realm of sin, for we have been translated into the realm of grace.

The idea that a Christian should yield to temptation and carnal passions is exceedingly hard to understand in the light of this. The idea that a Christian should have died to sin in order to live and then revel in it once again is utterly preposterous! Any Christian who abuses grace for sinning purposes is a creature of contradiction.

Living by the faith of Christ

(19) . . . I have been crucified with Christ; (20) and it is no longer I that lives, but Christ lives in me. And the life I now live in the flesh, I live by faith which is in the Son of God who loved me and gave himself for me. (21) I do not nullify the grace of God; for if righteousness is through the law, then Christ has died to no purpose.

When Paul says he died to sin and the Law, the means of that death was Christ's crucifixion. When Paul says he was crucified with Christ, he means it in two ways. Firstly, Paul was crucified with Christ in a legal and positional sense in regard to sin and the Law. Secondly, being crucified with Christ was a present experience for Paul. He now lived without any thought or reference to the Law and its rules, and viewed his daily Christian life through a new, radical perspective. He lived each day as if he was a walking dead man.

Having the knowledge that he was delivered from sin's power into the realm of God's grace, and knowing he was dead to the Law, Paul reflected on what this meant to his daily way of life. The continued use of 'I' in the text demonstrates this: I have been crucified, it is no longer I that live, the life I now live, I live by the faith of the Son of God. When Paul says he no longer lives, he means that his focus is no longer on himself. He no longer tries to be saved through works; he no longer puts any trust in his own faith, his own abilities and skills. He has decided to know only Christ and Christ crucified. His focus is on a new personality – Jesus Christ. Paul no longer lives, but Christ lives in him. It is all about the formation of Christ in his life.

When trying to explain this to Bible students in lectures, I usually ask them to try to imagine that while I was teaching I suddenly fell to the floor, dead. Bruce died and all that is left is my body. Then I ask them to imagine Jesus suddenly and supernaturally entering my empty dead body. I jump up, looking the same on the outside, but I'm not there on the inside – it's Jesus in my body. My teaching suddenly has a new note of authority, my anointing soars because Jesus is using my body and I'm not in it, I'm dead. The illustration is obviously only partially helpful, but it is true that Jesus really does live inside us by his Spirit. The important thing is that Paul yielded himself to the life of Christ within. He was dead to the flesh and alive to the Holy Spirit. In his daily life he deferred to Christ in all his words and actions. Paul is introducing us here to the concept of walking by the Spirit that he will teach us about in chapter 5.

How do you actually live by the faith of Jesus? Well, have you ever found yourself in a position where you are trying to have as much faith as possible for a situation in your life? Maybe you are trying to have faith for healing, and you are believing as hard as you can. Or you are facing a trial or a test and you need mountain-moving faith.

Relying on your own works of faith assumes that we all have an internal 'faith generator' that produces power for Christian living. But to live by the faith of Christ is not to generate our own faith, but rather to plug in to the current of his faith within us and allow it to flow through us. Like plugging an electrical appliance into the national grid, we can plug our lives into the grid of the Spirit of faith.

The anointing and the gifts of the Spirit are all manifestations of Christ working through us. We should be in total trust, drawing on Christ's overcoming faith which dwells within us. We are to be a conduit for his faith to flow through.

I remember when I used to pray for people in the healing lines at Kensington Temple. I tried so hard to believe, it was exhausting! Now all I do is to try to prevent unbelief, sin and thoughts of inferiority from becoming resistors to the current of Christ's faith that seeks to touch those who need a miracle. I just die and let him live. I remove the barriers to his faith and let him flow out of me.

I remember a situation facing one of my KT cell members. He was so under pressure from a particular circumstance in his life that he was convinced he would cave in. The next day was going to be so difficult for him that he didn't know how he would get through it. He said his faith was gone and he couldn't pray. He asked if I would pray and believe God on his behalf for the whole of the next day. He said, 'I believe that if my leader is praying and believing God for me the whole of tomorrow, it will all be OK, because I trust in your prayers and faith because you're a man of God.'

It wasn't the time to instruct him on the failings he obviously had not yet observed in my life, nor to tell him piously to trust in God alone. The man was desperate. I agreed and relief swept over his face as stress did over mine. 'You are now carrying my burden, Bruce, and I am ready to face whatever happens in the next twenty-four hours.' Well, I did my best the next day to honour my commitment, but unlike Jesus I don't live ever more to make intercession.

When I saw him at my next cell group, he said, 'It was as tough as I imagined, but every time I wavered I pictured you on your knees, Bruce, praying for me, and I knew it would be all right.' I smiled uneasily and told him not to mention it – after all, what are cell groups for if not for members to support one another?

Now, forgetting about my weakness and inability to live up to his full expectations of me, this is a picture of how we should live by the faith of Christ (and not 'by the faith of' our leader). We looked earlier at the man in Habakkuk 2:4 who was trusting in the faith or faithfulness of God to live his life, believing that God would not fail is in his promises. That is exactly what Paul is talking about when he says that he lives by the faith of the Son of God. It isn't about how much faith we have, it is about how much faith and faithfulness Christ has towards us (from his faith to our faith). That excites me because I can live by that. My cell member went on to mature and to put the same faith he had in a so-called 'man of God' into the Man who is God.

Didn't this happen also to Peter, whom Christ prayed for?

> Simon, Simon, behold, Satan has demanded permission to sift you like wheat; but I have prayed for you, that your faith may not fail; and you, when once you have turned again, strengthen your brothers. (Luke 22:31,32, NASB)

Our faith is, trusting and making a demand on his unfailing faithfulness. This isn't a mechanical action, and the illustrations I made are weak because really the closer and more intimate you are with Christ the greater your capacity to receive from his faith into your faith – that is, from faith to faith. This is Paul's point, that he is practically living in the flesh by energetically releasing Christ's faith into every part of his life. We will explain the role of the Spirit in this later on in Galatians 5.

> (21) I do not nullify the grace of God; for if righteousness is through the law, then Christ has died to no purpose.

Paul now brings the history of his argument with Peter in Antioch to a close. To retreat behind the boundaries of the Law, or to build moral regulations as walls of protection for grace, is unacceptable. Moral or religious codes do not protect the integrity of the gospel, but actually nullify the grace of God. The word 'nullifies' means 'render ineffective, inoperable'.

Jesus Christ has broken through all the boundaries that kept human beings from God. Christ did it all, but if we are not persuaded of this fact we render his saving work powerless in our lives. We must ratify his perfect faith by our faith. We must be convinced in our heart that we are saved by grace alone, otherwise we nullify its effect in our lives and enslave ourselves all over again.

7.

Receiving the Spirit with Power

(Gal. 3:1–5)

(1) You foolish Galatians! Who has bewitched you – you before whose eyes Jesus Christ was openly portrayed as crucified? (2) This only I want to learn from you: was it by works of the law that you received the Spirit, or by hearing with faith? (3) Are you so foolish? Having begun with the Spirit are you now made complete with the flesh? (4) Have you experienced so much in vain? If it is indeed in vain. (5) So I ask again, he who supplies the Spirit to you and works miracles among you, is it by the works of the law or by hearing with faith?

When Paul first addressed the Galatians, his frustration and anger were palpable. Now turning to speak directly to them once again, his feelings have not diminished. Paul turns from his own personal testimony to the testimony of the Galatians themselves.

Lost assurance

The Galatians had lost their assurance that they were saved by faith alone. The Judaizers had disturbed the Galatians's peace, making them believe that the only sure way to maintain God's acceptance was to be circumcised and follow the Law. Their stupidity in listening to the Judaizers astounded Paul. He tells them straight, in the vocative tense emphasizing emotion, 'You foolish Galatians!'

The Greek word for 'bewitched' is *baskaino*, and describes the Galatians as having fallen under a demonic spell. The scholar F.F. Bruce translated the phrase as 'who has hypnotized you?'

Hypnotize is a good translation because *baskaino* was historically connected to the power of the 'evil eye' (belief in the power that a person could harm someone with a glance). The Galatians had lost the clarity of their gospel vision. They had literally lost their spiritual sight, hypnotized by a false gospel. They were distracted by religious rules, and had taken their eyes off Jesus. How could their vision of the true gospel be restored? Only by having a fresh vision of Christ crucified would they be able to recover their assurance of faith.

A portrait of Christ crucified

Having accused the Galatians with the charge of being under a spell, Paul reminds them that the power to break the 'hypnotic' influence of the Judaizers is Christ crucified. Why couldn't they remember that before their very eyes Christ was portrayed as crucified? Paul had painted vivid images of Christ on the cross to the Galatians through his preaching. Using dramatic language to create a vision of Christ's death, Paul preached the gospel with passion. He understood that the actual proclamation of Christ's death has power to break the hold of sin and Satan over people's lives. We see the message of Christ crucified as central to his preaching in 1 Corinthians 1

> For the word of the cross is foolishness to those who are perishing, but to us who are being saved it is the power of God. (1 Cor. 1:18, NASB)

> but we preach Christ crucified, to Jews a stumbling block and to Gentiles foolishness, but to those who are called, both Jews and Greeks, Christ the power of God and the wisdom of God. (1 Cor. 1:23,24, NASB)

> For I determined to know nothing among you except Jesus Christ, and Him crucified. (1 Cor. 2:2, NASB)

The death of Christ is essential in Paul's understanding of the incapacity of the Law to save. At the heart of the Law was sacrifice, and the Jews relied on it to cover their sins and failings whilst walking according to the Law. The death of Christ fulfilled these sacrifices, and sacrifices of the Mosaic Law couldn't 'cover' sins any longer. The sacrificial system was merely a shadow and type of the cross – it had no power in itself, but only in what it anticipated. Since the coming of Christ, the Law no longer has recourse to atoning sacrifice. To follow the Law and be saved now entails 100 per cent obedience with no slip-ups, and Paul will make this clear (Gal. 3:10).

> For indeed Christ, our Passover, was sacrificed for us. (1 Cor. 5:7, NKJV)

Paul preached a life-changing encounter with the historic event of the cross. The death of Christ is at the heart of the gospel of grace and the Christian's experience of freedom from sin. Christ was crucified for our sins and we, by his death, have also been crucified and are dead to sin and the Law. The lifting up of the cross through proclamation actually releases divine supernatural power (1 Cor. 1:18). Jesus said

> As Moses lifted up the serpent in the wilderness, even so must the Son of Man be lifted up; so that whoever believes will in Him have eternal life. (John 3:14,15, NASB)

The striking thing about Jesus' reference to the serpent of Moses is that just as the poisoned Israelites had to look to the serpent high on the pole to be cured, so Jesus is saying that people need to look upon him crucified in order to be saved. Believing is looking to Christ crucified. Unbelief is taking your eyes off the cross and looking to other things for justification. In 2 Corinthians Paul parallels faith with sight and unbelief with blindness.

> And even if our gospel is veiled, it is veiled to those who are perishing, in whose case the god of this world has blinded the minds of the unbelieving so that they might not see the light of the gospel of the glory of Christ, who is the image of God. (2 Cor. 4:3,4, NASB)

So in Galatians 3, Paul rebukes the church for falling into a legalistic, hypnotic spell, blinding themselves to the portrait of Christ painted through preaching. It is back to basics for the Galatians, and there is nothing more fundamental in the Christian faith than Christ crucified.

The gift of the Spirit: God's promise

> (2) This only I want to learn from you: was it by works of the law that you received the Spirit, or by hearing with faith?

Paul asks the Galatians an astonishing question. He is so sure of the answer that he can base his whole defence of justification by faith alone on the expected reply. Indeed, this was the only question he needed to ask to win his case. Paul asked them about an experience that was common to them all, a supernatural encounter that couldn't be doubted – one that was personal in nature and yet also observable to others. This experience was the reception of the Spirit, also known as the baptism in the Holy Spirit or the gift of the Spirit. Paul appeals to this experience of the reception of the Spirit as evidence that the Galatians are justified without the Law.

The reception of the Spirit is the final stage in Christian initiation. Regeneration (being born again) leads to faith, bringing justification. Justification brings righteousness (right standing and total acceptance before God). Righteousness before God means that we can now subsequently receive, by faith, the gift of the Spirit.

The baptism in the Holy Spirit is not the beginning of the Spirit's work in a life. The Spirit is at work in the Christian's life long before he is even saved. The Holy Spirit works regeneration, conviction of sin, and he gives us the gift of faith. Any view stating that the Holy Spirit is not already actively at work in a Christian's life until the baptism in the Holy Spirit is false.

There have been endless discussions about whether someone can be justified but not yet have received the Spirit. Of course this is possible, but such a Christian would be a bizarre anomaly in the church of Galatia, and indeed in the New Testament age itself. As brand new Christians all the Galatians would have been taught to expect and receive the gift of the Spirit and that is why Paul could use it so effectively as an argument.

Because all the Galatians had received the Spirit, some assume that all Christians throughout history must also have received the Spirit automatically at the moment of their conversion. They conclude that receiving the Spirit is simply justification by another name. Yet receiving the Spirit is always an objective experience in the New Testament. This experience was common to all in the Galatian church and so self-evident that there could be no argument or confusion about it having taken place in their lives.

Receiving the Spirit is a conscious, charismatic encounter. You do not automatically receive the Spirit when you first believe (although the Spirit has been active in your life through regeneration and so on).

Paul is clear that the reception of the Spirit can be externally verified. People who believe that receiving the Spirit is equal to conversion are often at pains to make it a thoroughly subjective experience (or not an experience at all); after all, they could hardly make a believer's justification dependent on a charismatic experience such as speaking in tongues, could they? This is why one can indeed be saved but not yet baptized in the Spirit. Christ is the only assurance our faith ever needs, but as we will see, receiving the Spirit does bring us great assurance of salvation, and that is the point Paul is making to the Galatians.

This is really an important issue to ponder. Let me quote Professor James Dunn who believes that the baptism in the Holy Spirit is Christian conversion. The extract is taken from his concluding paragraph in his classic book, *Baptism in the Holy Spirit.*

> But there is an even more basic question which our conclusions raise, and one which must be answered before these other questions can be fully dealt with. Accepting that the gift of the Spirit is what makes a man a Christian, how does he and others know if and when he has received the Spirit? In what ways does the Spirit manifest his coming and presence? What indications are there that the Spirit is active in a congregation or in a situation? Clearly these are questions of the first importance at all points of Christian life and activity. And in case it should be thought that I have been less than just to the Pentecostals, let me simply add in reference to these questions that Pentecostal teaching on spiritual gifts, including glossolalia [speaking in tongues], while still unbalanced, is

much more soundly based on the New Testament than is generally recognised. But here and now I can only point out the rele-
vance of these issues, since to discuss the manifestations of the
Spirit is subject in itself.[1]

Professor Dunn rightly highlights a practical difficulty of identifying the baptism in the Holy Spirit with justification. For the
baptism in the Spirit or the receiving of the Spirit is indeed a
charismatic experience accompanied by supernatural signs. But
the baptism in the Holy Spirit is not regeneration, nor is it justification; it is subsequent to them both. In Ephesians 1:13,14 we
have a picture of what Paul is describing here in Galatians

> And you also were included in Christ when you heard the word
> of truth, the gospel of your salvation. Having believed, you were
> marked in him with a seal, the promised Holy Spirit, who is a
> deposit guaranteeing our inheritance until the redemption of
> those who are God's possession – to the praise of his glory. (NIV)

The major point here is that only *after* believing can you then
receive the promised Holy Spirit. If the Holy Spirit is a seal, then
there must be something already present for him to seal and that
is our justification. The Holy Spirit is a 'down payment', a deposit
guaranteeing our future glorification at Christ's return. He is the
first fruits of our salvation

> And not only this, but also we ourselves, having the first fruits of
> the Spirit, even we ourselves groan within ourselves, waiting
> eagerly for our adoption as sons, the redemption of our body.
> (Rom. 8:23, NASB)

Guarantee and seal

The Greek word used by Paul for guarantee or pledge is *arrabon*
(2 Cor. 1:22; 5:5; Eph. 1:14) and was used in commercial business
transactions. In selling and purchasing the *arrabon* was the
advance payment or deposit guaranteeing that the full payment
would eventually be made. The gift of the Holy Spirit is a foretaste

of the fullness of life that will be experienced in heaven – a pledge and guarantee that God will fulfil his promise of bringing the Christian into the fullness of glory. The baptism in the Spirit is the start of a lifelong experience of the first instalments of the kingdom of heaven. The future, full payment will result in literal glorification.

What is a seal? A seal is something that confirms or makes secure. We use phrases like 'signed, sealed and delivered' or 'he gave his seal of approval'. A law signed by a king would also carry the imprint of his seal ring in wax upon it. On jars of food we read 'Do not open if the seal has been broken'. The jar lid may be shut, but is it sealed, is it secure?

In his book *Flesh and Spirit*, William Barclay writes

> In the ancient world of trade a seal was commonly used much as a trade-mark is used today. It was the sign of ownership, or the proof that an article was the product of a certain man or firm. So, for instance, jars of wine were sealed with the seal of the owner of the vineyard from which they came. This, then, means that the possession of the Holy Spirit is the guarantee that a man belongs to God. The possession of the Spirit is God's trade-mark upon a man.[2]

The gift of the Spirit seals our salvation by giving us assurance. The gift of the Spirit Paul is referring to here in Galatians intensifies and magnifies what we already know by faith – that we are accepted by God. Here are some other passages that highlight the assurance aspect of the baptism in the Holy Spirit

> Because you are sons, God has sent forth the Spirit of His Son into our hearts, crying, 'Abba! Father!' (Gal. 4:6, NASB)

> and hope does not disappoint, because the love of God has been poured out within our hearts through the Holy Spirit who was given to us. (Rom. 5:5, NASB)

> For you have not received a spirit of slavery leading to fear again, but you have received a spirit of adoption as sons by which we cry out, 'Abba! Father!' The Spirit Himself testifies with our spirit that

we are children of God, and if children, heirs also, heirs of God and fellow heirs with Christ. (Rom. 8:15–17, NASB)

Now He who establishes us with you in Christ and anointed us is God, who also sealed us and gave us the Spirit in our hearts as a pledge. (2 Cor. 1:22, NASB)

All these passages speak about the assurance of being a child of God that the Holy Spirit gives to us when we receive him. To receive the Spirit is to receive the spirit of adoption. You are already adopted by the Father at your justification, but with the baptism in the Holy Spirit you receive direct witness by the Holy Spirit to your spirit that God is indeed your Father.

It is interesting that this experience speaks of an emotional 'crying out' of 'Abba! Father!' I wonder if this verbal utterance of assurance is linked to the gift of speaking in tongues that accompanies the baptism in the Spirit? The pouring of the Spirit into our hearts brings the guarantee that we are children of God, heirs with Christ with an eternal hope of glory. The Galatians had all experienced this, and that is why Paul knew that this argument was indisputable. They had all experienced the reception of the Spirit and his direct assurance, without having been circumcised and without the Law.

Remember that when Jesus was baptized by John and the Holy Spirit descended upon him, this was also accompanied by filial assurance from his Father in heaven

And the Holy Spirit descended in bodily form like a dove upon Him, and a voice came from heaven which said, 'You are My beloved Son; in You I am well pleased.' (Luke 3:22, NKJV)

Jesus already knew that he was God's Son, but this experience with the Holy Spirit must have been one of great assurance to him. The words of his Father sealed in his heart what he already knew. Note that the Father did not say, 'He is my beloved Son' but 'You are my beloved Son'. Jesus was given a direct experience of assurance by his Father – how amazing. This was a witness both to Jesus and, secondarily, to all present, that he was truly the Son of God. In Acts we see that Peter understood that the baptism

in the Holy Spirit was a witness not only to those who received
it, but also to those who observed it.

> While Peter was still speaking these words, the Holy Spirit fell
> upon all those who were listening to the message. All the circum-
> cised believers who came with Peter were amazed, because the
> gift of the Holy Spirit had been poured out on the Gentiles also.
> For they were hearing them speaking with tongues and exalting
> God. Then Peter answered, 'Surely no one can refuse the water for
> these to be baptized who have received the Holy Spirit just as we
> did, can he?' (Acts 10:44–47, NASB)

At the Council of Jerusalem, Peter made the case that the
Gentiles' baptism in the Holy Spirit was clear evidence that they
were justified without circumcision or the Law, and this is the
same argument being used by Paul here in Galatians.

Peter states

> Brethren, you know that in the early days God made a choice
> among you, that by my mouth the Gentiles would hear the word
> of the gospel and believe. And God, who knows the heart, testified
> to them giving them the Holy Spirit just as He also did to us; and
> He made no distinction between us and them, cleansing their
> hearts by faith. Now therefore why do you put God to the test by
> placing upon the neck of the disciples a yoke which neither our
> fathers nor we have been able to bear? But we believe that we are
> saved through the grace of the Lord Jesus, in the same way as they
> also are. (Acts 15:7–11, NASB)

Peter understood the gift of the Spirit as a *testimony* to the fact
that the Gentiles had clean hearts through faith, for they could
not receive the Spirit if they had not first been saved through
faith. The grace that saved them cleansed their hearts ready for
the baptism in the Spirit to take place. Receiving the gift of the
Spirit assured the Gentiles and the observing Peter that they were
indeed saved.

Initial evidence

There is a tremendous amount of ignorance regarding the initial evidence that accompanies the gift of the Spirit. I have said that both Paul and the Galatians were clear about the fact that they all received the Spirit through an experience which was not only internally, but also externally, verifiable. Here, in Galatians, Paul took it for granted that they all understood the nature and common experience of the reception of the Spirit.

Peter externally verified the baptism in the Spirit of the first Gentiles. He saw irrefutable evidence that convinced him that the reception of the Spirit had indeed happened amongst them. This evidence also persuaded the Jews that were with him at the time, and even later helped carry the day at the Council of Jerusalem.

The proof that the Gentiles had received the Spirit was clearly mentioned by Peter – that they spoke with tongues and exalted God. Some have thought that 'exalting God' without tongues would be evidence enough of the Spirit's reception. But what manner of so-called exaltations would be proof of the Spirit's reception? Any answer would be lost in mists of subjectivity. Had there been no speaking in tongues, Peter would not have had the objective evidence to convince himself, let alone Gentile-phobic Jerusalem, that the Spirit was being poured out on non-Jewish believers.

Peter and the apostles had also spoken with tongues when they received the Spirit on the day of Pentecost, and this is what Peter means when he says: 'And God, who knows the heart, testified to them giving them the Holy Spirit *just as He also did to us*' (NASB, emphasis added).

This is not the place to make a full defence of speaking in tongues as the initial evidence of the baptism in the Holy Spirit, for that would be a book in itself. And I am resisting the temptation to move to other verses that are not so directly related to Galatians 3. However, it must be said that the only indisputable initial evidence of the Spirit's reception in the New Testament is speaking in tongues.

Those who teach that the baptism in the Holy Spirit is accompanied by general 'supernatural signs' must further identify what these signs are. Over the years, I have seen supernatural phenomena occur in revival meetings that has affected not only believers, but unbelievers too. Can falling under the power of God be the evidence of Spirit-reception? Can shaking? Laughter and joy? Can healing be the evidence? I have witnessed all these manifestations happen to unbelievers in revival outpourings too, without them being converted. Now some or all of the above signs and more may take place at Spirit-reception, but it is only the gift of tongues that should be understood as normative.

The experience of the baptism in the Holy Spirit is so objectively recognized in the New Testament Christian community that reference to it can even settle theological debates – first Peter in Jerusalem and now Paul in Galatia. This is why I believe that speaking in tongues *is* the initial evidence of the baptism in the Holy Spirit. Whatever else might occur during Spirit baptism, the New Testament teaches us to expect speaking in other tongues.

Walking by the Spirit

The assurance of the gift of the Spirit is at the heart of Paul's argument in this chapter, but he also refers to other aspects of the baptism in the Holy Spirit.

> (3) Are you so foolish? Having begun with the Spirit are you now made complete with the flesh?

We have already mentioned that the reception of the Spirit is part of Christian beginnings. Paul explains to the Galatians that if they were justified and then sealed by the Spirit at the start of their Christian lives, why would they later turn to a righteousness of works? How foolish!

Many Christians today fall into the Galatians' error of beginning with the Spirit and then trying to progress by the flesh. They think that our faith must be expressed by our Christian works to be genuine. They would heartily preach that a person is justified by faith alone, but only to begin with. However, their discipleship teaching makes it plain that true saving faith is only validated by sustained works and obedience to moral law. If you find yourself trying to maintain your justification by works, by dos and don'ts, then you are just like the Galatians.

The Spirit was not just given for assurance; he was also given to live by. The Holy Spirit provides divine power and enabling for the whole of the Christian life. The 'flesh' stands for human frailty devoid of divine help; the flesh is self-serving, self-centred and self-indulgent. The gift of the Holy Spirit brings the believer into a new realm of supernatural living through a vibrant relationship with the Spirit.

Paul says that he is crucified with Christ and that the life he now lives is by the faith of the Son of God. This is the same as saying that the life he now lives is by walking in the Spirit. How absurd to receive the assurance of the Spirit and to then refuse his assistance in living the Christian life and, instead, turn to live by the Law's rules and regulations.

The Galatians had begun their Christian lives through an experience of the Holy Spirit. They were literally living in the Spirit through his presence and guidance. Now they wanted to substitute this life in the Spirit by living under the shadow of the Law and become subject to all its commands.

Receiving the Spirit with works of power

> And behold, I am sending forth the promise of My Father upon you; but you are to stay in the city until you are clothed with power from on high. (Luke 24:49, NASB)

> but you will receive power when the Holy Spirit has come upon you; and you shall be My witnesses both in Jerusalem, and in all Judea and Samaria, and even to the remotest part of the earth. (Acts 1:8, NASB)

There is a prevailing note of power for witness in these references to the reception of the Spirit. Paul refers to the works of power that the gift of the Spirit manifested through the lives of the Galatians here in verse 5

So I ask again, he who supplies the Spirit to you and works miracles among you, is it by the works of the law or by hearing with faith?

Paul now extends his defence of justification by faith alone by reference to the gifts of the Spirit. Everything that the Galatians had experienced from God had come by hearing with faith. To desire a life lived by the Law was to reject the life of faith completely. Paul is teaching in Galatians 3:1–5 that one is justified by faith, baptized in the Spirit by faith, that the Christian life is lived by faith, and that the gifts of the Spirit are also manifested by faith. There is no room for the Law in the Christian life.

This phrase 'hearing with faith' is the key to all of this teaching. Everything comes to the Christian by *hearing with faith.*

So faith comes from hearing, and hearing by the word of Christ. (Rom. 10:17, NASB)

Christians have absolutely no need for the Law because they have the Spirit. Paul points to the miracles and the constant supply of the Spirit experienced among them as demonstration that God is with them. The Galatians were Pentecostals about to trade their experience of the Spirit's power for legalism. This might seem bizarre, and of course it was, but the strange thing is that even the history of the present Pentecostal movement over the last 100 years is one that has been plagued by much turning from the Spirit towards legalistic rules and regulations. Pentecostals have often attached a 'holiness code' to life in the Spirit that effectively neutralizes his work among them. In some strands of Pentecostal teaching, even the reception of the Spirit was not taught to come by faith alone, but by works of repentance.

Interestingly, at Corinth, Paul would have to deal with the reverse problem. The Corinthians understood that the spiritual gifts operated through hearing by faith, but they were failing to live by the Spirit and abusing their freedom in the gospel, yielding to carnality. The Galatians were despising their freedom by seeking to enter into the bondage of codes, rites and religious rules.

In this section of his letter, Paul has shown us the signs of a healthy 'gospel' church. Such a church is focused on the message of Christ crucified, from which all spiritual life flows. It is characterized by faith, the baptism in the Holy Spirit, walking in the life of the Spirit, and a constant flow of spiritual gifts and manifestations of the Holy Spirit. All of these characteristics are based on the doctrine of justification by faith alone and are, in turn, powerful witnesses to it.

8.

The Blessing of Abraham

(Gal. 3:6–9)

(6) Just as 'Abraham believed God, and it was reckoned to him for righteousness'. (7) Know then that those of faith, they are Abraham's sons. (8) And scripture, foreseeing that God would justify the Gentiles from faith, preached the gospel beforehand to Abraham, 'In you shall all the nations be blessed'. (9) Consequently, those of faith are blessed with faithful Abraham.

The Galatians's own testimony showed that they were all justified and baptized in the Spirit by faith. The Judaizers insisted that the Galatians receive circumcision and obey the Law to become real Jews. Paul turns to the most Jewish person of all time, Abraham, as the ultimate example of a man who lived by faith and without the Law. Paul believed that if you really wanted to be Jewish, you needed to go back to the father of the Jews and see how he lived, and then follow his example.

The family of faith

The Judaizers had preached to the Galatians that they were deficient in their faith because they hadn't yet fully embraced Judaism. The Judaizers were tremendously proud of their natural heritage. They were born Jews, chosen people, direct descendants of Abraham with whom God made the covenant of blessing. If the Galatians wanted the blessing of Abraham, they were told, they had to become naturalized Jews through circumcision and obedience to the Law.

Both John the Baptist and Jesus confronted the view that the Jews were heirs of the Abrahamic covenant by natural descent alone.

John the Baptist said

> do not begin to say to yourselves, 'We have Abraham for our father,' for I say to you that from these stones God is able to raise up children to Abraham. (Luke 3:8, NASB)

In John 8 the Jews repeatedly told Jesus that they were sons of Abraham and therefore in covenant with God (John 8:33,39). Jesus told them

> Your father Abraham rejoiced to see My day, and he saw it and was glad. (John 8:56, NASB)

So the Jews believed that by virtue of their natural birth they were inheritors of the blessing and covenant of Abraham. Being the heir of Abraham is very significant, because God's promises to Abraham were not just for him, but also for his seed. When a rich man dies his family all desire to inherit his wealth and it was the sons, especially the first-born son, who received the inheritance of their father.

If you were able to choose to be the heir of any man in history, who would you choose? A famous king or a billionaire? Scripture tells us that the best man you could ever be heir to is Abraham. He was blessed in every way, both materially and, even more importantly, spiritually. To be an heir of Abraham's covenant of blessing with God is the richest inheritance anyone could ever hope for.

No wonder, then, that three of the world's major religions lay claim to be the legitimate sons and heirs of Abraham. The Jews believe they are his heirs by natural descent through Isaac. The Muslims believe they are Abraham's rightful heirs through Ishmael. But Paul believes that as Christians we are Abraham's true heirs by faith in Christ.

Abraham was justified by faith, and in both Galatians and Romans the key verse used is Genesis 15:6

Then he believed in the LORD; and He reckoned it to him as righteousness.

In Genesis 15, the Lord reveals himself to the pagan Abraham
and talks to him regarding his heir. Abraham was childless at the
time and worried that his servant Eliezer would inherit at his
death. The Lord told Abraham that his servant would not inherit, but that God would supernaturally provide him with a son.

Abraham was told to look up to the countless stars, because
that is how numerous his descendants would be. Abraham
believed what God said to him, and it was reckoned to him as
righteousness. His faith in God's word immediately changed
God's opinion of him. The Lord saw his faith and from that
moment considered Abraham as righteous before him. It is exciting that Abraham's justification was in the context of God prom-
ising him heirs. Abraham's justification is linked to the promise
of his future seed. This will be very important in Paul's later
argument.

When the Lord revealed himself to Abraham we must remember that he was not already a Jew. His father, Terah, was an idol
worshiper (Josh. 24:2) and Abraham was not circumcised.
Abraham was a 'Gentile' before he met the Lord.

> Is this blessing then on the circumcised, or on the uncircumcised
> also? For we say, 'FAITH WAS CREDITED TO ABRAHAM AS
> RIGHTEOUSNESS.' How then was it credited? While he was cir-
> cumcised, or uncircumcised? Not while circumcised, but while
> uncircumcised . . . (Rom. 4:9,10, NASB)

Circumcision is a term Paul uses as shorthand for a life lived
under the whole Law. Abraham was justified before the Law
even existed. It was important for Paul to establish that the
doctrine of justification by faith alone was not some new inven-
tion, but that it was there right at the beginning of God's
covenant with the father of all Jews, Abraham. The Jewish
covenant was initially founded on the doctrine of justification
by faith alone.

The simplicity with which Abraham was justified is spectacu-
lar. He simply believed God's word to him. His comprehension

of God was minuscule, yet his simple faith in responding to the Lord was acceptable. In many ways Abraham believed without understanding; he simply said yes to God. He did not prepare to be justified; he did not repent or seek the Lord through works of piety; he simply heard and believed. You see, you can't prepare for grace; it overtakes you right where you are.

Imputed righteousness

Abraham believed God, and righteousness was imputed or 'credited' to him. This word 'impute' is extremely important to us when studying justification. To impute simply means 'to ascribe to, to account to'. To impute to someone is to tell them what you really think of them; it is your estimation of them. If I was to describe to you my friend William and told you how generous and kind he was, I would be imputing to William the characteristics of generosity and kindness. Imputation is what God thinks about a person.

> Blessed is he whose transgression is forgiven, whose sin is covered. Blessed is the man unto whom the LORD imputeth not iniquity, and in whose spirit there is no guile. (Ps. 32:1,2, KJV)

In Romans 4:7,8 Paul quotes Psalm 32:1,2 in regard to Abraham's justification. God did not impute iniquity to Abraham even though he was a sinner. God did not impute (ascribe) to Abraham sin, but instead imputed to him righteousness when he believed the promise.

God imputes righteousness to you at that moment you believe in Christ. He treats you as being as righteous as Jesus himself. This is because Christ is our righteousness. So many Christians have problems with low self-esteem and live in the shadow of self-condemnation because they trust in their own righteousness. But the moment you have faith in Jesus, the Father has the highest opinion of you possible. Because you are in Christ and clothed with Christ, God treats you as being as righteous as his own dear Son. The moment you believe, righteousness is imputed to you forever.

(8) And scripture, foreseeing that God would justify the Gentiles from faith, preached the gospel beforehand to Abraham, 'In you shall all the nations be blessed'. (9) Consequently, those of faith are blessed with faithful Abraham.

Galatians 3:8,9 makes it plain that Abraham actually heard the same gospel that Paul preached. This reminds us of Jesus' words in John 8:56 about Abraham seeing his day and rejoicing. The gospel that Abraham heard was a gospel for the whole world, because through Abraham's seed all nations would be blessed. From the beginning, God's plan in choosing Abraham was to save the nations on the basis of faith. Paul was carrying out this mission by preaching the gospel to the Gentiles.

'Blessing' is a rich word meaning the bestowal of prosperity, peace, grace and wellbeing. Those who believe are the true sons of Abraham and receive his blessing. If you study Abraham's life, you will see a pattern for your own Christian life. Paul often uses Abraham as an Old Testament model for New Testament believers. He is a prototype for all who believe, for he is their father of faith.

The book of James teaches us that Abraham the prototypical believer also put his faith to work after he was saved. He became justified by works, which does not save a person, but gives them an experience of kingdom inheritance and God's rewards.

When Paul says we are blessed with faithful Abraham, he doesn't mean that Abraham's obedient lifestyle of faithfulness saved him. Actually, much of his believing life was a failure until he learnt to put his faith into action and overcome adversity. Paul means here that Abraham's faithfulness was simply trusting in God's promise to him. Abraham had faith in God's faithfulness.

9.

The Curse of the Law

(Gal. 3:10–14)

(10) For all who rely on works of the law are under a curse; for it is written, 'Cursed is everyone who does not abide by all that has been written in the book of the law to do it.' (11) And that by the law no one is justified before God is plain, because 'The righteous from faith shall live.' (12) But the law is not from faith, rather 'The one who does them will live by them.' (13) Christ has redeemed us from the curse of the law having become a curse on our behalf – because it is written, 'Cursed is everyone who has been hanged on a tree' – (14) in order that to the Gentiles the blessing of Abraham might come in Christ Jesus, in order that we might receive the promise of the Spirit through faith.

If you're not blessed, you're cursed!

Paul spoke about the blessing of Abraham which is received by faith. Now he turns to the negative cursing that comes from relying on works of the Law for justification. Faith brings the blessings of the Spirit, legalism brings a curse. We are either living under the blessing or under the curse and there is no third option. In verse 10, Paul quotes from Deuteronomy 27:26 which is found directly after the twelve curses pronounced by the Levites standing on Mount Ebal. To Paul, the curse was the exact opposite in every way to the blessing of Abraham. Where the blessing makes you an heir of the Abrahamic covenant, the curse cuts you off from it.

The Judaizers, who believed that the works of the Law defined you as a covenant son of Abraham, were hopelessly deceived. To rely on circumcision and food laws in order to be saved was ludicrous, as such works actually put you under a curse – for by the Law no one shall be justified. Paul, quoting from Habakkuk 2:4 reminds the Galatians that it is by faith in the promise of God that we receive salvation.

The real question here is what one trusts in order to be justified. The Judaizers believed in Jesus, but they also believed that the works of the Law saved and separated the believer from the cursed world of the Gentiles. Paul shocks the Galatians by turning the whole argument on its head. He says that the works of the Law actually separate you from God, not join you to him. Works of holiness, whether they be circumcision and food laws or Christian morality and good works, do not prove that you are saved. Indeed, if you rely on them to be saved, you are separating yourself from his blessing.

The dangerous position that the Galatians found themselves in was that they could find themselves living according to the cursed life. By 'living the cursed life' I am referring to two different types of people.

Firstly, there are religious people who rely on getting to heaven by such things as good works, penance, church attendance, charitable acts, sacraments or morality. These trust in their own works of righteousness to save them. In truth, they are actually non-believers and still under the full curse of separation from God's saving power.

The second type of people begin by being justified by faith and believing the gospel (just like the Galatians), but then become Judaized by legalistic pastors or preachers. These Christians fall into the deception of believing that faith must be demonstrated in works for it to be real, saving faith. They are living like slaves, even though they are free, bound by a cursed error. The curse they experience is not a loss of salvation, but a loss of liberty and assurance. For a Christian to lose their sense of liberty in God's saving grace and to be insecure about their eternal salvation is to be living a cursed life.

Christ died to set us free from the bondage of works and to make us secure in the unconditional acceptance of his Father's love. If you have lost your sense of faith's full assurance and freedom, you are living like a cursed person. You are an heir living like a slave, a prince living like a pauper, a freed person living like a condemned criminal, a blessed man or woman making their home among the cursed.

Over the centuries, many scholars have made the mistake of thinking that Paul had a very poor view of the Law. Some have presented his teaching on the Law as extremely negative, as if Paul saw the Law as an enemy to God's people. There is absolutely nothing wrong with the Law if we understand its role (see Gal. 3:19). The problem in Galatia was that the Judaizers wrongly thought that the purpose of the Law was to justify, but the Law was never intended to do that.

In response to Paul's quote from Deuteronomy 27, 'Cursed is everyone who does not abide by all that has been written in the book of the law to do it', the Jewish teachers believed that animal sacrifice would atone for any unfortunate non compliance. But Paul forcefully demonstrates here that the sacrifices in the Law for dealing with sin actually have no power to redeem us from the curse of the Law. The only way to be free from the Law's curse of separation from God is through faith in Christ's sacrificial death. Now that Christ has come, if we live without him we really are under the Law without atoning power – for Christ is the sacrifice for our sins.

Christ totally fulfilled the Law. He lived perfectly according to the Law, and he didn't need provision for sin because he was sinless. He also fulfilled the sacrificial aspects of the Law by his death on the cross. He became the Lamb of God who takes away the sins of the world. Christ lived the Law on behalf of all who believe and carried the curse that should have been upon us. If we have Christ then the demands and penalties of the Law have become both redundant and irrelevant to our lives. Christ is the end of the Law for all who believe, both Jew and Gentile.

The cross and the tree

Even the manner of Jesus' death is found within the Law:

> Because it is written, 'Cursed is everyone who has been hanged on
> a tree'.

This verse from Deuteronomy 21:23 is quoted by Paul to show
how Jesus became our substitute when he was crucified on a
wooden cross. The curse of the Law that separated us from God
was experienced in its totality by Jesus when he was separated
from his own Father during his crucifixion.

> And at the ninth hour Jesus cried out with a loud voice, saying,
> 'Eloi, Eloi, lama sabachthani?' which is translated, *'My God, My
> God, why have You forsaken Me?'* (Mark 15:34, NKJV)

For those who believe in Jesus, the Law has become obsolete.
This is because justification comes through faith in Christ, and
also because Christ fulfilled and completed the Law in his death.
Remember what Paul said in Galatians 2:19

> For I through the law died to the law, in order that I might live for
> God.

Finally, in this section Paul returns in verse 14 to reaffirm that
with the fulfilment of the Law there is now an even playing
field for Jew and Gentile in regard to knowing God. Having the
Law brings no advantage at all when it comes to being saved.
The blessing of Abraham comes to all, regardless of race or religious background, in the same way – through faith in Christ.
Christ became the curse in order to produce this new state of
affairs.

> (14) *in order* that to the Gentiles the blessing of Abraham might
> come in Christ Jesus, in order that we might receive the promise of
> the Spirit through faith.

The last will and testament of God (Gal. 3:15–18)

> (15) Brothers, I speak in human terms. Even a human will once ratified, no one sets aside or adds to. (16) But the promises were spoken to Abraham and to his 'seed'. It does not say, and to his 'seeds', as to many, but as to one: 'and to your seed' – who is, Christ. (17) My point is this: a covenant ratified beforehand by God, the law which came four hundred and thirty years later does not make void so as to render the promise ineffective. (18) For if the inheritance is from law, it is no longer from promise; but to Abraham God gave it freely through promise.

The promises of God remain

Struggling for an illustration to help explain the superiority of the promise over the Law, Paul turns to the example of a last will and testament. In everyday life, it was understood that when a man wrote his will and then died, the contents of that will could not be changed, amended or challenged. This will determined who would receive the dead man's inheritance.

The promises spoken to Abraham about all the nations being blessed were made to him and his seed 430 years before the Law. God's promise to Abraham to bless the Gentiles was, in effect, his 'last will and testament' to humanity. This meant that the Law had no right or power to amend or nullify God's former covenant with Abraham. Though this is a limited illustration, it is interesting to think that just as a human will is only executed at death, so God's last will and testament for humankind also needed a death for it to be enacted. It took the death of Jesus before the blessing of Abraham through the Spirit came to the Gentile nations.

Seed not seeds

We have already seen how the Jewish people considered themselves the exclusive descendants of Abraham. They believed that they were heirs of the blessing of Abraham through being his natural seed. Paul says that the natural bloodline means absolutely nothing when it comes to inheriting Abraham's promise. The promise was to two people alone: Abraham and his seed (singular). This seed is Jesus Christ himself. No wonder Abraham saw his day and rejoiced (John 8:56). It was too late for anybody to tamper with God's promise to Abraham and his seed, Christ. The Law has no power or authority over the promise. Faith in Christ can't be tampered with through laws and regulations. Salvation comes by the grace of God through faith in his promise. It is faith from start to finish.

Abraham's descendants are not perpetuated through procreation, but by spiritual regeneration. It is those who are born again who are the heirs of Abraham.

10.

The Purpose of the Law

(Gal. 3:19–25)

(19) Why then the Law? It was added for the sake of transgressions, until the coming of the seed to whom the promise was made, having been ordered through angels by the hand of an intermediary. (20) Now an intermediary means that there is not just one party; but God is one. (21) Is then the law against the promises (of God)? Not at all! For if the law had been given which could make alive, then righteousness certainly would be from the law. (22) But the scripture confined everything under the power of sin, in order that the promise might be given from faith in Jesus Christ to those who believe. (23) However, before the coming of faith we were held in custody under the law, confined till the faith which was to come should be revealed. (24) So that the law became our custodian to Christ, in order that we might be justified from faith. (25) But with faith having come, we are no longer under the custodian.

Why then the Law?

There are two questions that naturally arise from Paul's teaching on justification by faith alone. The first is, what is the point of having the Law if salvation comes through faith? The second question is, does the Law oppose the promises of God? Remember, Paul's style of writing is to ask a question, to anticipate the response, and then to answer what he already knows his readers will be thinking in reaction to his teaching.

Paul realizes that people might think that if salvation isn't through the Law, then it doesn't really have a function or a purpose. If the Jews had endeavoured to be justified through the Law for hundreds of years and they were now being told that it couldn't bring them righteousness, then wouldn't that make it both pointless and useless?

Paul explains clearly that the Law was added for the sake of transgression. The word 'transgression' in the Greek is *parabasis*. Paul chose this particular word rather than the more general term for sin, *hamartia*, which is applicable to all people without distinction. *Parabasis* refers to a specific stepping over of a defined boundary; it implies breaking a definite law.

In his later letter to the Romans, Paul makes a similar statement regarding the Law

> The Law *came in* so the transgression would increase; but where sin increased, grace abounded all the more. (Rom. 5:20, NASB)

The word used for 'came in' in the above verse literally translates as 'coming in through a side road'. It is as if the Law joined the highway of God's dealings with humanity by a slip road. The same word is also used in Galatians 2:4 to refer to the false brethren 'sneaking in' to spy out their liberty. The Law came in alongside the promise, but it did not replace it. The Law's purpose was entirely different to that of the promise. The Galatians were in danger of believing that obedience to the Law was part of God's plan to save humankind. But the Law only came in as a temporary digression, initially to deal with the wickedness of the children of Israel in the wilderness.

The purpose of the Law

It is amazing to think that for 430 years the descendants of Abraham lived by faith without the Law. That is a long time! It may be helpful to think that 430 years ago, Queen Elizabeth I was still on the throne of England. All that time the descendants of Abraham lived by covenant with God and the promise made to him and his seed. Moses recognized this point when he said,

The LORD our God made a covenant with us in Horeb. The LORD did not make this covenant with our fathers, but with us, those who are here today, all of us who are alive. (Deut. 5:2,3, NKJV)

Historically, the Law came in to deal with the great wickedness of the children of Israel during the Exodus. The story of Moses' generation was one of unbelief, ungratefulness and sin. Indeed, the children of Israel's rebellion in the wilderness is the example used in the letter to the Hebrews to illustrate the dangers of backsliding into unbelief and rebellion. This generation refused to live by faith, unlike their fathers who had walked by the promise made to Abraham. God had actually given the Exodus generation their own promises regarding the Promised Land, but they refused to believe them

> . . . they despised the pleasant land; they did not believe his promise. They grumbled in their tents and did not obey the LORD. (Ps. 106:24,25, NIV)

> Therefore, as the Holy Spirit says:
> 'Today, if you will hear His voice,
> Do not harden your hearts as in the rebellion,
> In the day of trial in the wilderness,
> Where your fathers tested Me, tried Me,
> And saw My works forty years.
> Therefore I was angry with that generation,
> And said, 'They always go astray in their heart,
> And they have not known My ways.'
> So I swore in My wrath,
> 'They shall not enter My rest.'
> Beware, brethren, lest there be in any of you an evil heart of unbelief in departing from the living God. (Heb. 3:7–12, NKJV)

Paul writes in Galatians 3:19 that the Law was given in response to the transgressions of the wilderness generation. The Law came in to make sin illegal. The Law revealed perfectly the nature of sin and codified it into legal offences with consequent punishments. It made sin into transgressions. Sin, of course, was around since the fall of Adam, and all people were separated from God because of it, but the Law revealed sin in all its forms, so that there was absolutely no dispute about what it was, and certainly no excuse for doing it.

> because by the works of the Law no flesh will be justified in His sight; for through the Law comes the knowledge of sin. (Rom. 3:20, NASB)

Dr R.T. Kendall, in his lectures on Galatians (his Friday night teaching series at Westminster Chapel, London, in 1977) puts it like this: 'The Law given on Mount Sinai made explicit the sin that had been implicit in man since the fall. The Law revealed sin by calling it by name.'

If the Israelites had walked in the footsteps of Abraham's faith like their fathers, I do not believe the Law would have needed to come in at this point in history. It was only added because of their outrageous sin and constant unbelief. The Law came in like a schoolmaster to bring a naughty class under supervision and control.

As well as revealing sin, the Law's punishments brought order and restraint to an unruly and disobedient nation. The Law was not just out to punish sin, though; it also fashioned a sacrificial system that allowed sin to be temporarily covered until it would ultimately be dealt with by Christ's death on the cross.

The Law is perfect and good. It was given to benefit and tutor the Israelites until the seed (Christ) came. But the Law is not of faith and has nothing to do with our justification, because that was never its God-given role.

Interestingly, because it is the nature of the Law not only to reveal but also to restrain sin, where it is preached it does have the capacity to scare and bully people into a form of outward obedience. This is the fatal flaw of many preachers today, who utilize the Law to produce obedience and moral conformity in their congregations.

Some Christians teach that the ceremonial and civil parts of the Law have been done away with, but the moral part of the Law remains and is to be obeyed by all Christians. This is nonsense. Scripture teaches that you are either under the whole Law or you are under grace – you can't pick and mix from the Law. Preachers who do try to mix Law with grace usually fear that the message of grace on its own will produce licentiousness, so they resort to the same method as the Law to restrain their congregation, cultivating obedience through fear of punishment. Their congregations demonstrate an outward form of obedience, but actually remain underdeveloped children of the Law instead of developing into mature adults of grace. Always remember this theological equation: Grace + Law = Law.

A temporary measure

The Law was only a temporary measure, whereas the promise to Abraham and his seed is an irrevocable oath (Heb. 6:17).

> (19) Why then the Law? It was added for the sake of transgressions, *until the coming of the seed* to whom the promise was made.

The Law was added until the coming of Christ. This does not mean that the Law replaced the Abrahamic covenant during that period, and neither does it mean that the faith of Abraham was put aside by the Law until Christ came. Hebrews 11 gives us a wonderful record of people who lived by faith, many even after the Law had come. These people had the faith of Abraham and were saved. They all lived by faith in God's promise, even though that promise was not to be fulfilled until the coming of the Christ.

> And all these, having obtained a good testimony through faith, did not receive the promise, God having provided something better for us, that they should not be made perfect apart from us. (Heb. 11:39,40 NKJV)

When Jesus came he fulfilled the Law and established the eternal priesthood of Melchizedek. Just as the Mosaic covenant had its sacrifices and Levitical priesthood, so the Abrahamic covenant has its priesthood of Melchizedek (Gen. 14:18–20). As the promise to Abraham preceded the coming of the Law, so too the priest Melchizedek preceded the coming of the Levites.

The Levitical priesthood was only a temporary and vague copy of heavenly realities. The sacrificial system pointed to Christ and provisionally covered sin until Christ came to deal with it decisively. When Jesus arrived, he became both the sacrificial Lamb of God and High Priest in the order of Melchizedek. By his blood, Jesus Christ has cleansed all who believe in him forever. The Law and its Levitical priesthood are now obsolete.

> For the Law, since it has only a shadow of the good things to come and not the very form of things, can never, by the same sacrifices which they offer continually year by year, make perfect those who draw near. Otherwise, would they not have ceased to be offered, because the worshipers, having once been cleansed, would no longer have had consciousness of sins? But in those sacrifices there is a reminder of sins year by year. For it is impossible for the blood of bulls and goats to take away sins. (Heb. 10:1–4, NASB)

Although the Law is obsolete for those who believe in Christ, it does remain the standard of judgement for all who do not believe. Unless faith comes to an individual they remain under the Law and will be judged by the standards of the Law.

The second-hand Law

Galatians 3:19,20 tell us that the Law was 'ordered through angels by the hand of an intermediary. Now an intermediary means that there is not just one party; but God is one.'

> you who received the law as ordained by angels, and yet did not keep it. (Acts 7:53, NASB)

> For if the word spoken through angels proved unalterable, and every transgression and disobedience received a just penalty . . . (Heb. 2:2, NASB)

Although the Law did come from God, it was given to Moses by angels. Moses then in turn delivered the Law to the Israelites. The Law thus came second-hand to Moses and third-hand to the people.

Moses was a mediator between God and people. He represented God to Israel, and Israel to God. The Law was thus given by God in an indirect manner. But God is one, and when it came to Abraham the promise was given directly and personally by him without any angelic or human mediation. This shows the superiority of the promise in comparison to the Law. The promise was so great that God gave it personally. Those Judaizers were offering a second-hand product to the Galatians, who had already received by faith the blessing of the Spirit directly from the Lord himself.

In competition

The Law could only really be against the promises of God if it was in competition with them. The Judaizers were in competition with the gospel because they proclaimed that without obedience to the Law you could not be saved. We have seen that the promises and the Law had two entirely different purposes and goals. If the promises and the Law both came from God, how could they actually be in conflict?

Interestingly, Paul uses the plural 'promises' not the singular 'promise'. Previously he had spoken about *the* promise of Abraham. The Christian life is lived by faith in God's promises from start to finish.

> For no matter how many promises God has made, they are 'Yes' in Christ. And so through him the 'Amen' is spoken by us to the glory of God. (2 Cor. 1:20, NIV)

For every need, circumstance and call in the Christian life there is a corresponding promise to be believed. The Christian lives by faith in the promises of God, just as the heroes of faith lived by them in Hebrews 11. Laws require doing, but promises require believing. For example, true sanctification comes by faith in God's promises, not by observance of the Law or even modern evangelical rules and regulations

> Therefore, having these promises, beloved, let us cleanse ourselves from all defilement of flesh and spirit, perfecting holiness in the fear of God. (2 Cor. 7:1, NASB)

Paul doesn't have a problem with the Law at all, and if a law had been made that could have given life, that would have been fine by him; but it hadn't. It is the Spirit alone who can give life.

Sin's universal imprisonment of humankind

> (22) But the scripture confined everything under the power of sin, in order that the promise might be given from faith in Jesus Christ to those who believe. (23) However, before the coming of faith we were held in custody under the law, confined till the faith which was to come should be revealed. (24) So that the law became our custodian to Christ, in order that we might be justified from faith. (25) But with faith having come, we are no longer under the custodian.

The whole world is in jail and living under a death sentence. Humanity has been found guilty, sentenced and imprisoned. Galatians 3:22 makes it plain that Scripture has confined all under sin. The Law exposes sin and pronounces judgement upon it

> What shall we conclude then? Are we any better? Not at all! We have already made the charge that Jews and Gentiles alike are all under sin. As it is written: 'There is no-one righteous, not even one; there is no-one who understands, no-one who seeks God. All have turned away, they have together become worthless; there is no-one who does good, not even one.' (Rom. 3:9–12, NIV)

> Now we know that whatever the Law says, it speaks to those who are under the Law, so that every mouth may be closed and all the world may become accountable to God; because by the works of the Law no flesh will be justified in His sight; for through the Law comes the knowledge of sin. (Rom. 3:19,20, NASB)

> This righteousness from God comes through faith in Jesus Christ to all who believe. There is no difference, for all have sinned and fall short of the glory of God, and are justified freely by his grace through the redemption that came by Christ Jesus. (Rom. 3:22–24, NIV)

In his commentary on Galatians, F.F. Bruce says this about Galatians 3:22

> But here the figure of speech is more vivid than in verse 8: the written law is the official who locks the law-breaker up in the prison house of which sin is the jailor . . . Those who come to their senses in the prison-house and recognise the hopelessness of their predicament will be the readier to embrace the promise of liberty and life: the law thus serves the interest of the promise – and of the beneficiaries of the promise.[1]

Others have seen a more positive image in regard to being held in custody by the Law. James Dunn sees the imagery revealing the Law as holding Israel in *protective custody* – the idea being that the Law was also protecting the people of God from the rule of sin until Christ came. This makes sense in our understanding of the role of the Law in both restraining sin and giving the benefits of sacrificial atonement. We can learn much from verse 22 through both of these approaches. It is to be noted that verse 22 can also be translated

> But the scripture confined everything under the power of sin, in order that the promise might be given from *the faith of Jesus Christ* to those who believe.

In this regard, see my earlier discussion on Galatians 2:16.

The Law as a guardian or teacher

In verse 24 there is a very interesting term used in reference to the Law. We are told that the Law became our 'custodian' or 'tutor' to bring us to Christ. The Greek word used is *paidagogos* and has been translated in the following ways: guardian, teacher, tutor, schoolmaster, custodian and trainer. I like the way that *The Message* version of the Bible translates this verse

> Until the time when we were mature enough to respond freely in faith to the living God, we were carefully surrounded and

protected by the Mosaic law. The law was like those Greek tutors, with which you are familiar, who escort children to school and protect them from danger or distraction, making sure the children will really get to the place they set out for.

The above is a good description because a *paidagogos* wasn't really a teacher at a school, but a trusted slave who would watch over the child until they reached the age of adult responsibility. I suppose in modern-day life the nearest thing to the role of a *paidagogos* is that of a nanny. Of course, unlike a *paidagogos*, a child usually outgrows a nanny well before adulthood.

This passage will be echoed later in Galatians 4:1–7 where the Law is described as the guardian and steward of Israel until it came to maturity with the advent of Christ. The important thing here is to understand that the Law was only temporarily in charge of the people of God until the fullness of the gospel arrived, then it was no longer necessary.

Can you imagine a grown man walking around holding his nanny's hand and being treated like a 6-year old? I have seen middle-aged men still tied to their mother's apron strings and that's bad enough. Is it possible for Christians to be in such a position? Most definitely! The Galatians were in the process of regressing from spiritual adulthood to legalistic infancy; back-sliding from freedom and responsibility to a stifling supervision by 'Nanny Law'.

There is much legalism in churches today, and many leaders who '*paidagog*' their congregations. Like ministerial nannies they espouse a horde of 'thou shalts' and 'thou shalt nots' as standards to be saved by. The result produces congregations that are spiri-tually insecure. They are children in bondage.

I am aware that Paul said much in his letters about right and wrong behaviour, but none of it was linked to the assurance of one's salvation. We need to allow our people to grow up and learn spiritually responsibility.

There is no way I would let my young son drive my car, but when he is old enough and has passed his test I will give him the keys. As an adult, he will then be responsible for careful driving. He may abuse that responsibility, but that's a risk I am willing to take to see him take his place in the adult world.

We don't need a nanny or a tutor. What we really need is a father. 1 Corinthians 4:15 compares the word *paidagogos* (translated 'guardians' here) to a father

> Even though you have ten thousand guardians in Christ, you do not have many fathers, for in Christ Jesus I became your father through the gospel. (NIV)

You never outgrow a true father. I think it is so apt that the Law is seen as a guardian, a steward or even a nanny, because by comparison Abraham is seen as a father

> Therefore know that only those who are of faith are sons of Abraham. (Gal. 3:7, NKJV)

> Therefore, the promise comes by faith, so that it may be by grace and may be guaranteed to all Abraham's offspring – not only to those who are of the law but also to those who are of the faith of Abraham. He is the father of us all. (Rom. 4:16, NIV)

We will never outgrow being sons of Abraham. We don't need a nanny any more because our Father in heaven is bringing up his children personally now.

Sons and heirs

> (26) For all of you are sons of God, through this faith, in Christ Jesus. (27) For as many of you as were baptised into Christ have put on Christ. (28) There is neither Jew nor Greek, there is neither slave nor free, there is no male and female; for you all are one in Christ Jesus. (29) And if you are Christ's, then are you Abraham's seed, heirs according to the promise.

Paul proclaims that all the Galatians are sons of God through faith in Christ Jesus. They no longer need a tutor or guardian because they have 'come of age'. The reference to being baptized into Christ and the denial that there is any racial, social or sexual distinction in him, is very close to what Paul also said in 1 Corinthians 12:13

For by one Spirit we were all baptized into one body, whether Jews or Greeks, whether slaves or free, and we were all made to drink of one Spirit. (NASB)

This verse sheds light upon what Paul is saying here in Galatians 3:26,27. Some have thought that Paul is talking about water baptism here when he speaks of the believers being baptized into Christ. This is certainly not his main emphasis, though. Paul is again referring to the doctrine of our union with Christ. I mentioned this teaching earlier in regard to Paul's claim to be 'crucified with Christ' in Galatians 2:20.

The baptism that Paul is talking about is the joining of the believer into union with Christ by the Holy Spirit during regeneration. This is not the baptism *in* the Holy Spirit – this is a baptism *by* the Holy Spirit into Christ. It is the Holy Spirit who regenerates us, convicts us, gives us faith and baptizes us into Christ. The word 'baptize', at it simplest, means to immerse: 'For as many of you as were immersed into Christ have put on Christ.'

Galatians 3:28 is reinforcing what was just said in verse 27: when it comes to salvation, the Galatians have already fully arrived. They are sons of God and united with everything Christ has done and everything that he is. A similar theme of being united and joined to Christ is found in Romans 6. We have 'put on' Christ. The phrase 'put on' means 'to be clothed'. We are clothed with Christ's righteousness, which means that when the Father looks at us he treats us just as he would his own Son – because we are now in Christ.

All people equal in Christ

Paul had been dealing with racism all the way through his letter. The Judaizers were trying to make what they believed to be inferior races into Jews. Paul was constantly defending God's decision to bless the Gentiles just as they were. Interestingly, there was a prayer that many Jewish men would pray each morning, thanking God that they were not born a Gentile, a slave or a woman. Paul was probably aware of this prayer when he wrote verse 28.

The gospel was affirming that not just Jews but all people have equal worth in Christ. In Christ there are no racial, class or sexual distinctions. In the ancient world in which Paul lived, these distinctions were entrenched at every level of society. His words were seeds that ultimately had the potential to turn society upside down as he taught the equality of all human beings. In Christ we are all part of God's upper class.

This was an amazing statement for Paul to make, and he didn't just attack the Judaizers' racial pride. He showed that the gospel recognizes the equal dignity of every single human being. The idea that there was neither slave nor free in Christ was a revolutionary principle that contravened the whole of ancient society at that time. Slaves were literally the property of their owners – they had no human rights. In Paul's letter to Philemon he deals sensitively with the issue of a runaway slave named Onesimus. He asks Philemon to receive him back as a brother, not a slave, for in Christ we become brothers and sisters forever.

Women were generally treated as second-class citizens during ancient times. Because heirs were usually male and men were so dominant in society, the birth of a female was often received with disappointment. Jesus himself was revolutionary in that he treated women with such respect. The high value that Jesus placed upon women even made some Pharisees question his morality.

It is important to emphasize here that Paul's main argument is that all people are equal when it comes to receiving salvation by faith. We are all sons of God and equal heirs of salvation, no matter what race, class or sex we are.

11.

Heirs of God

(Gal. 4:1–7)

(1) I tell you: as long as the heir is a child, he is no different from a slave, even though he owns everything. (2) But he is under guardians and stewards, until the time set by the father. (3) Thus also we, when we were children, were enslaved under the elemental forces of the world. (4) But when the fullness of time came, God sent his son, born of woman, born under the law, (5) in order that he might redeem those under the law, in order that we might receive the adoption. (6) And in that you are sons, God sent the Spirit of his Son into our hearts crying, 'Abba! Father!' (7) Consequently you are no longer a slave, but a son. And if a son, then also an heir through God.

If you compare the last six verses of chapter 3 with the first seven verses of chapter 4 you will notice a great deal of similarity in thought. Paul is expressing his argument again from a new angle. The recurring themes we find here are also very important.

Whenever you teach or preach and you come to something vital for your pupils to grasp, you won't normally only say it once – you will make the same point again and again in different ways until you know that it's been understood.

When Paul says 'I tell you', it is like he is driving home something of fundamental importance that his readers may not have grasped yet. As we look at these seven verses, revisiting what he has just written, we will find ourselves coming into a profoundly deeper understanding of that which Paul has already introduced to us.

From minor to major

We have already had an illustration of the Law being like a temporary custodian or tutor of God's people, and have seen that it became redundant when faith appeared. Now Paul depicts a child not yet old enough to inherit from his father. Paul uses different words than *paidagogos* here. The first word 'guardian' refers to someone legally responsible for the minor and appointed by the father to educate and oversee the child's development. The guardian would also manage the inheritance on behalf of the child until they reached their majority. The second term, 'steward' would normally refer to the role of a slave, who would oversee the child in much the same way as the *paidagogos* of chapter 3.

The status of the child, whilst in their minority, does not differ from that of a slave, even though as an heir they are master of all. In Roman society the role of the father was absolute. He had total power and control over everyone in his household. He even had power to sell his children as slaves.

In Roman law the household was viewed as a single unit that was financially and legally under the rule of one person, the father. This helps us understand the power of Paul's argument. Until the heir came of age, he had absolutely no legal power or say in the household. He had to obey his father's commands just like all the slaves around him. In fact, in accordance with his father's wishes, he had to take orders from the slaves watching over him; he was under their command.

In the same manner, Paul explains that we were also in a position of subjection and slavery. Fascinatingly, Paul does not say that we were in *bondage* to the Law, as we would expect here, but that we were enslaved under the *elemental forces* of the world.

Stoicheia is the Greek word for 'elemental forces' and can mean the fundamental substances of the world such as earth, water, air and fire. It can also refer to negative spiritual powers and cosmic forces. Finally, *stoicheia* can mean the basic and rudimentary teachings of any religion – for example, in Hebrews 5:12

> For though by this time you ought to be teachers, you have need again for someone to teach you the *elementary principles* of the

oracles of God, and you have come to need milk and not solid food. (NASB)

See to it that no one takes you captive through philosophy and empty deception, according to the tradition of men, according to the *elementary principles* of the world, rather than according to Christ. (Col. 2:8, NASB)

This reference from Colossians is most helpful in understanding what Paul is talking about in Galatians 4:3. The Law is being put into a general category of rudimentary religion that includes even the former paganism and philosophies of the Galatian Gentiles. Paul says that in comparison to the perfect gospel, the Law, along with pagan religions, is simple, primitive, ineffective and enslaving. The Law was as useless as pagan religion in regard to its ability to save from sin. Paul warns that for the Gentiles to put themselves under the Law would be comparable to them returning again to their old pagan religions.

The state of a Christian

The heir being no different to a slave, until he receives his inheritance, is a clear picture of the state of a Christian *before* coming to faith in Christ. We know that God in his sovereign mercy predestined and preordained each Christian to come to faith even before the creation of the world. God had signed our adoption papers even before he created the universe.

just as He chose us in Him before the foundation of the world, that we would be holy and blameless before Him. In love He predestined us to adoption as sons through Jesus Christ to Himself, according to the kind intention of His will, to the praise of the glory of His grace, which He freely bestowed on us in the Beloved. (Eph. 1:4–6, NASB)

But for each one of us there was an appointed time when we came to Christ. For some it was at a young age, for others it was later on in life. During the time that we were in unbelief we were in slavery, just like everyone else. We were, by nature, children of wrath and spiritually dead just like the others

> And you were dead in your trespasses and sins, in which you formerly walked according to the course of this world, according to the prince of the power of the air, of the spirit that is now working in the sons of disobedience. Among them we too all formerly lived in the lusts of our flesh, indulging the desires of the flesh and of the mind, and were by nature children of wrath, even as the rest. (Eph. 2:1–3, NASB)

Like the heir in Galatians 4:1 we were, in our pre-Christian days, no different to the rest who were slaves to sin. Yet the secret that we didn't know was that in God's eyes we were chosen heirs waiting to inherit salvation. God had his plan for us even while we were yet sinners. We were sons of God hidden amongst the slaves of sin until God revealed himself to us as our adoptive Father.

The gospel in a nutshell

Galatians 4:4–7 is the message of the gospel in its most concentrated form. Everything you need to know about the essentials of the gospel is found in these verses. It is a summary of the teaching of Paul so far in this section of the epistle that has been a defence of the gospel against the Judaizers.

> (4) But when the fullness of time came, God sent his son, born of woman, born under the law, (5) in order that he might redeem those under the law, in order that we might receive the adoption. (6) And in that you are sons, God sent the Spirit of his Son into our hearts crying, 'Abba! Father!' (7) Consequently you are no longer a slave, but a son. And if a son, then also an heir through God.

You can see many of the themes that we have been studying in chapters 3 and 4 summarized in these three verses.

Verse 4 is such a powerful statement about the person of Christ. So much truth is contained in it about the nature, mission and character of Jesus. The fullness of time underlines that God was always working towards the climactic moment of sending his Son to the earth. We have seen that the promise to Abraham and the giving of the Law were all necessary to prepare the global stage for Christ's entrance. Paul has been speaking about the wonderful moment in time when the heir inherits from his father. Everything has its time in the plan of God. The Lord is never too early and he is never too late.

> To everything there is a season. A time for every purpose under heaven. (Eccl. 3:1, NKJV)

Jesus was sent on a mission from his Father, and his sending was part of an eternal plan. He existed eternally before his birth and his sending involved being born of a woman. This verse teaches the doctrine of the virgin birth. Jesus was not the natural offspring of a human father, but he was the natural offspring of a human woman. He was always the Son of God, but when he was born of a woman he became incarnated – he became fully man – Jesus Christ, fully God, now also fully man, having been born of a woman.

Paul has already spoken about the seed of Abraham in Galatians. The seed always comes from the father (never the mother), and the father of all humankind was Adam. However, through Adam's sin his whole seed became corrupted, and sin became a *spiritually inherited disease* passed down through all generations. Jesus did not come from the seed of Adam and thus did not inherit the sin-contaminated Adamic seed. It was like God was starting all over again with a 'second' Adam, but this new seed, that was Christ, was uncontaminated by sin. Romans 5:12–15 compares Adam and Christ

> Therefore, just as through one man sin entered into the world, and death through sin, and so death spread to all men, because all sinned – for until the Law, sin was in the world, but sin is not imputed when there is no law. Nevertheless death reigned from Adam until Moses, even over those who had not sinned in the likeness of the offense of Adam, *who is a type of him who was to come.* But the free gift is not like the transgression. For if by the

transgression of the one the many died, much more did the grace of God and the gift by the grace of the one Man, Jesus Christ, abound to the many. (emphasis added)

This is one of the reasons why Jesus being born of a woman but not via human fathering is important – God's promise of blessing was to Abraham's seed and God provided that seed himself by sending his own Son, born of a woman. When we are regenerated or 'born again', instead of being children of Adam, who all received the contaminated and sin-corrupted seed, we become children of God whose seed is incorruptible. Christ is the seed of Abraham, and Galatians 3:29 tells us that if we are in Christ we too become Abraham's seed. We have died to the seed of fallen humanity and received the seed of redeemed humanity! This is what it really means to be born again, and we ought to learn to live in the light of this truth.

> for you have been born again not of seed which is perishable but imperishable, that is, through the living and enduring word of God. (1 Pet. 1:23, NASB)

> No one who is born of God practices sin, because His seed abides in him; and he cannot sin, because he is born of God. (1 John 3:9, NASB)

Next, Paul tells us that Jesus was born under the Law. This reminds us of his earlier teaching about Jesus' relationship to the Law, and how he took the curse of it on our behalf. It is amazing to think of the humility of the Son of God in subjecting himself to the Law. He could have been born over the Law; after all, it was he himself who gave the Law to Israel through the mediation of angels.

The Law had no claims on Christ, but he chose for our sake to submit to it. It was a delight not a burden for Jesus to walk according to the perfect Law of God. The Law was strict, though, and would be watching and monitoring his every single thought, word and deed. Not only would it be monitoring what Jesus did, but also checking to see if he omitted anything that he should have done. The Law was looking to accuse Christ 24/7, and one slip, one bad thought, one omission and it would all be over – he would have failed in his mission.

I doubt very much that any of us could walk according to the Law for even five minutes. Jesus did it faultlessly for thirty-three years. He not only lived perfectly according to the Law of God, but he fulfilled it completely. The Law was waiting for one person to come along and meet its demands and fulfil its purpose, and Christ did this for us. The Law has set an impossible test for us to pass. Thank God Jesus came and sat the Law's exam on our behalf, and by faith we are credited with his 100 per cent pass mark. He passed the test, we got the grade.

Jesus redeemed us from the curse of the Law. He paid the price, by his death on the cross, to purchase our redemption for sin and the curse of the Law. I want to emphasize that all unbelievers are under the curse and jurisdiction of the Law, whether they are Jewish or not. The Law is the universal standard by which all who do not believe in the gospel will ultimately be judged

> Now we know that whatever the Law says, it speaks to those who are under the Law, so that every mouth may be closed and all the world may become accountable to God. (Rom. 3:19, NASB)

Even though a Gentile may never have even heard of the Law and, indeed, may die without knowledge of it, they still have to produce works equal to its demands to be found righteous. You are a lawbreaker, whether you know what the Law says or you don't. Imagine if you drove your car in a foreign country, unaware of their speed limits, and the police pulled you over for speeding. Your ignorance of the law regarding the speed limit doesn't mean that you aren't guilty of breaking it. In all legal systems, ignorance of the law is not an excuse. So too with God's Law.

Permanent adoption

Redemption is not an end in itself. We were redeemed for a purpose, and that purpose was adoption. Here, in Galatians 4:5, we see that Jesus died in order that we might be adopted as sons of

God. God gave us his only Son in order that he might adopt many more sons. This adoption as children of God is often ignored by preachers and teachers today, yet it is the very purpose of the gospel message. It is Paul's gospel in a nutshell.

The first thing to say about adoption is that it is by the grace and initiative of God alone. Remember, the child never adopts his parents, the parents adopt the child

> he predestined us to be adopted as his sons through Jesus Christ, in accordance with his pleasure and will. (Eph. 1:5, NIV)

I myself was adopted as a 6-week-old baby. My mother tells the story about how she and my father had decided to adopt a child. They were informed by the Church of England adoption society about all the children who were available for adoption at that time. My father had set his heart on adopting a girl, but there were none available. I was presented as an alternative. My parents found it hard to make a decision because my dad was really hoping for a girl, so he told the adoption society worker 'no'. As the social worker left their house, my mother looked at my father and he suddenly exclaimed, 'I've made a mistake. He is the one for us!' They ran after the social worker, and subsequently adopted me three days later. I had absolutely nothing to do with that decision, even though it was all about me. It was 100 per cent the decision of my father and mother. God also chose to adopt you, and you had nothing to do with that decision. In fact, he signed your spiritual adoption papers before you were even born.

The legal adoption of a child has no 'opt out' clauses in it. When my dad signed my adoption papers, it did not read that I was adopted on the condition that I brushed my teeth each day, worked hard at school, gained my A levels, kept out of prison etc. I was adopted permanently and unconditionally, even before I had done anything of merit or discredit. I was adopted as a son for life.

What right, then, do people have to introduce conditions into our adoption by our heavenly Father? It is scandalous that religious teachers add legalistic requirements to our spiritual 'adoption papers' that were never originally there. Even worse, preachers concerned that other children of God might not live up to their standards put caveats into the adoption agreement, teaching that God has full rights to revoke the adoption if we do not meet certain standards of righteousness. One can never make the assertion that we are 'adopted by his grace on *condition* that we . . .' The moment grace becomes conditional, it ceases to be grace.

Adoption by God is unconditional, permanent and irrevocable. We can become good children or disobedient children of God, but children we will always remain. God is not fostering us for a trial period; he adopted us forever.

Full rights as sons and heirs

Jesus is the only natural son of God, but as adopted sons we receive full family rights and privileges. Adoption as sons of God entitles us to enjoy, inherit and experience the full blessing and authority of the kingdom of God. If we could only understand the full implications of this fact for our daily lives, it would revolutionize us. Of course, the term 'sons of God' refers to both male and female Christians. Paul says we are all 'sons' because in his day, only the male could inherit.

We must beware ending up like the brother of the prodigal son who sees his brother squander his inheritance as a son and then complains that he hasn't experienced any of his own birthright. The two sons in this parable were equally wrong. One abused his position of sonship by taking his father's kindness and inheritance for granted. The other son never understood the generous heart of his father or experienced the inheritance that was his to enjoy. He had a poor image of his father's generosity, and of his own status and rights. The father said to his older son

> Son, you have always been with me, and all that is mine is
> yours. (Luke 15:31, NASB)

Just because we are adopted sons doesn't mean that we automatically experience and enjoy our inheritance. Fear, unbelief, legalism, lack of assurance and understanding can prevent us from enjoying all the benefits that are rightfully ours and that God wants us to receive. So many Christians who are adopted sons of

God are still living as slaves, and that is why in verse 7 of this chapter, Paul has to remind the Galatians that they are no longer slaves, but sons and heirs of God. The Galatians were returning to a life of slavery, instead of enjoying the inheritance that they had come into.

Adopted and assured

(6) And in that you are sons, God sent the Spirit of his Son into our hearts crying, 'Abba! Father!'

You would think that after adoption we would have reached the end of Paul's *gospel in a nutshell* but there is still more. Paul returns to a theme he has already mentioned a number of times before: the believer's reception of the Spirit. God not only wants us to understand our position as adopted sons, but he also wants to us to intimately experience his fatherly love for us.

No one would legally adopt a child and not nurse it with parental love. Verbal and physical affection is one of the greatest gifts a parent can give to their child. Children thrive on the hugs, kisses and words of love from their parents. Our Father in heaven desires us to know the fullness of his love for us. He wants intimacy with us. After all, we are his adopted children and he wants us to experience his love and never doubt how much he adores us.

I remember listening to a sermon Heidi Baker preached at Kensington Temple, explaining how the Lord taught her about the difference between an adopted child and an orphan. Heidi and her husband, Roland Baker, are missionaries to Mozambique and have literally taken into their homes thousands of orphaned children.

Heidi spoke about watching the progress of the orphans as they gradually become aware of their new status as adopted children. The newly adopted children, fresh off the streets, constantly avoid eye contact and will often just curl themselves up in a ball away from the other kids. They will freeze when hugged, unable to comprehend what is happening. They will cower in fear when the family dogs come near them.

But, after days and weeks of receiving constant love, hugs, food, care and affirmation, Heidi said that there comes a distinct moment when an orphan grasps that they really are a true son or daughter. From this point their demeanour totally changes, their confidence begins to rise, they feel free to raid the fridge for food whenever they like, they shout at the dogs to sit, and they laugh when they obey. The orphan spirit has left them and they know they have become sons and daughters.

Heidi said that those that do not know Christ have the opposite to the Spirit of adoption working in their lives. They live under an orphan spirit, even though most don't realize it. To Heidi, the preaching of the gospel is simply calling all the spiritual orphans home to the Father, so that they might receive the Spirit of adoption into their hearts, crying, 'Abba! Father!' I wonder, have you come to that point as a Christian where God's love overwhelms you and your self-understanding shifts from orphan to son?

We know we are God's sons because we believe his gospel. The gospel message is our adoption papers, and we have faith in their validity. I know I am adopted by my parents because I have the adoption papers and I know they are legitimate. I don't need any more proof that I am their adopted son than these legal documents – and you don't need any more proof that you are saved than faith in the 'document' of God's gospel word. Having said that, wouldn't it be strange if my parents didn't also want to demonstrate my adoption through personal and intimate love?

The Father desires to seal the adoption of his children with a personal experience of the baptism of the Holy Spirit. I have explained much of this in my teaching on Galatians 3, but it is worth revisiting this topic again. Notice that we must first be sons before we receive the Spirit of sonship. Having become sons of God, the Father then desires to send his Spirit into our lives, crying out, 'Abba! Father!' In this section on adoption, Paul is emphasizing the assurance element of the baptism of the Holy Spirit, rather than the power-for-service dimension.

God desires intimacy with his children and the basis of such a relationship is trust and assurance. Children need to be assured they are loved unconditionally for them to develop healthily. When a child is not assured of the unqualified love of its parents, then doubt, fear and the drive to seek acceptance can become the root cause of a future broken life. A healthy Christian life must also be founded on the assurance of God's eternal love for his children. Without this, the believer will eventually turn to legalism or despair. Because we are his sons, God wants to magnify and intensify the assurance we have by faith with an ongoing experience of the Holy Spirit.

It is important to note that in verse 6 Paul says that God sends forth the Spirit *of his Son*. It means that the Father wants his adopted sons to have the same experience and assurance of his fatherly love as his only begotten Son, Jesus, does. Through Spirit baptism the same Spirit that is in Jesus is poured into our hearts to give us an experience and assurance of God's fatherly love. Imagine that! The same Spirit that cries out 'Father' in Jesus now cries out 'Abba' from our hearts too.

And it is into our hearts that the Spirit is sent during the baptism of the Holy Spirit. Romans 5:5 explains that the love of God has been poured out into our *hearts* by the Holy Spirit who was given to us. It is that overwhelming love that God wants us to experience, so that we never doubt our salvation again. In 2 Corinthians 1:22 it says that God sealed us and gave us the Spirit in our *hearts* as a pledge.

The 'heart' can have many different nuances of meaning in the Bible, depending on the context in which it is written. The best way of describing the heart is to say that it is the deepest part of who we are. The heart is the real *you*; the essential you. When all that is superficial or pretend in our lives is stripped away, we get to the heart of who we really are. This is why God is primarily concerned with our hearts. It is out of our hearts that good or evil flows. God does not judge by appearances, but by what we really are in our heart of hearts.

Into our hearts God sends forth the Spirit of his Son, right into the centre of our being. The baptism of the Holy Spirit is an amazing experience bringing full assurance of salvation and power to minister the gospel. This experience also produces a response from us as we cry, 'Abba! Father!'

One of my greatest personal delights is to hug and cuddle my severely disabled daughter who can barely speak five words. As I pour out my total love and affection into her life she often can't help herself, she lets out a squeal of delight and it needs no interpretation. She knows she is adored, loved, and she cries out. The phrase 'cry out' is used both here in Galatians and also Romans 8:15–17

> For you have not received a spirit of slavery leading to fear again, but you have received a spirit of adoption as sons by which we *cry out*, 'Abba! Father!' The Spirit Himself testifies with our spirit that we are children of God, and if children, heirs also, heirs of God and fellow heirs with Christ . . . (NASB, emphasis added)

Krazo, the Greek word used for 'cry out' in the New Testament, refers to a spontaneous and emotional eruption that flows out from the heart and comes out of the mouth as a cry. When Peter was sinking on the water he 'cried out' to Jesus to save him. When Jesus entered Jerusalem, the crowds 'cried out', 'Hosanna!' When Jesus died on the cross he 'cried out', 'It is finished!'

The passage in Romans says that when we receive the Spirit we ourselves cry out 'Abba! Father!' Here in Galatians it says that the Spirit himself cries out, 'Abba! Father!' The Spirit cries out and we cry out. He witnesses to what we experience, and we cry out together. When a football crowd witnesses their team scoring, they all cry out testifying to the goal. Both our spirits and the Holy Spirit cry out together, testifying that we are children of God. It is 'Abba! Father!' that we cry out. The only time we witness Jesus using the phrase '*Abba*' is in the Garden of Gethsemane:

> And He was saying, 'Abba! Father! All things are possible for You; remove this cup from Me; yet not what I will, but what You will.' (Mark 14:36, NASB)

Abba is the Aramaic word a child would use to address their father. It is an intimate word, like 'Daddy'. The everyday language that Jesus spoke was Aramaic. In the Garden of Gethsemane, Jesus was at his most serious in his communion with his Father. The use of *Abba* shows the intimacy of his relationship with the Father, but also reveals that the term is not frivolous or some form of baby talk – it can be deeply serious as well as profoundly intimate. Paul's use of *Abba* underlines the fact that as adopted children, we are as much sons of the Father as Jesus.

His relationship with his Father is now ours. God the Father loves you as much as he loves Jesus.

The baptism in the Holy Spirit is not a one-off experience, but a doorway into a life of assurance and a Father-child relationship with power for service. Some teach that the sealing of the Spirit is an utterly sovereign act that one may or may not receive, depending on God's will. They teach that only in times of sovereign revival can we expect the majority of Christians to receive the Holy Spirit. There is no evidence for this position. I think people who teach this view have often experienced so little of the baptism of the Spirit in their own circles of influence that they assume it must be some rare sovereign act. Galatians 3 makes it clear that Spirit reception is received by hearing with faith, just like justification. It is available for all sons of God, and all the Galatians had experienced it. The baptism of the Holy Spirit is a promise to be appropriated by faith.

In order to see the sealing of the Spirit among the children of God it must be preached and taught to them, and it rarely is. We preach the power part of the baptism in the Holy Spirit, but rarely the experience of assurance it also brings. I have noticed that since I have preached the assurance and the power of the baptism in the Spirit, people have been experiencing both elements of it. We know that one cannot receive salvation without hearing the message of the gospel with faith, and very few will receive assurance unless they hear its message and believe God for this experience.

The Father's Blessing

The Toronto Blessing, or 'the Father's Blessing' as John and Carol Arnott prefer to call it, was a move of God that started in Canada in the mid 1990s. It is, in many ways, a movement demonstrating this assurance of the Spirit crying 'Abba! Father!' in the believer's life. Literally hundreds of thousands of people received an experience of the Father's love that not only revolutionized their relationship with God the Father, but freed them to serve the Lord in a new and fruitful way. For some, I am sure it was the first time they were baptized in the Holy Spirit. For others, it was part of the ongoing pouring out of God's love into their hearts. The sealing of the Spirit is not a self-centred, introverted experience. It is a freeing, releasing, empowering experience. It releases one from constant introspective examination to be able to focus better on the lives of others.

I remember my experience of the Fathers' Blessing at John and Carol Arnott's church in Toronto in 1994. For five days I witnessed people receiving powerful experiences of God's love. I had been sealed by the Spirit a few years before then, and had never since doubted my status as a child of God. Often, during the all-night services, I felt a little bit removed from what was going on, because I wasn't having the powerful experience that many others were. On the last night, one of the ministers came up to me in the prayer line and simply said, 'I see by the Spirit that you are a minister. The Lord wants you to know that it is you he loves and it is you he wants, and your ministry and its success means nothing to him compared to this.' Well, this word hit me like a hammer that breaks a rock. I received a new dimension of assurance that meant that subsequent failures in ministry would never affect my knowledge of God's everlasting devotion to me. I know of many ministers who need this type of revelation today.

There is an initial sealing of the Spirit that opens us up to a life of encounters with the Father's love. We are assured by God so that we can be confident enough to minister in power, self-sacrificially. Assurance allows us to be delivered from our insecurities with God and from self-indulgent 'navel-gazing'.

I have already said that speaking in tongues is the initial evidence of the sealing (or baptism) of the Holy Spirit. Peter's evidence of the Gentiles' Spirit baptism was that they spoke in tongues and praised God just as he did on the day of Pentecost. There are two types of gifts of tongues in the New Testament: *personal tongues* that we receive at our sealing, and tongues that come only *as and when the Spirit desires* for interpretation and the edification of the church. The tongues problem in Corinthians was that they were mixing up these two separate gifts. The tongues that you receive when you receive the Spirit are personal and addressed to God. Once received, you may speak in this tongue any time you wish to edify your life:

> For one who speaks in a tongue does not speak to men but to God
> . . . (1 Cor. 14:2, NASB)

How do we speak 'Abba! Father!' at our reception of the Spirit? We do it by spontaneously speaking in tongues with praise. The cry of the Spirit of adoption is not a silent one.

Lost assurance

The Galatians had lost the assurance that they had once experienced. Not only had they lost this experience, but of even more concern, they had also lost the assurance that comes from faith alone. By looking to the Law for assurance of salvation they had fallen from the path of grace. Instead of living as adopted sons of God, they were sliding back into slavery. The Galatians had transferred the ground of their assurance from Christ to the Law, and from the witness of the Holy Spirit to their own works.

I would like to make the point that it is also possible for believers to lose their sense of assurance without backsliding like the Galatians did towards the Law. Sometimes the trials and tests that we go through in life can squeeze out almost every ounce of the sense of assurance that dwells within us, and we can be left just hanging on to the promise of God's love by faith. Sometimes God even seems to hide his face from us and we can feel as if we have been abandoned. In those times, all we have left is faith in the promise of Christ. We must remember that these tests and trails are ultimately designed to strengthen and enrich our relationship with God, not to destroy it.

> Consider it pure joy, my brothers, whenever you face trials of many kinds, because you know that the testing of your faith develops perseverance. Perseverance must finish its work so that you may be mature and complete, not lacking anything. (Jas 1:2, NIV)

The doctrine of the assurance of the Spirit does not replace our walking by faith. The reception of the Spirit does not change our Christian faith into a feelings-based religion. Sometimes our assurance of God's love is tested so that it can develop to become even deeper in our lives. This reminds me of growing up under the care of my mother and father, who adopted me. Like every child, my relationship with my parents went through tests and trials, but today my bond with my Mum and Dad is better and deeper than ever because our relationship has matured through the years. Sometimes it is the hardest trials of life that bring a child and their parents closest together. It can be the same with our relationship with our heavenly Father.

In Galatians 4:7, Paul concludes this section of his teaching by addressing the condition that the Galatians found themselves in, having lost their assurance. Having known that they were saved through faith, the Galatians were now entering into an awful situation of assurance by self-examination. In order to be assured of salvation they would now need to be circumcised, obey the food laws and the Sabbath and feast days. They would have to obey all the precepts of the Law to be confident that they were acceptable to God.

In this life of legalism, Christ could have no place. It was either the Law or Christ; faith in him or faith in their own works; trust in repeated, ineffective animal sacrifices, or faith in the once and for all atoning death of the Lamb of God. There could be no mixing of the Law with faith, because the two are mutually exclusive.

Paul still addressed the Galatians as sons despite all of their backsliding from the gospel. He had been present at their adoption by God, seen their profession of faith and witnessed their baptism in the Spirit. When Paul wrote to the Thessalonians, he reminded them how the New Testament gospel was not just one of words, but one of power and assurance through the subsequent sealing of the Spirit:

> For our gospel did not come to you in word only, but also in power, and in the Holy Spirit and in much assurance . . . (1 Thess. 1:5, NKJV)

The Galatians may have lost sight of who they were, but Paul hadn't. He spoke to them according to their nature and not their present experience. He was calling them back to sonship, and telling them to stop acting like slaves.

12.

No Turning Back

(Gal. 4:8–20)

(8) Formerly, however, when you did not know God, you were in slavery to beings that by nature are no gods. (9) But now that you have come to know God, or rather to be known by God, how is it that you are turning back again to the weak and beggarly elemental forces? Do you want to be in slavery to them once again? (10) You are observing days and months and special times and years. (11) I am afraid that perhaps I have laboured for you to no avail.

The Galatian déjà vu

The Galatians thought that by embracing the Jewish Law they were advancing in their knowledge of God. The Judaizers taught them that in order to mature in their faith they had to embrace the observances and traditions that had been handed down through successive generations of Jews since Moses. Paul, in Galatians 4:8–11, argues that the Galatians were not advancing in their knowledge of God, but were, in fact, returning to a situation not dissimilar to when they were unconverted. Paul was effectively saying, 'Can't you Galatians see that all this legalism is really déjà vu? You have seen and experienced all this before as pagans.'

Paul contrasts the condition of the Galatians before and after their conversion. He asks them to recall how that before the gospel came to them, they had absolutely no idea who God was. Paul uses two Greek words translated as 'know' in verses 8 and 9. The first word, *oida*, is used in verse 8 in regard to their lack of knowledge of God as pagans. The second word is *ginosko* and is used in verse 9 to describe knowing God personally and being known by him as a believer. A brief comparison of the two words will explain exactly the difference in the Galatians' understanding of God before and after salvation. The comparison also shows the present danger of them losing the second kind of *ginosko* knowledge by returning to a religion of works, laws and rites.

Ginosko often refers to a personal, intuitive, progressive and intimate knowledge of a truth or person, whereas *oida* refers to a more factual, observable knowledge or perception. For example, John 14:7

> If you had known [*ginosko*] Me, you would have known [*oida*] My Father also; and from now on you know [*ginosko*] Him . . . (NKJV)

We can see in the above verse that personal and intimate knowledge of Jesus would bring an awareness of the fact of reality of the Father – and knowledge of this fact would then lead to a personal knowledge of the Father.

Oidas can be likened to the fan of a famous star knowing all the facts about their life and career and yet never meeting them in person. *Ginosko* is like becoming that star's personal, intimate friend with knowledge of them in that sense. Before the gospel came to the Galatian Gentiles, they didn't even *oidas* God, let alone *ginosko* him. They were ignorant of the true and living God; they didn't even know of his existence. However, when they believed in the gospel they came to *ginosko* God intimately and personally. The Galatians had forgotten the pitiful state of ignorance they were formerly in, and the wonderful experience of getting to know God that began when they first had faith in Christ.

In verse 9 we notice Paul making a remark, then pausing, rethinking what he has just written and then clarifying it

> But now you have come to know God, or rather to be known by God . . . (NASB)

Many times, as Christians, we invite unbelievers to come and *know* God. We appeal to them to respond to the gospel and rightfully so.

But salvation is not ultimately about us finding God, but God finding us

> For those whom He foreknew [*proginosko*], He also predestined to become conformed to the image of His Son, so that He would be the firstborn among many brethren; and these whom He predestined, He also called; and these whom He called, He also justified; and these whom He justified, He also glorified. (Rom. 8:29,30, NASB)

In Romans 8:29 we see Paul using the word *pro-ginosko* to describe God's foreknowledge of who would believe, even before they actually come to faith. This knowledge is not simply a factual knowledge (*oidas*) by God that certain people would one day believe. Rather it is the loving knowledge (*ginosko*) and desire of the Father who foreknew his future children individually and personally. This intimate foreknowledge energizes the whole of salvation, guaranteeing not only our justification, but also our future glorification at Christ's return. God's intimate knowledge of us and our progression in the knowledge of him is at the heart of the gospel message.

With these things in mind, it seemed incredible to Paul that the Galatians wanted to replace their personal knowledge of God with obedience to rules, Sabbaths, special feast days and outward observances of the Law. We know that the Jewish Law was viewed by Paul as just as much a part of the *stoicheia* or elemental forces of the world as paganism in respect to its ability to save (Gal. 4:3). It is true that the Jews under the Law did have an *oida* knowledge of God, unlike the Gentiles, but in all other respects, when it came to a saving knowledge of God, it was no different than paganism – it simply could not deliver righteousness to humankind.

These weak and beggarly forces could enslave, but they could not save. In comparison to the riches of the gospel, the elemental forces were spiritually impoverished and bankrupt. Paul fears that he has laboured in vain amongst the Galatians. He used this word 'vain' back in Galatians 3:4

> Have you suffered so many things in vain – if indeed it was in vain? (NKJV)

Paul desired to see Christ formed in believers through discipleship. Just a few verses later (v. 19) Paul speaks of labouring in birth again until Christ is formed in the Galatians. They had been through so much and if they continued with the Judaizers, the church of Galatia that had started so well would end up shipwrecked and desolate. Anyone who has ever been involved in the work of church planting (and at Kensington Temple we started over one hundred and fifty churches in the 1990s) knows the joys of a flourishing new church, but also the pain of seeing a church that begins so strong and full of promise deteriorate into the final throes of death. Paul was jealous over his children.

The future of the church in Galatia was hanging in the balance, and in Galatians 4:12–20 Paul reminds them of the incredible relationship and fellowship that they shared together in the gospel before the Judaizers attempted to spoil it

> (12) Become as I am brothers, I beg you, because I also became as you are. You have done me no wrong; (13) for you know that it was on account of the weakness of the flesh that I preached the good news to you earlier; (14) and you did not despise or spit at what was a provocation to you in my flesh, but welcomed me as an angel of God, as Christ Jesus. (15) Where then is your blessing? I testify on your behalf that if it had been possible you would have torn out your eyes and given them to me. (16) So now I have become your enemy by telling you the truth? (17) They are zealous over you for no good purpose, but wish to shut you out, in order that you might be zealous over them. (18) It is always good when zeal is displayed in something good, and not only when I am present with you. (19) My children, over whom I am again in the pain of childbirth until Christ is formed in you; (20) I was wishing I could be present with you now and could change my tone, for I am at a loss in your case.

Throughout Galatians Paul has defended the supremacy of faith over works. His arguments have come from autobiography, from incidents that took place in the early church, from the Galatians' own experience and from Scripture. Now he reminds them of the incredible fellowship that they had personally enjoyed together in the gospel.

There is very little in church life that is as upsetting as seeing once intimate and fruitful relationships for Christ turning sour over doctrine or matters of vision and direction. In this deeply personal and emotional section of the letter we see how spiritual relationships, often closer than even family ties, can be tested to breaking point. The relationship Paul had with the Galatians was one of a father to his children. Paul had nothing natural in common with the Galatians – it was the gospel message that had united them as brothers and sisters in Christ. Now that the gospel was being undermined, so also was the relationship that had sprung from it.

Paul had challenged the Galatians, saying that perhaps everything they had experienced was in vain, but now he pleads with them as brothers. He is asking them to open their hearts, to remember the 'good old days' of grace. He is appealing to them to become like he is, for he had become like they were. He is asking the Galatians to put themselves in his shoes. They were travelling in the opposite spiritual direction from Paul, aspiring to place themselves under the same Law that Paul had died to years ago. Paul had become as they were: living as a Gentile believer free from the Law. Now they wanted to live like he had in the past, as Jews under it! Paul is saying that therefore they should follow him and now die to the Law by faith in Christ as he had.

An eye for an eye?

Paul told the Galatians that they had done him no wrong. He appealed to the benefits of their past relationship, but he was not going to deal with this present situation out of a feeling of personal offence. Of course, he was deeply pained by the whole condition of the Galatian church, and in many ways they had indeed done him wrong. But he now acted out of concern for their perilous position. If Paul acted out of feelings of offence it would not only cloud the issues that were at stake, but also be entirely counterproductive. If only leaders in the midst of church disputes today could follow the model of Paul here, much harm and hurt could be avoided. It is unfortunate that in many church disputes people very soon lose sight of the actual issues and degenerate into personal power struggles fuelled by deep offence. Paul was determined to avoid this.

He remembers the wonderful way in which the Galatians got to know him. When he first met them he was far from at his best; it seems that he was struggling from a physical weakness. This may have been a sickness. If so, the question is whether Paul had travelled to the Galatian highlands because the environment would be healthier for him, or whether it meant that he stayed there for longer than he expected because his illness prevented him from travelling.

However, this physical condition of Paul's was probably not an illness at all. He was probably recovering from having recently been stoned and left for dead in Lystra

> But Jews came from Antioch and Iconium, and having won over the crowds, they stoned Paul and dragged him out of the city, supposing him to be dead. But while the disciples stood around him, he got up and entered the city. The next day he went away with Barnabas to Derbe. (Acts 14:19,20, NASB)

Can you imagine the physical state of Paul, having been stoned so badly by his persecutors that they assumed he was dead? His appearance must have been horrific for months, his disfigured face bruised and battered. This would certainly explain his distasteful appearance and his reference to the Galatians being prepared to pluck out their eyes for him, along with his need for recuperation and rest. It would also explain their deep affection for him in his physical circumstances, for the gospel he preached was not just in words and power, it was written into his body.

Perhaps Paul was keen to remind the Galatians at this point in the letter about these physical badges of honour. For instead of being disgusted by his appearance, as one might expect, the Galatians were acutely touched by his infirmity. They received him like an angel, as if he was Jesus Christ himself. They were so impacted by his gospel message and his visible commitment to die for Christ that they responded by not only believing, but also desiring to tear out their own eyes (as Paul's had nearly been torn out by stoning) and give them to Paul as a gift. In other words, they wanted to share in his sufferings for the gospel.

This unity and strong emotional fellowship in the gospel makes what Paul writes in verse 16 all the more striking: 'So now I have become your enemy by telling you the truth?' How ironic – it was the truth that had made them friends, and now it was the same truth that was making Paul their enemy! Paul hadn't altered one bit; he had remained constant in the same gospel and the same truth. It was the Galatians who had changed.

Paul then turns to the real enemy – the Judaizers and their attempt to deceive the Galatians. As in all attempts to break up a fruitful relationship, the Judaizers had attempted to separate and isolate the Galatians from Paul. The Judaizers were extremely zealous about determining who was and wasn't a genuine Christian. It was adherence to the Law, especially circumcisions and food laws, that proved someone was a true believer. To them it was all about inclusion and exclusion, who was in the covenant and who was outside.

> (17) They are zealous over you for no good purpose, but wish to shut you out, in order that you might be zealous over them.

Like the Judaizers, modern-day cults use the same technique of separating and isolating their adherents from former influences. 'Love bombing' is a technique where spiritual leaders attempt, in a short period of time, to pour out attention and affection upon the individuals they are seeking to control and deceive. Whilst lavishing attention on the victims, they also begin to encourage the individuals to separate from and cut off all former friends, family and mentors in their lives. The end result is a cult member who shuts out all influences from the past and lives a life controlled by an isolated community.

Members of a cult trust no one but their own leaders and those who follow its rules, teachings and regulations. Paul was doing his best to de-programme the Galatian disciples from these Judaizing zealots. He so wished he could be with them, but he was suffering the disadvantage that the Judaizers were there 24/7, and because of this his tone had to be strong, immovable and aggressive to wrench them out of the clutches of these deceivers.

(19) My children, over whom I am again in the pain of childbirth until Christ is formed in you.

Paul appeals to them as a true father in the gospel, and he uses a powerful analogy of labouring in birth for them again until Christ is formed. It was not that Paul was referring to them being born again-again or being twice regenerated. Paul understood the Galatians to be both regenerated and justified already.

You in Christ and Christ in you

It is helpful at this point to understand that Paul in his epistles teaches a difference between us being in Christ and Christ being in us.

'Being in Christ' refers to our position and union in him. We looked at this doctrine back in Galatians 2:20. A great study of Paul's use of 'in Christ' can be found in Ephesians 1:1–15 where 'in Christ' is used eleven times in fifteen verses. All the backslidden Galatian believers were 'in Christ' because they had genuinely been converted. Being in Christ refers to our regeneration and justification. It refers to our status in Christ as believers.

But Paul also refers to 'Christ in you' or 'being formed in you'. Paul was not so concerned about them being in Christ, but was more anxious about the formation of Christ's likeness in them. Paul recognized that salvation should also work through our lives in a process of spiritual maturing and sanctification. He will criticize the fleshly Corinthians for being babes in Christ, only able to receive milk and not solid food. The Galatians were in an even worse state than the Corinthians because legalism is a more dangerous sin than even carnality. That is why Paul was so much tougher on the Galatians, because their sin actually perverted the very gospel message itself. In Corinth, Paul did not have to fight for the gospel message, rather he confronted fleshly lifestyles. The Galatians tampering with the gospel message was so serious that they were in danger of not even being recognized as Christian babies. The Corinthians couldn't digest spiritual solid food, only baby milk, but the Galatians were actually allowing the spiritual milk itself to become poisoned.

When Paul says he is labouring in birth for the Galatians again, he is referring to the work of re-establishing the ABCs of the gospel in their lives. They thought they were superior by turning to the Law, but actually they had so regressed in their faith in Christ that the next step forward for them was to become babes in Christ all over again.

The reference to the pains of birthing a child show how deeply and intimately Paul felt the pains of the situation in Galatia that he was addressing. The picture of him bringing the Galatians to birth a second time also brought a sharp contrast to the Galatians' own view of themselves – that by adhering to the Law they were actually maturing as believers. The childbirth imagery also connects with his earlier teaching on sonship and inheritance, and anticipates his next teaching on the birth of Isaac and Ishmael. Paul knows that the Galatians are children of God, but he reminds them that he is also, in a sense, a spiritual parent to them. There is a motherly association that he has with them in the gospel that the Judaizers could never share.

And, like a spiritual mother, Paul wished that he was present with his children so that he could change his tone. Paul was aware of the limitations of a letter as a vehicle for communication. We know that in 2 Corinthians 10:10 Paul was criticized by some for being bold in letter and weak in presence

> For they say, 'His letters are weighty and strong, but his personal presence is unimpressive and his speech contemptible.' (NASB)

Face to face is always the best way to deal with conflict if possible. It is amazing how tempers can flare and positions harden between two parties who are in conflict through only the medium of letters, emails or even a third party. But there is nothing like being face to face with someone when dealing with a major issue. It brings openness, and an opportunity to swiftly deal with misconceptions. No wonder Paul wished he was present with the Galatians in order to dispel the concerns he had about them.

13.

Your Mother From Above

(Gal. 4:21–31)

(21) Tell me, you who want to be under the law, do you not listen
to the law? (22) For it is written that Abraham had two sons, one
by a slave girl, the other by a free woman. (23) But the son of the
slave girl was born in accordance with the flesh, whereas the son
of the free woman was born through the promise. (24) Such things
are to be interpreted allegorically. For these women are two
covenants; one from Mount Sinai gives birth into slavery – such is
Hagar. (25) This Hagar – Sinai is a mountain in Arabia; she belongs
to the same column as the present Jerusalem, for she is in slavery
with her children. (26) But the Jerusalem above is free; such is our
mother. (27) For it is written: Rejoice, you barren one who bears no
children, break forth and cry aloud, you who experience no labour
pains, because many are the children of the deserted wife, more
than of her who has her husband. (28) And you, brothers, like
Isaac are children of promise. (29) But just as then, the one born in
accordance with the flesh used to persecute the one born in accordance with the Spirit, so also now. (30) But what says the scripture? 'Throw out the slave girl and her son; for the son of the slave
girl will never inherit with the son of the free woman'. (31)
Wherefore, brothers, we are children not of the slave girl but of the
free woman.

Having addressed the Galatians as his little children for whom he
was giving birth all over again, Paul turns to the account of two
mothers giving birth to two sons. His tone and style shifts from a
personal appeal to a pictorial and symbolic representation of his

argument so far. Many scholars feel that the allegory about Sarah, Hagar and their respective sons was unnecessary, as he had already fully argued his case against being under the Law. But one of the key questions that Paul addresses in the letter is who has the right to call themselves sons of Abraham (Gal. 3:29). Both the Judaizers and Paul are claiming to be the legitimate heirs of Abraham, so Paul turns to the story of Abraham and his sons to explain that it is those of faith who are the rightful heirs of Abraham. Those following the Law have become 'Ishmaels' and are to be cast out from the Abrahamic family.

In verse 20, Paul wishes he could change his tone to them, and in the next verse he does. He taunts them, sarcastically asking if they truly desired to be under the Law, then why did they not listen to the Law? In the Greek, the word for 'listen' is based on the word for hearing, *akouo*. You can see the similarity between the two words in the Greek. Obedience literally means 'under hearing'. The Law or Torah was not just used for the entire corpus of Jewish Law, but also as shorthand for the first five books of the Old Testament (also known as the Pentateuch). Paul was saying 'OK, you Galatians want Law? I'll give you Law! Listen and obey this . . . For it is written!' Paul then hits them hard with the allegory taken from the book of Genesis, which was also part of the Torah that they wanted to be under.

Paul's allegory

Paul's description of the two wives of Abraham and their sons is allegorical (v. 24). An allegory takes people, objects and actions in a tale and then uses them to represent something outside of the storyline. A metaphor is when you compare two different things by linking them directly to each other. For instance, she is a rose, he is a pig, the world is a stage. Allegories are really extended metaphors and were very popular in both Greek and Hebrew teaching during New Testament times. Unlike parables, which usually illustrate one major truth, allegories can often represent a number of different ones.

Not everyone had the logical mind of Paul, and this allegory supplements his early teaching by putting his position into an

easily recognized, understood and remembered story. This allegory captures so much of the heart of the letter to the Galatians
that it is extremely valuable in giving us a new dimension of
Paul's message. To those of us who think better in pictures than
in abstracts, Paul's allegory helps enormously.

It begins by describing Abraham as the father of two boys. We
know that Paul has argued about who is the genuine seed and
heir of Abraham. Whoever is the true heir of Abraham receives
the benefits of his covenant blessing. Paul claims that the true
descendants of Abraham are those of faith not works

> Therefore, be sure that it is those who are of faith who are sons of
> Abraham. (Gal. 3:7, NASB)

The question is: Which one of his sons was of faith, and which
one was of works or the flesh? In the allegory there is one father
but two wives, bearing two sons in two different ways. The wives
were very different to one another; indeed, they were exact oppo-
sites. Sarah was a free woman, but Hagar was a slave girl.
Although the women shared the same husband, they didn't share
the same status or position. Both women gave birth to sons, but
the way that their sons were born couldn't have been more dissimilar. Ishmael was born according to the flesh; Isaac was born
through the promise.

It is sufficient to say here that the flesh symbolizes unbelief, disobedience, reliance on human effort and surrender to our base and
carnal instincts. The flesh is the opposite to living by faith in God's
promises by the power of the Spirit. So when Paul tells us that
Ishmael was born according to the flesh we can sense the poor,
weak, feeble and negative circumstances that the boy was born
into. Ishmael was the product of human thinking, human working
and, even worse, he was the product of unbelief. In this allegory,
'flesh' really equates to unbelief. Ishmael was not part of God's
plan for Abraham; he was completely unnecessary. If Abraham
had remained faithful to God's promise, Ishmael would have
never been born. Abraham's unbelief spawned a wholly negative
series of events – it was a human counterfeit of a divine plan.

Contrast Isaac, born through the promise of God. How different were the circumstances of the birth of the son of promise. Paul

has emphasized the importance of God's promise to the Galatians in his letter, especially in Galatians 3:16–22, and how the Law had absolutely no effect on the promise given to Abraham and his seed. Isaac was the result of God's grace, promise and divine activity.

It is interesting to compare this section of Galatians with Romans 9:6–13

> But it is not as though the word of God has failed. For they are not all Israel who are descended from Israel; nor are they all children because they are Abraham's descendants, but: 'THROUGH ISAAC YOUR DESCENDANTS WILL BE NAMED.' That is, it is not the children of the flesh who are children of God, but the children of the promise are regarded as descendants. For this is the word of promise: 'AT THIS TIME I WILL COME, AND SARAH SHALL HAVE A SON.' And not only this, but there was Rebekah also, when she had conceived twins by one man, our father Isaac; for though the twins were not yet born and had not done anything good or bad, so that God's purpose according to His choice might stand, not because of works but because of Him who calls, it was said to her, 'THE OLDER WILL SERVE THE YOUNGER.' Just as it is written, 'JACOB I LOVED, BUT ESAU I HATED.' (NASB)

We can see that Paul is expanding on this theme in Romans concerning the nature of the descendants of Abraham. Here again we have the children of the flesh and the children of the promise. Even with Isaacs's sons there was a distinction between the son of the promise and the son of the flesh. Esau sold his birthright due to his unbridled appetite for food, whereas God promised that the older would serve the younger. God's choice and promise make us into children of Abraham.

In Galatians 4:24, the allegorical interpretation of the two mothers is that they represent two covenants. Hagar represents the Law given on Mount Sinai which gives birth to bondage. Sarah represents the Jerusalem above and is the mother of all who believe. The reference to geographical places is important because Sinai lies outside the promised land of Canaan, and thus outside the realm of God's promise to the Exodus generation. Like Ishmael, the Law wasn't necessary for those who believed the promise, it was added because of the transgression of those who did not believe. In the allegory Paul puts Hagar and the Law into the same category, even though Hagar had no more knowledge of the Law than either Abraham or Sarah. Both Hagar and the Law came onto the scene through unbelief and sin; both produced bondage and that is why they are classed together.

The Jerusalem 'from above' is contrasted with Hagar and Sinai. In Hebrews 12:18–24 we see the Jerusalem from above seated on Mount Zion and compared to Mount Sinai and the giving of the Law

> For you have not come to a mountain that can be touched and to a blazing fire, and to darkness and gloom and whirlwind, and to the blast of a trumpet and the sound of words which sound was such that those who heard begged that no further word be spoken to them. For they could not bear the command, 'IF EVEN A BEAST TOUCHES THE MOUNTAIN, IT WILL BE STONED.' And so terrible was the sight, that Moses said, 'I AM FULL OF FEAR and trembling.' But you have come to Mount Zion and to (the city of the living God, the heavenly Jerusalem, and to myriads of angels, to the general assembly and church of the firstborn who are enrolled in heaven, and to God, the Judge of all, and to the spirits of the righteous made perfect, and to Jesus, the mediator of a new covenant, and to the sprinkled blood, which speaks better than the blood of Abel. (NASB)

We can see in this passage the difference between the two covenants. The Law brought fear, darkness and judgement. Even if a beast touched the mountain it would be stoned. But the heavenly Jerusalem is the city of the living God, full of righteous inhabitants sprinkled clean by the blood of Christ's sacrifice.

The main characteristic of the Jerusalem above is freedom. This liberty bears fruit and joy. The characteristic of the blessing of God is fruitfulness and multiplication, but often in Scripture fruitfulness comes out of a terrible place of barrenness. We think not only about the example of the barrenness of Sarah, but also of Rachel, Hannah and Elizabeth. Paul was, in a sense, the mother of the Galatian churches through the power of the gospel. The Galatians had been spiritually born through regeneration. They were children of Abraham because they had been born of the Spirit. They had been 'born from above' (see John 3:3).

Out of this allegory, Paul quotes from Isaiah 54:1 a promise of fruitfulness in the midst of barrenness. In its original context, Isaiah was prophesying to the exiled Jews carried off to Babylonian captivity. Jerusalem had been left desolate, without walls or inhabitants. Isaiah promised that one day the barrenness would end and Jerusalem would be more populous than ever before. Present barrenness is dealt with by a promise of future blessing, and the expected response of the people is to have faith in that promise.

In Isaiah 51:1-3 the exiles are asked to look to Abraham and Sarah in their barrenness to encourage them that God's promise for fruitfulness would always eventually come to pass.

> Listen to me, you who pursue righteousness,
> Who seek the LORD:
> Look to the rock from which you were hewn
> And to the quarry from which you were dug.
> 'Look to Abraham your father
> And to Sarah who gave birth to you in pain;
> When he was but one I called him,
> Then I blessed him and multiplied him.'
> Indeed, the LORD will comfort Zion;
> He will comfort all her waste places.
> And her wilderness He will make like Eden,
> And her desert like the garden of the LORD;
> Joy and gladness will be found in her,
> Thanksgiving and sound of a melody. (NASB)

So, even during the Babylonian captivity of Israel, God was giving promises of blessing and fruitfulness to his desolate and barren people. This is the way that God deals with his people. He brings them a promise in the midst of defeat, a word of life into a sterile environment, and he expects people to believe in his word of promise.

The way to deal with barrenness in our lives and ministry is not by leaning on the arm of the flesh; it is not by manufacturing the semblance of success by human means, or giving birth to our own version of Ishmael. How do you know whether you are birthing Ishmael or Isaac? Well, how do you deal with the barrenness in your life? How do you cope with disappointment and disillusionment?

Over the years I have met many Christian leaders who have had their 'faith edge' blunted by barrenness, fruitlessness and desolation. Such leaders may become cynical about promises yet unfulfilled. Hope deferred can definitely make the heart sick, and the heart is the seat of faith. Their faith and expectation rises no higher than their natural experience. They laugh at the idea of an Isaac being born. They have become fleshly, empowered by human reason and natural resources alone. The best they can hope for is an Ishmael to be born.

But Paul has a word for those in barrenness: 'Rejoice, you barren one . . .' This is the rejoicing of faith whilst we are actually still in barrenness – the shout of victory whilst not even in the process of birthing our promised Isaacs. Walking by the promises in contrary circumstances – that is the single proof that our Isaacs will eventually come forth

> For this reason it is by faith, in order that it may be in accordance with grace, so that the promise will be guaranteed to all the descendants, not only to those who are of the Law, but also to those who are of the faith of Abraham, who is the father of us all, (as it is written, 'A FATHER OF MANY NATIONS HAVE I MADE YOU') in the presence of Him whom he believed, even God, who gives life to the dead and calls into being that which does not exist. In hope against hope he believed, so that he might become a father of many nations according to that which had been spoken, 'SO SHALL YOUR DESCENDANTS BE.' (Rom. 4:16–18, NASB)

So we see that the gospel comes with a promise, and when it is believed it brings fruitfulness, whereas the Law can't bring life to anything or anyone (Gal. 2:21). As children of Abraham we live by the promises of God, just as he did.

(28) And you, brothers, like Isaac are children of promise.

The Galatians were asked to identify themselves with Isaac, for they were born of the promise of God. The promise that birthed them spiritually was also the promise that would raise them to spiritual maturity. The Judaizers were of the flesh, the Galatians were born of the Spirit. Paul had been persecuted by Judaizers right from the beginning of his ministry to the Gentiles. It is very possible that Paul's 'thorn in the flesh' was, in fact, the legalists plaguing him and his ministry at every turn, trying to turn the liberty of the gospel into the bondage of the Law.

Kick out Ishmael!

(30) But what says the scripture? 'Throw out the slave girl and her son; for the son of the slave girl will never inherit with the son of the free woman'.

Paul knew exactly what the Galatians needed to do. They had to expel these Judaizers from their midst. This is a reference to Genesis 21:8–13

The child grew and was weaned, and Abraham made a great feast on the day that Isaac was weaned. Now Sarah saw the son of Hagar the Egyptian, whom she had borne to Abraham, mocking. Therefore she said to Abraham, 'Drive out this maid and her son, for the son of this maid shall not be an heir with my son Isaac.' The matter distressed Abraham greatly because of his son. But God said to Abraham, 'Do not be distressed because of the lad and your maid; whatever Sarah tells you, listen to her, for through Isaac your descendants shall be named. And of the son of the maid I will make a nation also, because he is your descendant.' (NASB)

The Galatians had turned from Isaac to Ishmael, from beginning in the Spirit to attempting to be perfected in the flesh. In Galatians 5:17 we shall see how the flesh and the Spirit are in absolute opposition to one another. There can be no partnership between flesh and Spirit in any way whatsoever. Ishmael mocked Isaac, and Sarah saw this as a threat to the promised inheritance. Sarah's insistence that Ishmael and his mother be driven out greatly distressed Abraham.

It is possible in our Christian lives and ministries to have strong attachments that are motivated by natural rather than spiritual affections – love of traditions or an excessive attachment to a form or model of church, past or present. Anyone who has ever operated at a high level of Christian leadership will attest to the fact that some of the hardest decisions are the ones we have to make about people or the direction of ministry that goes against natural affections, instincts and relationships. Abraham loved Ishmael with all his natural fatherly affection. He would even be prepared to overlook his bullying of the promised child just to keep him around.

I remember one new believer at KT who was growing well in the Lord, but the problem was she could not break away from her Ishmael. Her Ishmael was her unbelieving boyfriend who had abused her psychologically many times in the past. She had such a fleshly attachment to him that she just kept going back to him. As a result, a cycle of abuse, break up, Christian progress and then backsliding again occurred. She was counselled and warned by her cell leader to cast out this Ishmael from her life once and for all, but she just could not do it. In the end, the girl totally backslid to this unbelieving man and left the church. We must understand that we can never have both Ishmael and Isaac, no matter how much we try. In the end, one or the other must prevail in our life.

Paul understood this principle and wrote in Galatians 5:29 that that which is born of the flesh always persecutes that which is born of the Spirit. Abraham had to crucify his natural affections for the sake of spiritual ones. It was one of the hardest things he ever had to do, to cast out Ishmael. How much easier it would have been if the boy had never been born.

How much better for the Galatians if they had never heard of the Law, but they were growing in natural affection towards circumcision, food laws and living by the Law for their assurance. They were casting out Isaac in preference of Ishmael! Paul reminds the Galatians that they are children not of Hagar, but Sarah. As we shall witness later in Galatians, there is an all-out war declared by the flesh against the Spirit, and vice versa. As Christians we aren't to mediate or negotiate a peace between flesh and Spirit, for that is unachievable.

14.

Liberated for Freedom

(Gal. 5:1–6)

(1) For freedom Christ has set us free. Stand firm, therefore, and do not be subject again to a yoke of slavery. (2) Look! I, Paul, say to you that if you are circumcised, Christ will benefit you not at all. (3) I testify again to everyone who is being circumcised that he is obligated to do the whole law. (4) You have been estranged from Christ, you who are seeking to be justified by the law; you have fallen away from grace. (5) For we by the Spirit, from faith, are awaiting eagerly the hope of righteousness. (6) For in Christ Jesus neither circumcision counts for anything, nor uncircumcision, but faith operating effectively through love.

The whole message of the letter to the Galatians is summed up in verse 1. This verse also transitions us from the teaching of justification by faith alone into the teaching of sanctified living. Paul has, by this point in the letter, firmly established the truth that Christ is the sole foundation of salvation. Once we truly believe in him we have forever passed from death to eternal life, we are adopted into the family of God and secure in our eternal salvation. Christ has forever set us free from the realm of sin, the condemnation of the Law and the power of Satan. By faith we are in Christ, and everything that happened to him has also happened to us. We are even seated with him in heavenly places. It is a done deal, we are eternally set free.

Paul is quite clear that we have been set free and this is our unassailable position. But we have been set free for a purpose on earth, not just qualification for heaven. It is for freedom that we have been set free. Paul understands that it is possible to have been set free and yet not properly experience this freedom in daily life – like a slave being given a legal document of freedom and then returning to the cotton fields. The slave is free but he doesn't enjoy his freedom; he doesn't know how to. When we were justified through faith alone, we were legally set free. But God doesn't just want us legally free, he wants us to experience that freedom right now.

The Galatians had been set free. Paul was in no doubt of this, for he had just called them children of the promise and children of the free (Gal. 4:28,31). Yet the Galatians were stepping into one of the very bondages they had been set free from, namely the Law. It was not for bondage that Christ had set them free, but for true Christian liberty.

Paul's teaching on justification by faith so far has begged the question of how a Christian should live life practically. He has been unyielding in his view that morality, supremely demonstrated in the Law, has absolutely no place in our justification. Salvation by grace through faith alone can't be affected by any external factors, including our good or even bad actions. It was Christ who set us free and even our faith was a gift from him (Eph. 2:8,9).

If you have properly understood the message of Galatians so far, your response might be to think that the gospel Paul preached was an antinomian one. The word 'antinomian' means 'against the Law' and refers to Christians who believe that they have been freed to enjoy whatever they want, including sin and the works of the flesh. Paul was often accused of preaching antinomianism. His opponents said that because he taught that there was unlimited grace for the believer, that he implied we are therefore free to continue in sin (Rom. 6:1). If we demolish the Law, including the Ten Commandments, the question is, what do we put in its place? How do we live? How do we know what is right or wrong? Galatians 5 answers these questions.

What is freedom?

Most people who misunderstand the gospel have a faulty understanding regarding the nature and meaning of biblical 'freedom'. We live in a Western world that is dominated by the term 'freedom'.

We talk of freedom of religion, freedom of conscience, democratic freedom, personal freedoms, freedom of choice – we even fight wars for 'freedom'.

To Western minds, total freedom means to have the power to do whatever we want. True freedom is seen as the sovereignty of the human will to do what it likes, when it likes, how it likes. There is an ancient Greek saying that states, 'A free man is one who lives as he chooses.'

The power of choice is central to the Western concept of freedom. The doctrine of 'free will' lies at the heart of both the extreme teachings of antinomianism and legalism. Unfortunately, the teaching of free will is the *a priori* starting point for most people's study of salvation. '*A priori*' means something that is self-evident, obvious, beyond question and not open to discussion.

People often think that the freedom of the human will is an absolute truth. It is presupposed that humans are free agents, going through life making independent and entirely free decisions. The sovereignty of the human will is behind much of the modern-day Christian's self-centred theology. Yet a proper study of the Bible shows that far from being free to choose, the human will is in reality not free at all. Cliff Richard sang a song called 'Under the Influence' and in it he made the point that no one is really free or lives in a vacuum. All of us are under the influence of somebody all of the time. We are constantly being influenced for good or for evil. The Scriptures never speak of the concept of sovereign human free will

> What then? Shall we sin because we are not under law but under grace? May it never be! Do you not know that when you present yourselves to someone as slaves for obedience, you are slaves of the one whom you obey, either of sin resulting in death, or of obedience resulting in righteousness? But thanks be to God that though you were slaves of sin, you became obedient from the heart to that form of teaching to which you were committed, and having been freed from sin, you became slaves of righteousness. (Rom. 6:15–18, NASB)

This passage teaches us that we are either slaves to sin leading to destruction, misery and judgement, or we are slaves to God. We are never our own master. To be a slave of righteousness brings liberty, joy, peace and the blessings of the kingdom of God. This is true freedom. Some theologians talk about the 'free agency of man' i.e. that human beings are free moral agents. But according to Scripture fallen humanity is not free, we are not moral and we are not the agent.

Before we were saved we were the slaves of sin and we didn't even realize it. We would not and could not obey God. Our Adamic nature was entirely enslaved by the power of sin, Satan and the Law. We were powerless to break free and were ruled by the 'god of this world'. We were blinded to the things of God. Our enslaved will could not do anything else but obey its masters. We were running at 100 miles per hour in the wrong direction, towards eternal destruction, and we couldn't even see it. And there was no excuse for our actions because we willingly accepted this bondage, having no desire to change.

God in his mercy regenerated us and brought us out of the realm of sin by his irresistible grace, justifying us by faith in Christ. Now we stand free from condemnation. We are in Christ and are liberated, saved once and for all from the eternal consequences of sin. Galatians 5 is all about bringing this objective truth into our daily Christian experience. For it was for a life of freedom that Christ set us free.

Before we were redeemed we were unable to resist the power of sin, but now we are saved we are free *not* to sin. We have died to sin and have freedom to walk in the Spirit and in obedience to God. I have heard so-called grace teachers preach powerfully about the fact that salvation is a free gift and that it cannot be lost by anything that we do or don't do. This is true, but some teachers spend their whole time emphasizing the fact that Christ has set us free, but never go on to explain how this practically works in our daily lives. It is like they have never studied Galatians 5 and 6.

I have also listened to some almost boast in what the Christian can get away with and still be saved. To them the freedom of the gospel is to do whatever we want. These teachers shy away from the responsibility to serve God sacrificially, because they feel condemnation if any type of pressure is put on them to obey God – especially in areas where their flesh doesn't want to. It is as if any call to obedience will somehow interfere with their freedom and put them back in bondage and guilt all over again. This type of person claims that God did it all and that because there is now no condemnation, we can pick and choose whatever we want to do for God. They misunderstand freedom, thinking that our freedom must be to do what we want, when we want and how we want.

Freedom and obedience

I remember one former member of Kensington Temple complaining to me that although we preached salvation by grace alone, KT was in error because we put too much pressure on the congregations to evangelize and be active disciples. He said that this active call to service made him feel guilty and that this pressure to obey was robbing him of the freedom and joy that he felt when he had first heard the grace message. This man was clearly in bondage to the flesh and self-centredness, but he couldn't see it. He didn't understand that Christ had set him free from the old master to serve a new Lord, and that to actually experience more freedom one must choose to grow in obedience. He thought to obey Christ was to lose his freedom.

The more you live for God the freer you become. We all know of times when, as Christians, we have lived in periods of great sacrificial obedience to the Lord, and these are often the greatest times of joy, peace and satisfaction. It sounds a contradiction, but we know it to be true. The more we lay down our life for him, the more we will find it. Isn't it true that the times when we have followed our self-serving flesh, we soon find ourselves unhappy in our soul, frustrated, unsatisfied, and with less and less control over our lives as we fall from the power of grace and back into the bondage of the flesh?

This ex-KT member thought he was set free to serve himself. He didn't realize that as a slave of God his freedom was to serve Christ. An obedience that flows out of an experience of God's love is the key to receiving the wonderful liberty and blessings of the kingdom of heaven.

Who are you yoked to?

In Galatians 5:1, Paul commands Galatians to

> Stand firm, therefore, and do not be subject again to a yoke of slavery.

The Galatians had been yoked to the slavery of sin and false religion before receiving the gospel, and now they were in danger of yoking themselves to the Law. Paul's command to stand firm is like that of a standard bearer, rallying the troops to resist the onslaught of the enemy. We need to stick the bloodstained banner of the crucified Lord in the soil of our hearts and refuse to come under enemy control. The word 'to stand' in the Greek language also means 'to establish'. It is so important that we establish these teachings of Paul in our lives, because if we don't we will be building our Christian lives on shifting sands rather than a solid Rock.

The picture of a yoke is a good picture of what Christian freedom is like. Oxen were yoked to pull together, then they always moved together in the same direction. But one had to make sure that the oxen were of even strength, or else the weaker one would just be pulled around and dominated by the stronger. When we were sinners, we were in a heavy and unequal yoke with sin and Satan. Even if we thought at the time that we were making our own decisions in life, actually we were being pulled this way and that by a malevolent master far too powerful for us to resist.

When we were converted, the yoke of sin's slavery was broken and we were set free for a new life with a new yoke-fellow – Jesus. It is impossible for a human to ever be yoke-free and totally independent – we just weren't created that way. It is *who* we are yoked to that determines whether we are free or bound.

The Galatians had been freed from the elemental forces of sin and false religion. They had experienced the freedom of being yoked to Christ through the Spirit. Now they were turning to the yoke of the Law which was a return to the *stoicheia* or elements that enslave (Gal. 4:3). Jesus tells us the kind of liberty and freedom of living we can expect when we choose to walk with him as a yoke-fellow

Come to Me, all who are weary and heavy-laden, and I will give you rest. Take My yoke upon you and learn from Me, for I am gentle and humble in heart, and you will find rest for your souls. For My yoke is easy and My burden is light. (Matt. 11:28–30, NASB)

Galatians 5:1 does not just say that Christ has set us free. It says Christ has set us free *for freedom.* That freedom is the ability to walk in the Spirit and obey our new master, Jesus. Biblical liberty is the freedom to serve God.

Into the very cement of the foundation of justification by faith alone the Judaizers had mixed obedience to the Law. This was not freedom! This was to live under the crushing, condemning demands of the Law. The Galatians were becoming entangled and snared by the yoke of it. How tragic for legalistic Christians not even to have the foundation of salvation by grace alone to stand on. What bondage to live day by day in fear of falling from holiness and believing that your adoption papers may be ripped up at any moment by your own heavenly Father.

Both legalistic and fleshly Christians are equally backslidden because they are equally self-obsessed. Together they fail to pursue true Christian liberty. Both of these extremes must be rejected.

Cutting off the wrong flesh

(2) Look! I, Paul, say to you that if you are circumcised, Christ will benefit you not at all. (3) I testify again to everyone who is being circumcised that he is obligated to do the whole law. (4) You have been estranged from Christ, you who are seeking to be justified by the law; you have fallen away from grace.

The Galatians were looking for a new sense of belonging. When they came to Christ, the ensuing social upheaval must have been enormous for them. Their pagan religion had been not just a belief system, but part and parcel of their communal, social, business, political and family life. Pagan rituals, ceremonies and festivals brought a sense of social cohesiveness and belonging to the followers. Even those Gentiles who didn't believe in the deities still adhered to the forms of worship, for not to do so was to exclude yourself from so much of community life.

The Galatian believers were struggling with their own type of identity crisis. They were the pioneer believers in their region and the challenge was for them to build a brand new community through the Holy Spirit without the old pagan culture. The Judaizers came with a pre-packaged, religious and cultural identity to offer them. Even better, this identity could be bolted onto the gospel message, giving them an established ritual, civil and moral pattern of identity and community. The Galatians could simply move from pagan temples to Jewish synagogues, from food sacrificed to idols to Jewish food laws, from pagan licentiousness to Jewish morality, from a Hellenistic culture to a long-established Jewish heritage. The Judaizers offered a seemingly easy cultural quick fix for the Galatians to adopt.

All this was summed up in the supreme act of Jewish identification – circumcision. This rite was the entrance to a new way of living for the Galatians. Through it they would become Jews.

If we stop for a moment and reflect on contemporary Christian culture, it may be that we also fall into the same trap that the Galatians were falling into. When some think of Christianity they think of church buildings, rituals, festivals, sacraments and services, pulpits and pastors, holy places of pilgrimage, the Ten Commandments etc. Like the Galatians, we can fall back on a form of religious Christian culture that replaces the role of the Holy Spirit. We can have religious communities devoid of the Spirit, a morality that is a dark shadow of true spirituality. When a church is no longer seeking, first and foremost, to become a charismatic community that seeks to be filled and led by the Holy Spirit, it must decline into a culture of tradition leading inevitably to legalism.

This is why Paul struck at the heart of Judaism, for he knew that to wipe out circumcision was, at the same time, to cancel out the Law which was at the heart and soul of Jewish identity. Paul did not want to see built up again what the gospel had torn down (Gal. 2:18). It wasn't about being Jewish or Greek, male or female, slave or freedman (Gal. 3:28) – it was about a brand new community of disciples of Christ who were to live a new and radical life of freedom under the direct influence and leadership of the Holy Spirit.

The Galatians were dealing with the wrong type of flesh. They were considering cutting off their foreskins to become sanctified, when they should be crucifying the flesh of self-centeredness, worldliness and unbelief. Paul uses the full force of his authority as an apostle, saying, 'Look! I, Paul, say to you . . .' The apostle was identifying so strongly with his next statement that to reject what he was about to say would also be an outright rejection of his own apostolic authority.

Paul said that if the Galatians became circumcised, Christ would profit them nothing. He would no longer be of benefit to them. Some have thought that this statement and the one in verse 4, where Paul speaks of the Galatians having become estranged from Christ, is proof that a Christian may be 'de-justified', or lose their salvation.

Those who are adamant that a Christian can lose their salvation are often bound by a form of legalism themselves. Some teach that we are saved by grace, but that we stay saved by obedience to the moral Law. Yet Paul makes it plain that it was this type of obedience to Law that was the cause of the Galatians falling away. If you follow one part of the Law you must follow all of it.

Note that most people who think a believer can lose their salvation usually suppose it occurs by breaking one of the Ten Commandments – through idolatry, adultery, stealing etc. But Paul is saying exactly the opposite here. He is saying that Christ becomes of no effect if we try to *keep* the Law, not if we break it.

Remember that the Judaizers and backslidden Galatians still considered themselves Christians. They believed in Christ. They understood that he had been crucified and raised from the dead to save them. If you asked them how they were saved, they would undoubtedly have said through faith in Christ. However, and this is the point, if you asked them how they remained saved, they would say by obedience to the Law.

Often, legalistic Christians say that they are saved by faith in Christ, but then they tell you all the commandments that one must keep to prove that you have real faith. It often sounds like this: 'If you really had saving faith, you wouldn't do this and you wouldn't do that – and if you really had saving faith you would be obedient in this and in that . . .' Often they use spiritual language to cloak their legalism – we obey the law by faith, they can be heard to say.

You can't mix faith with the Law

But you can't mix faith with Law, ever! Faith, to a Christian legalist, simply becomes outward obedience to moral codes. The Judaizers would say to the Galatians, 'If you really had faith in Christ, you would be obedient and become circumcised. If you really believed in him you would follow the Law.' But we have learnt in Galatians that saving faith is not tied to works of obedience.

In chapter 2 we saw that the apostle Peter backslid in a very similar way to the Galatians. He too was intimidated and persuaded by the Judaizers. Peter withdrew from table fellowship with the Gentile believers because of the issue of circumcision. His return to the Jewish table fellowship laws was a confirmation of his return to trusting in circumcision (and thus the Law) for holiness.

Peter knew he was saved by faith, but he was persuaded to live by the Law. It was the fact that the Gentile believers were not circumcised that caused him to consider them too unclean to fellowship with. No one, least of all Paul, thought that Peter had lost his salvation and Peter surely didn't consider the Gentiles of Antioch unsaved. After all, they had recently attended the Council of Jerusalem, confirming that Gentiles did not need to be circumcised.

Peter withdrew because he considered the Antioch Gentile Christians unsanctified. This is why he was playing the hypocrite. Peter's actions were incompatible with the gospel he had believed and preached. Peter had started out in the Spirit, but was trying to live out holiness through means of the Law. Peter had been set free by justification, but he was no longer living free when he withdrew from table fellowship with uncircumcised believers. His position was totally inconsistent with the gospel, but at the time he just couldn't see it.

Being set free from the realm of sin and death is Christ's work. Christ has set us free. It is the ongoing sanctification of the believer that is the big issue of chapter 5. Never mix justification and sancti-fication together, or you will find yourself in the same mess as Peter and the Galatians.

Modern-day legalists

How can we compare modern legalistic Christians with the Galatians? After all, even the most legalistic Christians of today would never insist on circumcision or even adherence to food laws to remain saved. Galatians and Romans are so clear on these issues that no one could ever demand them again. However, Christian traditions have set up new types of 'circumcisions'. There is the modern circumcision of abstinence to proscribed substances and activities. Just as the Judaizers taught that to remain saved you had to be circumcised and follow laws, so we have seen in church history Christian groups claiming that if we don't abstain from alcohol, tobacco, the cinema, dancing (or whatever) we will lose our salvation. They aren't simply teaching that we will be unsanctified by doing these things, but that we can actually lose our salvation.

Throughout Galatians we have seen that Paul has consistently affirmed the justification of the Galatians. He has called them sons of God (3:26; 4:6,7); he has referred to them as children of the promise (4:28), and even children of the free (4:31). All this, just three verses before saying they have fallen from grace. How could he one moment call them justified and then the next, unjus-tified? Paul is not talking about justification in verses 2 to 4 of chapter 5, but sanctification.

It is true that if we choose to look to the Law to perfect or com-plete our salvation, Christ is of absolutely no benefit to us in the process. He will not help us live by the Law. He will not bless our legalistic obedience. He will not recognize circumcision as a fruit of a holy Christian life. And he will not accept food laws as an act of worship and obedience. Christ will not help or aid us in our future Christian living through any external type of law-keeping.

Christ won't help legalists

This refusal of help is in the future tense – 'Christ *will* profit you nothing' – and it isn't a reference to a future judgement, because we who believe have already passed from judgement to life – past tense. We died with Christ and were raised with him 2,000 years ago. It's a done deal. Nevertheless, Christ will not profit us in our future Christian living if we look to legalism and outward moral laws to keep us saved and sanctified. If we do, he can't and won't help us, and we will remain underdeveloped in our faith as fleshly Christians.

Paul firmly reminded them that everyone who became circumcised was obligated to obey the whole Law – all of it – ceremonial, civil and moral. We have mentioned that some Christians today believe that the moral part of the Law is still applicable and should be lived by. But this is false teaching. It is the whole Law or no Law at all. You can't carve up the Law or pick and choose portions of it. Either follow the whole Law or reject the whole Law. These are the only two options open to us.

Fallen from grace

In verse 4, Paul tells the Galatians that in seeking to be justified by the Law they have become estranged from Christ and fallen from grace. The way the phrase 'estranged from Christ' is translated can heavily influence its meaning.

> You who are trying to be justified by law have been alienated from Christ; you have fallen away from grace. (NIV)

> You have been severed from Christ, you who are seeking to be justified by law; you have fallen from grace. (NASB)

> For if you are trying to make yourselves right with God by keeping the law, you have been cut off from Christ! You have fallen away from God's grace. (NLT)

> Christ is become of no effect unto you, whosoever of you are justified by the law; ye are fallen from grace. (KJV)

The translations that speak about being 'severed' or 'cut off' from Christ give the impression that the Galatians (who only four verses before were called children of the free) have now lost their salvation completely. But these translations of the Greek word *katargeo* are uncalled for. The word means 'to render useless or unproductive, to make ineffective or powerless, to be estranged from, to be released from or set aside.' This word can just as easily fit into the view that the Galatians remained saved, but had become totally unproductive in respect to their Christian walk. By seeking to remain saved through the Law, they were distancing themselves and turning their back on Christ and his grace. They thought that they could have Christ and live the Law, but Paul is showing beyond a shadow of doubt that this could never work.

The Galatians were turning away from a life of freedom to become entangled in a yoke of bondage. They were children of the promise, heirs of grace and freedom who were saved to enjoy freedom. But instead they were locking themselves in a prison of legalistic living. And whilst in that self-confinement, Christ would be absolutely no use to them in their practical Christian living.

In trying to be justified by the Law, the Galatians had fallen from grace. Confusion about what Paul means by falling from grace can occur if you don't realize that three Greek words are used in the New Testament for 'falling'. The first word is *apostasia* from which we get the English word 'apostasy'. This word is used in 2 Thessalonians 2:3 regarding the major falling away of nominal Christians during the end times.

Falling away in the book of Hebrews

In Hebrews 6, the word used for 'falling away' is *parapipto*, meaning 'falling away with no hope of return'. This is referring to judgement on persistent backslidden Christians who actually come to the place where they lose their inheritance for good. Hebrews uses the Israelites in the wilderness as an example of how this can happen. They were disqualified once and for all from entering the Promised Land. The generation of Moses was left to wander in the wilderness until they died, never experiencing the destiny that God had prepared for them. Even Moses failed to enter into his inheritance. This can happen to Christians, too. Persistent backsliding can result in a permanent state of spiritual deafness to the present and ongoing voice of the Holy Spirit.

Hebrews warns us a number of times to listen to what the Holy Spirit is saying and not to harden our hearts to his words, lest we receive judgement. This judgement can mean ultimately that the backslidden Christian may enter a state where he will no longer return to the Lord during the rest of his life on earth. In this state, the Holy Spirit no longer speaks to him and the backslidden Christian isn't troubled by this. When he dies, he becomes like the person saved by fire in 1 Corinthians 3:15. This falling away is the worst thing that can happen to Christian. But remember, if you are ever concerned or fearful that this judgement has happened to you, your very concern is proof positive that it hasn't. This only occurs when God, in all his patience, has finally had enough of rebellion in a believer's life. When this judgement takes place, the believer isn't aware of it, nor do they worry about it, because they are so backslidden of heart they aren't even bothered about such matters any more.

The third Greek word used for 'falling away' is *ekpipto*, which is the word that Paul uses here in Galatians. This word means 'to fall off', like a bottle falling off a wall. This word is used in Acts 12:7 about the chains falling off Peter in prison. It can also mean to drift off course or run aground like the ship that Paul travelled in (Acts 27:17,26,29). This word is also found in 2 Peter 3:17

> You therefore, beloved, knowing this beforehand, be on your guard so that you are not carried away by the error of unprincipled men and fall from your own steadfastness. (NASB)

Peter warns Christians not to backslide or be led astray by the error of the wicked. The Galatians had fallen away from living by grace. They had drifted right off the course of freedom and run aground on the Law. Paul, in saying that they had fallen from grace, was accusing them of being backslidden. They were living according to the flesh. The Galatians hadn't seen this. They falsely believed that they would live the Law through the grace of God, and that the Holy Spirit would now help them live in obedience to the commands of the Law.

Modern Christian legalists also unwittingly cover their legalism with a so-called 'grace that works'. The teaching is that we are indeed saved by grace alone, but that same grace must work sanctification in us to be authentic grace. The error of fusing justification with sanctification by a false understanding of grace is very common in our churches today. The Judaizers had said that works of grace equated to our obedience to the Law. 'You will live the Law by grace and faith and thus be truly saved,' they had told the Galatians, who in turn had fallen for this deception. They had fallen from real saving grace to embrace a false grace that really was another way of binding them to the Law.

Misunderstanding James

I want to refer at this point to the teaching found in the book of James, because legalists often use it to back up their teaching that true faith must be demonstrated in works. That is, if we can't show our works then our faith is fake and we are not saved. James 2:14–16 is the passage used to teach that saving faith without works is dead and doesn't save us. The precise list of these saving works are not often expressed in any detail by legalists. But this teaching says that whatever these works are, we had better produce them or we aren't saved; we have counterfeit faith.

Actually, the context of the passage shows that James is saying that faith without works can't clothe or feed a person in need. Faith without action can't profit the needy. He is not referring to saving faith at all. James is talking about a second and different type of justification that has nothing to with salvation. He is talking about justification by works (faith put into action) that brings deliverance from trials, rewards and inheritance in the kingdom of God. This faith demonstrates visibly and publicly that we are a friend of God. If we don't put our faith to work, it is dead (Jas. 2:17,20), of no profit (Jas. 2:16) and it is useless.

James 2:21 is mistranslated 'dead' by some versions of the Bible, but the actual Greek word used simply means 'useless'. This also helps us understand what James means when he did use the word 'dead' in verses 17 and 20. If we don't rise up in faith, we will not see the power of faith in our lives. If we don't put our faith to work in life, then it might as well be dead. Our faith becomes useless if it is not put into practice.

The Galatians could not live their lives by trying to mix Law with faith. As we have seen, the Law is the enemy of faith. Grace and faith can never enter into a coalition with the Law in order to rule our lives. The Galatians had fallen from the power of grace by seeking to live under the Law.

Faith operates through love

> (5) For we by the Spirit, from faith, are awaiting eagerly the hope of righteousness. (6) For in Christ Jesus neither circumcisions counts for anything, nor uncircumcision, but faith operating effectively through love.

Verse 5 can also be translated

> For we through the Spirit by faith wait for the hope of righteousness.

Or

> We eagerly await the hoped for reality that righteousness brings.

Paul, having told the Galatians they have fallen from grace now introduces the alternative to living by the Law, which is the Spirit-filled life. We, through the Spirit by faith, have a hope of righteousness. This righteousness can't mean saving righteousness, because we already have that

> for with the heart a person believes, resulting in righteousness. (Rom. 10:10, NASB)

The righteousness that Paul is referring to is righteous living and sanctification. The Galatians were hoping to live righteous lives through the Law. Paul says we live righteous lives through walking by the Spirit. In Romans he teaches that having been justified, we are called on to present ourselves as slaves of righteousness.

I am speaking in human terms because of the weakness of your flesh. For just as you presented your members as slaves to impurity and to lawlessness, resulting in further lawlessness, so now present your members as slaves to righteousness, resulting in sanctification. (Rom. 6:19, NASB)

We are righteous before God, and we should now also become righteous in our lifestyles. In the above passage we see that if we present ourselves as slaves to righteousness, we have the hope of resulting sanctification. It seems to me that many of us lose hope of living life at a high level of righteousness. Disappointed and disillusioned by past failure, we tolerate low levels of sanctification and consecration. Hope must be restored to us. Faith will give us hope and the Holy Spirit will stir our faith. We will never become perfect in holiness in this life, but we can become mature in righteous living. Paul begins to explain that life in the Spirit can restore hope, and this hope will bring an experience of righteous changes to our lives. Later on in this chapter he will explain this more fully.

It is possible, of course, to interpret verse 5 to mean hope in the future sense of Christ's return. On the day of resurrection, the full reality of righteousness will certainly be experienced in our bodies and souls. However, Paul is dealing with the 'here and now' and then moves on to talk of the absolute inability of circumcision to help the Christian in any way, shape or form. In Christ, circumcision is meaningless, it produces nothing. What really works is faith working through love.

This is the answer to those who ask how you live without the Law. It is faith working through love. We have mentioned James, when he wrote about faith without works being dead or useless. He, like Paul, understood that faith works in the Christian life through love. The examples of faith-works that James gave to illustrate this point were feeding the hungry and clothing the naked, which, of course, are acts of faith working through love.

Faith works through love – love for God and love for people. Love gives faith its power. The Greek word used for 'works' is where we get our English word 'energize' from. Love energizes, activates and directs our faith. We will return to this theme in greater depth when we reach verses 13 and 14.

15.

Love Your Neighbour

(Gal. 5:7–15)

(7) You were running well. Who hindered you in not being persuaded regarding the truth? (8) That persuasion is not from him who calls you. (9) 'A little leaven leavens the whole lump of dough.' (10) I am persuaded with regard to you in the Lord that you will not think otherwise; but he who troubles you will bear his judgement, whoever he is. (11) And I, brothers, if I still preach circumcision, why am I still persecuted? In that case the stumbling block of the cross has been removed. (12) Would that those who are upsetting you might also get themselves castrated. (13) For you were called to freedom, brothers; only not the freedom for opportunity to the flesh, but through love serve one another. (14) For the whole law is fulfilled in one word, in the well-known, 'You shall love your neighbour as yourself.' (15) But if you bite and tear at one another, look out lest you are consumed by one another.

The Galatians had started out with such promise. The comparison Paul uses is that of a running race. The Galatians came out of the starting blocks, sprinting. They had begun in the Spirit, but something happened to them. The word for 'hindered' in the Greek comes from the verb that means 'to cut in on'. The illustration is of a fellow competitor cutting in on their running line and causing them to trip, taking them out of their stride. It was the Judaizers who were obstructing the Galatians. It was their legalism that had tripped them up and slowed them down in their obedience to the gospel. Paul reiterates that the Judaizers' message is a false gospel and not from God.

A little yeast . . .

Paul liked the metaphor of leaven, and used it again in a later letter to the Corinthians. Paul compared the Corinthians' sexual wickedness and licentiousness to leaven. Leaven, or yeast as we would say today, is used in the process of bread-making. You only need a very small piece of yeast in the fermentation process of bread. During baking, the tiny yeast cells aerate the dough by producing bubbles of gas, causing the bread to rise. Paul was concerned that in the church of Corinth, immorality would have the same effect as yeast in bread – that it would spread and develop throughout the whole church. He told them to clean out the old leaven so that they could become like unleavened bread, sincere in faith, and true

> Your boasting is not good. Do you not know that a little leaven leavens the whole lump of dough? Clean out the old leaven so that you may be a new lump, just as you are in fact unleavened. For Christ our Passover also has been sacrificed. Therefore let us celebrate the feast, not with old leaven, nor with the leaven of malice and wickedness, but with the unleavened bread of sincerity and truth. (1 Cor. 5:6–8, NASB)

The problem in Galatia, of course, was not sexual immorality, it was legalism. Its teaching was spreading throughout the Christian community like yeast through dough. Like immorality, unchecked legalism (and both are as bad as each other) will not simply be contained in one area of a church, for according to its yeast-like nature, it will spread. Paul was cleaning out the leaven of the false gospel and purging the Galatian church of its cancerous spread.

Mess with the gospel at your peril

Paul is confident that his letter has already burst the bubble of the false gospel preachers. He has faith that the Lord will use his arguments to bring the Galatians back to their senses and back to the gospel. But he makes it clear that the Judaizers will not get away with their actions towards the Galatians. God will judge them. This pronouncement of judgement takes us back to Galatians 1:8,9 where Paul proclaimed anathema over anyone who preached a different gospel from that which he received from Christ. The curse and the pronouncement found here is a giving over of these false prophets into the judgement of God.

When you study church history, you find periods when false doctrine arises and threatens the whole church. Its increase in popularity seems unstoppable at the time. These false teachers in Galatia would be claiming success and pointing to the increasing numbers of their followers as proof that they were right. It is strange but true that God sometimes allows the success of false teaching for a time, as part of his actual work in judging it. He gives people over to their own lies and falsehoods. Paul knows that one day God will judge these false gospellers, and he believes that ultimately God will sort this situation out and deal with the troublemakers himself. This faith in God as ultimate judge kept him from attempting any fleshly acts of retribution against his enemies. Vindication is always the Lord's and never our own.

A proof of Paul's authentic ministry and gospel is that he suffered persecution. Before Christ he was a preacher of circumcision, and no one was more zealous regarding the Law than he. There would have been no way that the old Saul would have allowed any Gentile to be a follower of Judaism without being circumcised. Remember, when Paul talks about preaching 'circumcision' he is using the word as shorthand to mean obedience to the whole of the Law. In his pre-conversion days, Paul was the persecutor, but now he finds himself as the persecuted. The Galatians should remember the battered state in which Paul first came to them, having been all but stoned to death outside Lystra. This was a result of preaching the gospel – it would have never have happened if he was still a preacher of the Law.

The offence or stumbling block of the cross is a theme Paul speaks about in 1 Corinthians 1:22,23

> For indeed Jews ask for signs and Greeks search for wisdom; but we preach Christ crucified, to Jews a stumbling block and to Gentiles foolishness. (NASB)

The idea that the true Messiah would be crucified was unthinkable to most Jews. It was generally thought that the Messiah would come and restore Israel as a political kingdom by the sword. Also, the message of the cross is the exact opposite of all that circumcision stands for. The cross broke down the barrier between Jew and Gentile that circumcision had upheld for so long. Christ crucified is at the heart of the gospel and the Galatians' pursuit of the Law was seen as abandonment of the message of the cross that Paul had preached to them (Gal. 3:1).

You can tell that Paul is starting to get passionate again. Probably the memory of his persecutions and the price he paid for the gospel now being opposed in Galatia was stirring him up. And it was all due to these Judaizers. Paul then makes a very severe comment

> (12) Would that those who are upsetting you might also get themselves castrated. (NASB)

Many feel embarrassed about this verse which is often softened in translation. The New King James version, for example, says, '. . . would even cut themselves off!' Some think that this is an attempt at humour from Paul, but the mood in this passage is not one of hilarity.

Paul is shockingly honest here about the Judaizers. In practice he would not condone the turning of these Judaizers into eunuchs, but his blood was boiling. It is a bit like when people say, 'I could knock their heads together!' or 'I could give them a good butt-kicking!' We don't actually mean that we would physically do those things (I hope not, anyway), but such phrases express our exasperation with the people concerned.

However, this is more than just Paul blowing off steam. His statement is staggering, but also extremely pertinent. The Galatians were in danger of going under the knife of circumcision and having their foreskins cut off. This was supposed to make them members of God's covenant people according to the Judaizers. But just one slip of the knife could make them eunuchs and Deuteronomy 23:1 disqualifies the castrated from entering the assembly of the Lord:

No one who is emasculated or has his male organ cut off shall enter the assembly of the LORD.

In the Law, eunuchs are actually excluded from joining the people of God. Many Romans viewed the rite of Jewish circumcision with great disdain and considered it a type of castration. Ironically, it was the very Judaizers who were insisting on circumcision who were now outside of God's covenant people. They were the 'eunuchs' of the New Covenant. The preaching of circumcision which had previously been the entrance to the assembly of the Lord was now the very barrier to admission.

Liberty

> (13) For you were called to freedom, brothers; only not the freedom for opportunity to the flesh, but through love serve one another.

This verse is one of the most exciting in the whole letter to the Galatians. It echoes the sentiment of the first verse of this chapter, where the nature and character of true freedom is presented. This freedom in the gospel that the Galatians received could be used responsibly or irresponsibly; it could be esteemed or abused.

For Paul, the Law was like a nanny or a schoolmaster overseeing the Jews until they came to spiritual adulthood. To live in freedom from the Law entails growth in spiritual maturity. Adults are responsible for the children under their care, but when they reach the age of adulthood they become fully responsible for their own actions. To live apart from the Law is to embrace the responsibility of freedom.

Have you ever seen naughty children who are kept in line by strict parental discipline? They refrain from misbehaving only because they know they will be punished. The threat of being grounded or having pocket money stopped or, in past times, being spanked is a great deterrent to wayward kids. I remember the story of one parent commanding their child to sit down, and the child refusing to obey. The parent threatened to spank the child and, in the light of impending punishment, the child sat down. As the child took his seat he muttered, 'I may be sitting down on the outside, but I am standing up on the inside!' This is a picture of how legalism works – it produces whitewashed tombs

> Woe to you, teachers of the law and Pharisees, you hypocrites! You are like whitewashed tombs, which look beautiful on the outside but on the inside are full of dead men's bones and everything unclean. (Matt. 23:27, NIV)

When a child matures into an adult and leaves the strict supervision of its parents, a whole host of opportunities and freedoms suddenly present themselves. The young adult knows that it is their responsibility to choose what they do, for they are no longer under their parents' twenty-four-hour supervision. They are free to do things against their parents' wishes without fear of punishment, but hopefully they have learnt the wisdom to live in a responsible manner. If not, trouble will soon be on the horizon.

During my first term at university, it was fascinating to be a part of a whole intake of students living, for the first time in their lives, away from the daily scrutiny of parents or boarding school teachers. We felt like we had all been freed from prison. We had so many new freedoms; we could go to bed any time we wanted without parental intervention, and drink as much alcohol as we wanted whenever we wanted. No parents and no punishment!

Of course, some students went totally wild and out of control, abusing their first taste of real adult freedom, and eventually getting themselves and others into some terrible situations. One student got drunk and fell off a bridge during Freshers Week whilst doing tricks, and was so badly injured that it was a whole year before he could return to his studies. Another got pregnant and had to drop out of university altogether. Most, however, realized that the freedom they now had should be handled responsibly. We all made mistakes, but we grew in our maturity and learnt not to abuse the freedoms of adulthood.

Paul teaches that it is possible to abuse freedom. To the immature, free grace could mean freedom to sin. It is possible to be in Christ and use your freedom to live a fleshly life. This possibility terrifies some church leaders who don't actually believe that their flock can cope with the responsibility of grace. They take it for granted that if the average church member is given an opportunity to abuse grace, they will.

An opportunity to sin?

Paul exhorts the Galatians not to turn their freedom into an opportunity for the flesh. The Greek word *aphorme* translated 'opportunity' was used in a military sense to refer to a headquarters for operations, or the base camp for an expedition. It carries the meaning of a starting point for further action.

The way of the flesh is a slippery slope that leads to destruction. To yield to the lust of the flesh will allow the enemy to establish a base camp in our lives from which he will attempt to strike and destroy us. To use grace as an opportunity for the flesh gives sin and Satan a foothold in your life. We don't have the power to play fast and loose with sin and the flesh, for it will entangle us, dominate us and ultimately cause us and others to come to ruin. In verse 16 we shall see how the works of the flesh in Galatia were wreaking havoc among the Galatian community as they consumed one another in fleshly conflict.

This opportunity for the flesh is an important concept to grasp. Without the opportunity to abuse grace, we will never know how sanctified we really are. A legalistic Christian always has in the back of their mind the fear that if they break a 'Christian law' they will lose their salvation. This external fear of losing our salvation is used by many preachers to keep their flock in order. It is their belt and braces approach to producing righteousness in their congregation. The people are encouraged to live righteously out of love for the Lord, but behind this is the fall-back position that clearly proclaims that if we don't live right we will lose our salvation.

This external pressure to conform is exactly how the Mosaic Law worked to restrain Israel's sin, through fear of punishment. Not every legalistic Christian turns from sin solely due to the fear of hell – many genuinely desire to live righteously and serve the Lord out of love. Many of the strictest Pharisees also had a deep passion and love for God. My point is that if we ultimately believe that we can lose our salvation by carrying out the desires of the flesh, then we can never clearly measure our true motivation for holiness. Would we still be holy if we knew we could get away with it and still go to heaven? This is the question that grace asks us, and our answer reveals the true state of our heart.

Legalistic preachers oppose Paul's message of grace because they fear that if it is taught to their people there will be a mass falling away into fleshly sin. The criticism of Paul's message of grace is that his teaching of once saved always saved means that Christians would be so sure of going to heaven that they would effectively have a license to sin from God. 'Who cares if I sin, there is always more grace!'

Opponents of Paul's teaching believe that the vast majority of Christians would backslide if only they could get away with it. Someone once accused my own teaching of being nothing more than a 'Get Out of Jail Free' card, to which I replied that I didn't need such a card since as far as I was concerned, God had destroyed the jail itself. I am free from the prison of eternal condemnation forever.

What we need is a righteousness that exceeds that of the Pharisees – an obedience from the heart, not obedience to laws and fear of punishment. To walk in the Spirit is not outward conformity to rules, but rather a voluntary overflow of righteousness from a truly free heart.

The opportunity for the flesh will reveal your true spiritual condition. Sin and the flesh are our real enemies. They are the way to misery, pain and destruction in life. It is this understanding that makes the flesh repugnant and the ways of the Spirit so attractive.

Freedom to serve others

Legalism promotes introspection, but grace and freedom promotes servanthood. The choice for Christians is fleshly, self-centred living, or becoming our brother's keeper. Spirit-filled living is always focused on serving others. The way to enjoy our Christian liberty is to become primarily concerned about the needs of others. Modern Christians are far too wrapped up in themselves. If you look at bestselling Christian books or teaching CDs, they are always about the individual, their needs, their growth and their personal walk with the Lord. But the New Testament priority for us is all about serving others. We will see that the fruits of the Spirit are mainly to do with the quality of relationships we have with others.

Our liberty, freedom and purpose in life is all about serving God and other people. Jesus spoke about this principle of Spirit-filled living

> just as the Son of Man did not come to be served, but to serve, and to give his life a ransom for many. (Matt. 20:28, NIV)

> But the greatest among you shall be your servant. (Matt. 23:11, NASB)

Paul is starting to teach us how a Christian is to practically live a life free from the Law.

> (14) For the whole law is fulfilled in one word, in the well-known, 'You shall love your neighbour as yourself.' (15) But if you bite and tear at one another, look out lest you are consumed by one another.

In verse 14, Paul gives us the key principle for Christian living, which is to love our neighbour as ourselves. This is the only rule we need – everything else in the New Testament about practical Christian living is but an illustration and explanation of this one principle. Paul restates this theme in the next chapter (6:2) when he says

> Bear one another's burdens, and so fulfill the law of Christ. (NKJV)

We see the law of Christ reiterated in what is popularly known as the 'Golden Rule'

> So in everything, do to others what you would have them do to you, for this sums up the Law and the Prophets. (Matt. 7:12, NIV)

Paul and Jesus have summed up the Law in the same way. The scriptures above are the foundation for the Spirit-filled life. Before Paul can talk in detail about the fruit of the Spirit, he has to first establish the context in which walking in the Spirit is to be lived, which is that of love. Walking in the Spirit, as we shall see, is never an individualistic or private affair, but all about the health of our relationships.

Paul quotes here in Galatians from Leviticus 19:18

> You shall not take vengeance, nor bear any grudge against the sons of your people, but you shall love your neighbour as yourself; I am the LORD. (NASB)

This verse speaks of a forgiving, gracious attitude towards people, treating them as you would like to be treated, loving them as you would like to be loved. In the same chapter of Leviticus, this principle is repeated in terms of dealing with strangers to the community of God

> The stranger who resides with you shall be to you as the native among you, and you shall love him as yourself, for you were aliens in the land of Egypt; I am the LORD your God. (Lev. 19:34, NASB)

A divine love

Paul establishes the loving of one's neighbour as the basis of Christian living, but he also realizes that this can't be achieved through natural effort. This is so important to stress, because even outside the church people often quote 'love your neighbour as yourself' as something laudable and to be pursued by all. But this love is not a natural love, it is a *supernatural* love. It can't be produced by the unbeliever, because it is actually a fruit of the Holy Spirit himself.

The word that Paul uses for 'love' is the famous Greek word *agape*. This word is often used in the New Testament to define the love of God, or the God-kind of love. It is only by the grace of God and the power of the Spirit that we can love one another in the way Christ wants us to. We should be both surprised and amazed at the levels of love and service we walk in, because it should be a thoroughly supernatural work of the Spirit. Here are a selection of scriptures that show the supreme importance of loving and serving one another as Christians

> A new commandment I give to you, that you love one another, even as I have loved you, that you also love one another. By this all men will know that you are My disciples, if you have love for one another. (John 13:34,35, NASB)

> and may the Lord cause you to increase and abound in love for one another, and for all people, just as we also do for you. (1 Thess. 3:12, NASB)

> Now as to the love of the brethren, you have no need for anyone to write to you, for you yourselves are taught by God to love one another. (1 Thess. 4:9, NASB)

> and let us consider how to stimulate one another to love and good deeds. (Heb. 10:24, NASB)

> Since you have in obedience to the truth purified your souls for a sincere love of the brethren, fervently love one another from the heart. (1 Pet. 1:22, NASB)

> Above all, keep fervent in your love for one another, because love covers a multitude of sins. (1 Pet. 4:8, NASB)

> For this is the message which you have heard from the beginning, that we should love one another. (1 John 3:11, NASB)

> This is His commandment, that we believe in the name of His Son Jesus Christ, and love one another, just as He commanded us. (1 John 3:23, NASB)

> Beloved, let us love one another, for love is from God; and everyone who loves is born of God and knows God. (1 John 4:7, NASB)

Now I ask you, lady, not as though I were writing to you a new commandment, but the one which we have had from the beginning, that we love one another. (2 John 1:5, NASB)

These scriptures demonstrate the incredible importance of love and service for the Christian life. This love is supremely expressed in the life, death and resurrection of Jesus himself. We don't need the Law any more because Christ himself is our example. We look to him and his model life. Jesus himself has replaced the Law, for it has found its fulfilment in him. The plan of God is that Christ, not the Law, will be fashioned within us.

We must grasp that this love is the God-kind of love. It is a supernatural fruit of the Spirit. We should not read the command to love one another as a simple moral directive to be obeyed out of human strength alone. Walking in love is also walking in the Spirit. Love begins and ends in the Spirit. The love of God was poured into our hearts by the Holy Spirit (Rom. 5:5). The love of God is to be soaked into the very centre of our being. In order to properly love others, we must ourselves be experiencing God's love on a daily basis. Communion with God is vital if we are to walk in love by the Spirit. You can only love others to the degree that you are personally encountering God's love for yourself.

Experiencing the presence of the Spirit of God must be a daily occurrence – to soak in his presence and to be touched by his glory. In 2 Corinthians 3, Paul talks about the glory that Moses experienced in the presence of God

> But if the ministry of death, in letters engraved on stones, came with glory, so that the sons of Israel could not look intently at the face of Moses because of the glory of his face, fading as it was, how will the ministry of the Spirit fail to be even more with glory? (vv. 7,8, NASB)

Paul spoke of the veil that Moses wore over his face because of the radiating glory of God that it reflected. The Israelites couldn't bear to look at the glory upon him, so he covered his face. Paul said that there was a corresponding veil over the hearts of the unbelieving Jews that prevented the glory of God's word from breaking through (vv. 14,15). Describing the condition of a believer, Paul writes but whenever a person turns to the Lord, the veil is taken away. Now the Lord is the Spirit, and where the Spirit of the Lord is, there is liberty. But we all, with unveiled face, beholding as in a mirror the glory of the Lord, are being transformed into the same image from glory to glory, just as from the Lord, the Spirit. (2 Cor. 3:16–18, NASB)

The Holy Spirit brings the glory, grace and love of God into our lives in a way that is even more powerful than he did for Moses. This glory of the New Covenant is an ongoing experience, transforming us from within to become more Christlike.

A theology of experience

When I survey much of the literature on Galatians, I am often struck by the way in which references to spiritual experiences are played down. Paul's references to charismatic experiences with God are often ignored by commentators. But Galatians is full of references to conscious experiences of the Spirit and his love.

To walk in the Spirit has, sadly, sometimes been portrayed as basically a set of ideals and a new moral framework to live by. Some have even taken the 'moral' part of the Law of Moses as the pattern for walking in the Spirit. But walking in the Spirit is an *experience* rather than a new set of moral guidelines.

Walking in the Spirit is not just a matter of intellectual understanding and exerting our willpower. We must appreciate that our feelings and emotions are just as important as our intellect when it comes to knowing God. Sometimes our intellect can be way behind our emotional or even physical experience of God. We can have a powerful experience of God's love and presence that transcends our understanding. God can impact our spirit in ways that our mind cannot comprehend. Truth can be experienced emotionally and physically, as well as intellectually. The Word of God is the framework in which we can safely experience the Holy Spirit and the glory of God.

The Word of God is not the sole domain of the intellect. When Jesus said, 'The words I have spoken to you are spirit and they are life' (John 6:63, NIV) he was talking about an experience, an encounter with Scripture that includes but also transcends the intellect.

This overemphasis on reason and intellect can often be seen in Christian teaching today. We are told that love is a 'command' not a 'feeling', but actually it is both. We are told to control our emotions, as if they were inherently fleshly, but emotions can be powerfully touched and used by the Holy Spirit to bring about real change and transformation in our lives. When we talk about walking in and by the Spirit, we mean a walk that is full of experiences and encounters with God which impact the human spirit, soul and body.

Fulfilling the Law is not a new way to obey it

Paul's teaching regarding the Law in this section of the letter is often totally misunderstood. Certain teachers say that Paul, having taught that we have died to the Law, is now encouraging Christians to live by it – not, of course, for assurance of salvation, but as a new pattern of Christian living. They believe that Paul is restoring the Law's role in the Christian's life with a new purpose. The Law is now to be understood through the guiding principle of 'loving our neighbour' and become our guide in righteous living.

This view teaches that we look at the Law through the cross, which filters the relevant from the irrelevant. Thus we can jettison such things as circumcision, food laws, and the ceremonial and civil parts of the Law, but not the moral commandments of the Law, for they come 'through' the cross to become the pattern for walking by the Spirit. The idea is that the Jews under the Law are required to obey all its requirements at every point, but the believer, freed from the Law, doesn't need to obey any of it to be justified; however, they will walk by its moral commandments to be sanctified. The Jews obey the Law, and we fulfil it. The Law is rehabilitated in a new role as a tutor, aid and guide for the Christian life.

Such commentators often quote Romans 13:8–10 to show how the Law applies to the Christian's life

Owe nothing to anyone except to love one another; for he who loves his neighbor has fulfilled the law. For this, 'YOU SHALL NOT COMMIT ADULTERY, YOU SHALL NOT MURDER, YOU SHALL NOT STEAL, YOU SHALL NOT COVET,' and if there is any other commandment, it is summed up in this saying, 'YOU SHALL LOVE YOUR NEIGHBOR AS YOURSELF.' Love does no wrong to a neighbor; therefore love is the fulfillment of *the* law. (NASB)

The idea that Paul is somehow rehabilitating the Law in order to give it a new role in the believer's life couldn't be more wrong. There is no place for the Law in the Christian life! We have learnt how Abraham and his descendants lived for 430 years completely ignorant of the Law. They did not know it, neither did they need it. Are we therefore saying that the true seed of Abraham in Christ need the Law to help them walk in the Spirit? Certainly not!

When Paul mentioned the Ten Commandments in Romans 13:8–10, he was not commanding us to follow them, he was explaining how unnecessary they are for the one walking in the Spirit. The Ten Commandments are superfluous for the one who walks in the Spirit and in love.

Paul is further strengthening his previous argument that the Law is fulfilled, done away with and completely redundant for the Christian. Apart from Galatians 5:14 and Romans 13:8–10, the only other place that Paul speaks about the Christian fulfilling the Law is Romans 8:4

so that the requirement of the Law might be fulfilled in us, who do not walk according to the flesh but according to the Spirit. (NASB)

All the language used in these three scriptures about the Christian fulfilling the Law is in the perfect tense, meaning something that has already been accomplished in the past but which still has an association to the present. Neither in Romans 8:4 nor Galatians 3:14–26 is the Law being recommended as a guide for Christian living. Rather, walking in the Spirit is portrayed as the viable alternative to the Law. Walking in the Spirit is totally different to walking by the Law. We should never confuse or attempt to mix the two; they are mutually incompatible. Like oil and water, they never mix.

The Christian has no need of the Law whatsoever, because even the Law's best intentions are fulfilled in the Spirit-filled life. The Law is now completely redundant. When we walk in the Spirit, we are actually fulfilling the greatest aspirations of the Law. What the Law hoped to do but couldn't, we can now do through walking in the Spirit. When we obey the law of Christ, we are living at a level of righteousness that is totally beyond that of the Law. The Mosaic Law has nothing of any value to offer us in this respect. Paul is finishing off his argument that we have totally and utterly died to it.

Ben Witherington III in his exceptional commentary, *Grace in Galatia* puts it like this

> The intent or basic aim of the Law was to produce a unified people of God, unified on the basis of love toward the one true God and toward each other. This is still the will of God for the people of God, even though they are no longer under the Mosaic Law covenant. Thus it is that Paul can speak of the basic substance of the Law being fulfilled in the community of Christ, not because the Law continued to be the rule for believers' behaviour and not by them submitting to that Law. Rather this fulfilment is what happens quite naturally when Christians follow the example and teaching of Christ. If the Galatians will continue to walk in the Spirit, pay attention to the Law of Christ, and run as they had been running, they will discover that a by-product of this effort is that the basic aim and substance of the Law has already been fulfilled in their midst. They thus need not worry about submitting to the Law, when its whole aim is already fulfilled in their midst.[1]

The Christian who is led by the Spirit will fulfil the Law accidentally, coincidentally and as a side effect. Paul is not rebuilding here what he has just dismantled in the last four chapters.

We do not need the Law because we have Christ, his words and life for our pattern of living. I love those wonderful wrist bands with W.W.J.D. embroidered on them (What Would Jesus Do?). They are so theologically profound. Paul said earlier in Galatians that he no longer lived, but Christ lived in him. And he was in intense spiritual labour that Christ would be formed in the

Galatians. Why look to the Law for guidance when we can look to Christ who fulfilled the Law and took it away?

With our lives founded on the Golden Rule and our eyes fixed on Jesus, the Holy Spirit can now guide and empower us to live victorious Christian lives.

Do unto others before they do it to you

> (15) But if you bite and tear at one another, look out lest you are consumed by one another.

Paul knew that the Galatians were quarrelling and arguing. Legalism always produces self-righteousness and arguments. The Galatians were not walking by the Golden Rule, but rather, 'Do unto others before they do it to you.'

Paul uses the imagery of vicious animals biting, tearing and devouring one another. Fear will make us manipulate and treat people around us as potential enemies. Life is not a chessboard where we anticipate each other's moves and strategize to dismantle one another's strong points piece by piece to get a checkmate. Life is trusting God and loving people. Most of the works of the flesh are simply the selfish use and abuse of other people. The Galatians were engaged in a fleshly, dog-eat-dog struggle with one another. In the end, we only have two alternatives as Christians: to trust God, releasing us to love and serve one another, or to try to make life work by biting and devouring one another.

16.

How to Be Led by the Spirit

(Gal. 5:16–18)

(16) I tell you walk by the Spirit and you will not satisfy the desire of the flesh. (17) For the flesh desires against the Spirit, and the Spirit desires against the flesh; for these are opposed to one another, to prevent you from doing those things you want to do. (18) But if you are led by the Spirit, you are not under the Law.

Having established that the law of Christ is to love your neighbour as yourself, we are now free to walk in the Spirit. Verse 18 is the key scripture of the whole epistle. If we understand what it is to be led by the Spirit, we have understood everything that Paul is trying to teach us. This is because those who are led by the Spirit are not under the Law.

(16) I tell you walk by the Spirit and you will not satisfy the desire of the flesh.

What a liberating verse! After the warning to the Galatians about devouring one another, Paul then encourages them that they can indeed have victory over the desires of the flesh.

The desire of the flesh

Unfortunately, the New International Version in all but its latest edition[1] mistranslates the word 'flesh' as 'sinful nature' in this passage (as it does in 5:13), translating the verse as

So I say, live by the Spirit, and you will not gratify the desires of the sinful nature. For the sinful nature desires what is contrary to the Spirit, and the Spirit what is contrary to the *sinful nature.* (emphasis added)

The actual Greek here is not 'sinful nature' at all, it is the simple word 'flesh' (the Greek word '*sarx*'). I have done some research into how people understand the concept of 'sinful nature' and most think that it and the 'born again nature' are locked in a lifelong battle. The struggles and failures of life suggest to them that the two combatants are pretty evenly matched.

This is such a wrong understanding of what Paul is trying to convey to us. We do not have a sinful nature any more – our 'old man' was crucified and buried with Christ (see my comments on Gal. 3:19). We do not have two closely matched opposing natures in combat with one another. The Holy Spirit is like the heavyweight boxing champion of the world taking on the flesh, which is akin to some geriatric amateur flyweight. Please don't think I am underestimating the power of the flesh – I know it is all too real in our lives – but I suspect most of us overestimate the power of the flesh because firstly we don't know how to defeat it, and secondly we are still having the same thought patterns of the old, unsaved nature that was truly enslaved by it.

The idea that a Christian has a sinful nature has contributed to a generally low expectation of how free from sin we can actually live in this life. There is an extreme view, commonly known as Christian Perfectionism, that teaches that the eradication of the sinful nature (our Adamic nature) means that we should never struggle with sin ever again. This is false, because Paul makes it clear in this chapter that there is indeed a conflict between the flesh and the Spirit in all Christians' lives.

So what is the flesh, if it is not the sinful nature? I introduced the concept of the flesh earlier on, but here we will dig a little deeper into its meaning.

The term 'flesh' can mean a number of things, depending on the context in which it is used. Firstly, 'flesh' can simply mean humanity or humankind

God looked on the earth, and behold, it was corrupt; for all flesh had corrupted their way upon the earth. (Gen. 6:12, NASB)

A voice says, 'Call out.' Then he answered, 'What shall I call out?' All flesh is grass, and all its loveliness is like the flower of the field. (Isa. 40:6, NASB)

And the Word became flesh, and dwelt among us (John 1:14, NASB)

since by the works of the Law no flesh will be justified. (Gal. 2:16, NASB)

Even in this neutral use of the word 'flesh', there is often the sense in which humanity as flesh is highlighted as weak, frail and mortal.

Secondly, it can simply refer to the physical body in the same way as we use the word in English

the life which I now live in the flesh I live by faith in the Son of God, who loved me and gave Himself up for me. (Gal. 2:20, NASB)

For our struggle is not against flesh and blood, but against the rulers, against the powers, against the world forces of this darkness, against the spiritual forces of wickedness in the heavenly places. (Eph. 6:12, NASB)

Thirdly, the term 'flesh' can refer to the unregenerate state of the unbeliever. When Paul refers to being 'in the flesh', he means when we were unconverted and enslaved to it.

For when we were in the flesh, the sinful passions which were aroused by the law were at work in our members to bear fruit to death. (Rom. 7:5, NKJV)

Fourthly, flesh is often translated as 'carnal' in the New Testament, to refer to actions and attitudes that are in direct contrast to the work of the Holy Spirit. It refers to unbelief, self-centeredness and sensual worldly pleasures. Unbelief and self-ishness generates carnality.

And I, brethren, could not speak to you as to spiritual people but as to carnal, as to babes in Christ. (1 Cor. 3:1, NKJV)

for you are still carnal. For where there are envy, strife, and divisions among you, are you not carnal and behaving like mere men? (1 Cor. 3:3, NKJV)

Fifthly, and most relevant to this passage of Galatians, the flesh can refer to the *sinful leftovers that still affect us from the old life.* The flesh is the residue of the old life, but as I have said, it is not the 'old man' or sinful nature, because we have been delivered from that.

The body of sin

In his letter to the Romans, Paul uses the body of sin to refer to the flesh. They are one and the same thing.

knowing this, that our old self was crucified with Him, in order that our body of sin might be done away with, so that we would no longer be slaves to sin. (Rom. 6:6, NASB)

Therefore do not let sin reign in your mortal body so that you obey its lusts. (Rom. 6:12, NASB)

and do not go on presenting the members of your body to sin as instruments of unrighteousness; but present yourselves to God as those alive from the dead, and your members as instruments of righteousness to God. (Rom. 6:13, NASB)

For while we were in the flesh, the sinful passions, which were aroused by the Law, were at work in the members of our body to bear fruit for death. (Rom. 7:5, NASB)

So now, no longer am I the one doing it, but sin which dwells in me. (Rom. 7:17, NASB)

but I see a different law in the members of my body, waging war against the law of my mind and making me a prisoner of the law of sin which is in my members. (Rom. 7:23, NASB)

Wretched man that I am! Who will set me free from the body of this death? (Rom. 7:24, NASB)

If Christ is in you, though the body is dead because of sin, yet the spirit is alive because of righteousness. (Rom. 8:10, NASB)

for if you are living according to the flesh, you must die; but if by the Spirit you are putting to death the deeds of the body, you will live. (Rom. 8:13, NASB)

In Romans 6:6, we see that the body of sin is actually contrasted with our 'old man' or sinful nature. The Adamic sinful nature was crucified. It is dead and buried in Christ and has absolutely no part in the Christian's life any more. It was taken away so that the body of sin may now be dealt with successfully.

Some translations of this verse incorrectly talk about the 'old man' being crucified with him in order that the body of sin might be 'destroyed'. This is misleading. A better translation would be 'that the body of sin might be rendered ineffective or put out of action'. The body of sin is something that still affects the believer even after conversion. Before we were saved, it totally dominated us, but now we are born again we have power to render it ineffective.

The 'body of sin' is a reference to our physical body. In order to understand how sin works through the flesh, we have to remember that salvation relates to the past, present and future. We have been saved, we are being saved, and we will be saved.

Once we believed in Christ we were eternally justified before God, saved for ever. Righteousness has been imputed to us by God. I am regenerated, born again, and my spirit is 100 per cent saved – I am a new creation in Christ. My born again spirit exists in the realm of grace and cannot be touched or affected by the dominion of sin at all.

We are also still *being saved*, for we can choose to walk in the Spirit and allow imparted righteousness to bring us into an experience of powerful holy living. Remember when I wrote about the difference between being in Christ (imputed righteousness) and Christ being in us (imparted righteousness)? As we walk by the Spirit, our lives are being sanctified and we can neutralize the power of the body of sin (flesh). God's plan for us is to become increasingly sanctified throughout our lives on earth.

However, in relation to our physical human body, salvation is ultimately in the future. Our bodies are not yet saved. We still suffer sickness, death and corruption. Divine healing and health are signs that Jesus is Lord over the body, and that one day our bodies will be raised incorruptible, saved and glorified. Until the day of resurrection, our bodies remain in a fallen, unsaved state. Sin tries to dominate the believer's life through the access point of our fallen bodies. But as believers we have the power to nullify the effect of sin in our lives.

We are told not to let sin reign in our mortal bodies to obey its lusts (Rom. 6:12). Sin attempts to reign through the channel of our bodies. We are told not to yield the members (parts of our physical body) as instruments of unrighteousness, but instead present them to God. Sin is still dwelling in our mortal bodies, and that is the place where it must be dealt with. Sin certainly isn't in our born again spirit, which has been totally freed from its power and influence.

The human body includes everything pertaining to the physical, including our brains, minds and emotions. Anything in our life that is not part of our spirit is part of the body of sin and needs to be renewed. Often, as Western Christians, we separate the mental from the physical, but in Paul's teaching there is no separation. We can have fleshy thinking as well as fleshly actions. That is why mental illness can exist – because the mind and intellect are part of our physical life. We should steer clear from Greek philosophical thinking which separates the mind and intellect from the realm of the body.

The body is *not* sinful

I want to make this crystal clear: *Your body is not, in and of itself, sinful or evil.* Our body is a wonderful part of who we are. It is to be cherished, looked after and respected. Jesus spent much of his time on earth ministering to people who were suffering physically, demonstrating how important our physical lives are to him. After all, our body is the very temple of the Holy Spirit. God loves our bodies so much that he is going to glorify them one day. The body is an essential part of who we are.

The problem is that in its weakened state, it is subject to the influence of sin, and the sinful residue of the past seeks to remain there. The body has yet to be redeemed. The flesh retains the inclinations of our old life. Dr Martyn Lloyd-Jones uses this analogy

> Sin remains in its influence upon the body. I myself as a being, a spiritual being, am entirely and eternally outside the realm of sin's influence; but it has pleased God in his eternal wisdom to leave sin in the body. There is a kind of parallel with this in the Old Testament. God delivered the children of Israel out of Egypt. He took them across the Red Sea, through the wilderness, across the Jordan, and gave them the Promised Land. But he left certain of the nations in that Promised Land, and his people had to struggle with them. It seems to me that we have a very wonderful parallel there between God's way of dealing with his ancient people on that level, and God's way of dealing with his people now on the spiritual level. The body is not yet delivered from the effects of sin and the Fall – but I am delivered.[2]

Jesus was the Word made flesh. He has all the aspects of a human body that we do because he is fully human. He experienced all our physical instincts, faculties, inclinations, urges and desires, and yet his body was not fallen and subject to sin like ours. All of the bodily desires and instincts of Jesus were perfectly balanced and thoroughly in order. The natural drives and powers of our body are God-given; Jesus had them. Satan could thus tempt Christ through his bodily desires, and yet he resisted. He was tempted, just as we are, but remained without sin (Heb. 4:15).

The difference between Christ and us is that we were born with fallen bodies, and our urges, desires and instincts were biased and distorted towards sin from the start. These warped bodily inclinations were dominated by sin and we had no power to resist.

What are these inclinations of our fallen, weak bodies that sin used to master us? Here are a few of them: the appetite for food, the sexual instinct, the desire to rule, the drive for success, prosperity, multiplication, the need for affirmation, the seeking for comfort, the urge towards pleasure . . . These are just a few examples. Interestingly, the works of the flesh (Gal. 5:19–21) are all rooted in sinful attempts to satisfy such instincts.

These bodily instincts are not wrong in themselves. There is nothing wrong with sexual desire in its rightful place between husband and wife. But if we look at the world today, sexual passions are totally out of control. Many people have sexual addictions or deviations that dominate their lives; many become one with their perversions. This is sin working through the weaknesses of the body – it is the flesh at work. Look at how legitimate hunger turns into gluttony and obesity. The desire for comfort turns into greed. The desire to rule becomes inflamed through anger, violence and war. People are dominated by out-of-control cravings, and they live according to the flesh. Those in the flesh are dominated by self-gratification. But the redeemed should not live this way.

Though the body may be deadened by sin, the spirit is alive. That is why we can now effectively deal with the flesh.

> If Christ is in you, though the body is dead because of sin, yet the spirit is alive because of righteousness. (Rom. 8:10, NASB)

> for if you are living according to the flesh, you must die; but if by the Spirit you are putting to death the deeds of the body, you will live. (Rom. 8:13, NASB)

Having investigated how the body of sin is another term for the flesh, we can now return to our study of Galatians with a better understanding of what this flesh is that we must deal with.

Winning the war on the inside

> (16) I tell you walk by the Spirit and you will not satisfy the desire of the flesh. (17) For the flesh desires against the Spirit, and the Spirit desires against the flesh; for these are opposed to one another, to prevent you from doing those things you want to do.

Paul explains how we can nullify the body of sin or flesh through walking by the Spirit. Having seen that the flesh has powerful passions, it is remarkable to see in verse 17 that the Spirit too has strong desires and passions. The word used for the desires of the flesh and the Spirit is *epithumia*, meaning 'earnest desire' as when someone sets their heart on something they are absolutely determined to have.

The King James Version talks about the flesh lusting against the Spirit, and the Spirit against the flesh. In the English language today, lust almost always has negative connotations, but at the time when the KJV was produced lust was a neutral word meaning a strong desire. You could just as easily lust after God and righteousness as you could lust after immorality.

We all know what it is like to feel the pull of both the flesh and the Spirit in our lives. Even non-Christians feel the pull of their conscience concerning sinful behaviour. The unbeliever's conscience is fallen, yet it retains a broken and highly imperfect sense of good and evil. As a rule, unbelievers allow their conscience to be increasingly seared by sin as they go through life. Their conscience loses feeling as they become more and more sin-hardened. Romans 7:7–25 is a picture of Paul before he was converted, struggling with his conscience. His conscience could affirm that the Law was good, but at the same time he was absolutely powerless to obey it. At that time he was an unconverted man. The passage is very interesting because it shows us the best one can hope for as an unbeliever, devoid of the Spirit, to conquer the flesh.

But Paul is not talking about being led by our conscience; he is talking about being led by the passionate desires of the Holy Spirit. Everything the flesh desires the Spirit opposes, and everything the Spirit yearns for the flesh hates. They are in utter opposition to one another. We must understand the absolute enmity between the Holy Spirit and our flesh. We have all felt the intense passions of the flesh, but we need to seek the glory and presence of the Spirit in and on our lives so that we can come under his divine passions for love, holiness, righteousness and kingdom power.

It is only the influence of the Spirit in our lives that can countermand the lust of the flesh. Self-discipline is something we should learn to practice, but ultimately even that is not the answer to neutralizing it. Only an ongoing encounter with the Holy Spirit will enable us to overcome it. To experience his glory is to begin to know the intense passions of the Holy Spirit that will leave the lusts of the flesh whimpering in darkness and defeat.

Walking by the Spirit

So many Christians are sin-focused. Often we spend more time looking at what's wrong in our lives than what's right – and this isn't healthy. 'Sin lists' abound everywhere, and we can end up living in guilt, disappointment and discouragement when we see how many sin 'boxes' we continue to tick day by day. Repentance is not some sort of act of penance, where we constantly chastise ourselves for our failures; it is a joyful, positive experience. It is simply turning yourself over to the life of the Spirit. There is a sense in which we do give attention to crucifying the flesh, as we shall see, but Paul's emphasis for living righteously is not focused on sin, but rather Christ and his Spirit.

Spirit-filled living is not discovering a new list of New Testament dos and don'ts to replace the Law, and then trying to live by them. Spirit-filled living is an immediate and ongoing personal experience with the Holy Spirit. Paul does not tell us to walk by the Word, but by the Spirit. Bear in mind that Galatians was one of the first New Testament letters to be written. The believers there were not walking around with pocket New Testaments; they didn't even have access to the four gospels. There was no Romans, no Ephesians, no Timothy, no John . . . Imagine being in that situation – a new believer without a New Testament. They really did need the continuous help of the Spirit to deal with the complexities of daily life. Certainly they had been taught the gospel by Paul, and perhaps much that would be written in later epistles, but the emphasis on living the Christian life was through the immediate leading and witness of the Holy Spirit.

Think back to Galatians 3 which gave us a picture of the Galatian church in its heyday. The key to its success was always found in the Spirit. They had heard the gospel of Christ and received the Spirit. Having begun their Christian lives this way, God supplied them with a constant flow of the Holy Spirit and with supernatural miracles. The Holy Spirit was all they needed.

The leading of the Spirit in our lives is direct, instantaneous and continuous. The Greek verb for 'walk' is in the present continuous tense. This means that we keep on walking and continue to walk by the Spirit. Now, Paul had not taught the Galatians New Testament laws, but principles, and had provided illustrations of how the Spirit works, his values and his character. The Scriptures exist as a framework or safe environment *within* which to live the Spirit-filled life; they are not a tightrope on which we precariously walk. The Word of God is there to inform, correct and reprove, but it is the Spirit who leads us – even guiding us into the truth of the Word – and we must go directly and personally to him. We need, above all things in life, to be Spirit-conscious!

For the Spirit-led believer, the Bible is a wonderful resource of illustrations and principles of godly living – but never laws. Obedience is not outward conformity to New Testament directives. Let's not reinvent legalistic living. The righteousness that exceeds the Pharisees (including Christian 'Pharisees') is the pen of the Holy Spirit constantly and continually writing his will on our hearts (2 Cor. 3:3). He is doing it right now, this instant, and if you take the time to look into your heart he will immediately begin speaking to you and leading you.

Have you ever texted someone, or tweeted on Twitter, or given an update on Facebook? In modern terms, the pen and ink of the Holy Spirit can be likened to these types of communication. The Holy Spirit texts our hearts, tweets our spirits, posts updates on the profile of our inner person throughout each day, and all we have to do is listen.

> And the Holy Spirit also testifies that this is so. For he says, 'This is the new covenant I will make with my people on that day, says the LORD: I will put my laws in their hearts, and I will write them on their minds.' Then he says, 'I will never again remember their sins and lawless deeds.' (Heb. 10:15–17, NLT)

> But this is the new covenant I will make with the people of Israel on that day, says the LORD: I will put my laws in their minds, and

I will write them on their hearts. I will be their God, and they will be my people. And they will not need to teach their neighbours, nor will they need to teach their relatives, saying, 'You should know the LORD.' For everyone, from the least to the greatest, will know me already. And I will forgive their wickedness, and I will never again remember their sins.' (Heb. 8:10–12, NLT)

Jeremiah 31:31–33 is quoted twice in Hebrews, referring not only to the imputed righteousness of a total 'sin wipeout' for the believer, but also the imparted righteousness of walking by the Spirit. The Holy Spirit inscribes his will on our hearts and minds, giving us inward knowledge of God. The Spirit is leading his people not through external commands any more, but inward fellowship.

An illustration of the Spirit-filled life

The Sermon on the Mount is a perfect illustration of the Spirit-filled life. It deals with principles and illustrations of the law of Christ. To love your neighbour as yourself is not lusting in your heart, not being angry, having the kind of attitude that would give a spare shirt to someone in need, a prayer life known only by God in the secret place, one that values reconciliation with a brother, even over worship. Anyone walking in the Spirit knows these things intuitively. They are applications of the law of Christ and the Golden Rule. But these illustrations serve to confirm, illuminate and resonate with our life in the Spirit.

No one could obey the Sermon on the Mount legalistically, otherwise we would all have to give to everyone who asked us, lend to all who required something, be 'happy slapped' until we were blue in the face, and yield to all manner of unrighteous suing. No, it is the demeanour behind these examples (not laws) that illustrate the kind of obedience to the law of Christ that the Spirit will inspire.

Look to Jesus

Of course, the greatest example of walking by the Spirit is Jesus himself. Christ walked perfectly in step with the Holy Spirit throughout his time on earth. He is our model. As you read the gospels, you see the flawless way that Christ walked in the Spirit, overcame the devil's testing, loved his Father with all his heart and his neighbour as himself. Jesus did unto others as he would have them do to him. He carried the burdens of humankind; he walked in immaculate love. Paul was praying that Christ would be formed in the lives of the Galatians. It is Christ in us that is our hope of glory (Col. 1:27).

We have the internal leading of the Spirit, but we also have the external example of Jesus to look to – and both are essential in cultivating the Spirit-filled life. Being led by the Spirit involves repeatedly asking ourselves the question, what would Jesus do?

It is important for us to meditate on the gospels because as we look to Christ as our pattern for living, his life will actually be imparted to us. Looking to Jesus is not just about learning about his powerful example and emulating it – it is far more supernatural than that. The very act of looking at and meditating on Christ actually has spiritual power to change us.

The razor blade-wielding Spirit

The Word of God may be used by the Spirit to highlight to us fleshly and carnal actions

> Therefore let us be diligent to enter that rest, so that no one will fall, through following the same example of disobedience. For the word of God is living and active and sharper than any two-edged sword, and piercing as far as the division of soul and spirit, of both joints and marrow, and able to judge the thoughts and intentions of the heart. And there is no creature hidden from His sight, but all things are open and laid bare to the eyes of Him with whom we have to do. (Heb. 4:11–13, NASB)

The Spirit uses the Word of God to lay us bare before God. How incredible! The context of this verse is a warning to believers not to harden their hearts towards the Spirit's immediate voice, his voice of 'today' (3:8,13; 4:7). The Holy Spirit can take the written Word of God and cause it to come alive with razor-blade sharpness. When the Spirit of God wields the razor blade of the *rhema* word in our hearts, it will have dramatic and life-changing consequences – but only as long as we are willing to walk daily with him.

We can't allow ourselves to hide before God any longer. We must be prepared for our inner lives, attitudes and motives to be stripped naked before God. Are you prepared to be spiritually naked before God? Exposed, laid bare?

I tell you one thing for sure: if you don't have a powerful knowledge of your imputed righteousness you will never have the confidence to bare all in the light of God's glorious Spirit. You will be too ashamed, and you will cover up with rags of excuses and self-justification, even attributing, at times, your self-protective measures as the leadings of the Spirit himself. But when you know the safety and security of being in Christ and that our Father always treats you as being as righteous as his Son, you can, in confidence and trust, open yourself for Holy Spirit examination.

If you want to walk in the Spirit you *must* be humble before God. I am not talking about the kind of self-examination that is usually unhelpful, I am talking about opening our hearts to the searchings of the Spirit and the torchlight of the Word. Regrettably, it is very possible for Christians to walk in the flesh and call it the Spirit. I like what John F. MacArthur says in his book on Galatians, *Liberated for Life*: 'By walking in the Spirit "you will not carry out the desire of the flesh." If you walk in the Spirit, you have God's power, energy and strength working in you. The Holy Spirit works through us and in us in a way that never violates ourselves, never violates others, and never violates God.'[3]

The razor blade of God's Spirit-coated Word is likened to a scalpel in the hand of a surgeon, which can divide even between joints and marrow. The Spirit uses the scalpel of the *rhema* word to divide between what is Spirit and flesh in our lives. It judges the intentions of the heart. If we want to walk by the Spirit, we have to accept that there are major blindspots in our life where we can't discern the flesh from the Spirit. Unseen planks lie in our spiritual sightlines. Do we really want the Spirit to show us our true motivations? Sometimes we need to stop reading the Word, and let the Word read us.

How does the Spirit lead us?

The Spirit leads us in many different ways. Walking by the Spirit should be the most liberating experience of our life and yet, at the same time, the most challenging. Being led by the Spirit should be the exact opposite of a legalistic and rule-based lifestyle. Freedom, liberty, joy, strength and power all lie ahead for the believer who walks the paths of the Holy Spirit.

The law of Christ is the basis for the life of walking in the Spirit. This law of Christ or Golden Rule tells us to love our neighbour as ourselves, and to do unto others as we would have them do to us. When we talk about being led by the Spirit, some people become quite introspective. They think that walking by the Spirit is all about them and their needs; that it is essentially the Lord leading them to personal success. But this is just a by-product of walking in the Spirit, it is not his central purpose. The Holy Spirit's main concern in guiding us is to deliver us from the flesh and empower us to bless others. Being led by the Spirit is really more about how we treat others than it is about our personal needs. The path of the Spirit is one of servanthood.

The majority of the works of the flesh and the fruits of the Spirit are relational in nature. The sexual sins of the flesh are abuses of others for selfish pleasure. Anger, jealousy and envy, all directed towards others, violate the law of Christ and grieve the Holy Spirit. The fruit of the Spirit, such as love, patience, kindness and gentleness, are focused on other people. Simply put, the way you treat others will demonstrate how well you are walking in the Spirit.

The Holy Spirit will lead us and speak to us in many diverse and surprising ways, but remember, because we are children of God we will often instinctively know how to walk in the Spirit in any given situation. The more we soak in the Scriptures, the more we will become attuned to the mind of Christ. I want to emphasize this spiritual 'instinct' we have for walking in the Spirit before talking about the diverse ways in which the Spirit speaks to us, because some people actually turn 'walking in the Spirit' into a new form of bondage.

Some think that being led by the Spirit is to constantly wait for a specific word from God for every situation. I have known people seek the leading of the Spirit on what clothes they should wear each day, which service they should go to and what food they should buy. I have seen people not turn up for appointments because they had a 'check in their spirit' at the last moment not to attend. These things aren't wrong in themselves, for the Holy Spirit is our best friend. I have often whispered to him about whether he has any recommendations regarding what I would like on the menu at some restaurant, and sometimes he gives me a response. But when I ask him about such relatively mundane matters, it is out of a relationship of ease and grace, not some manic, intense super-spirituality. The more driven and intense we are about hearing the Spirit, the less we will. We will end up in bondage and fear, terrified that we might miss his leading. This is not the way of the Spirit of grace.

When my son asks me a silly question, or about something he can solve himself, I often respond by saying, 'Well, what do you think?' and leave him to it. Walking by the Spirit is not like walking on a tightrope, fearing that if we miss our next step, our whole life will plunge into disaster. I have learnt that some of my greatest mistakes were eventually used by God to get me into some of the greatest spiritual places. Walking in the Spirit is stepping into an environment of love, grace, freedom and liberty.

We are sons of God, and it is our confidence in being sons that allows us to enjoy the freedom of the Spirit. The Holy Spirit will often lead us purely through our own righteous instincts. He can carry us along in life like a boat sailing down a river. He carried the men who wrote Scripture in such ways. Because they lived consciously in the presence of the Spirit, when they wrote Scripture they wrote the very Word of God, yet in a naturally-supernatural way. Paul did not fast and pray for days before writing each verse of Galatians; he wrote personally and instinctively because he was yielded to the Holy Spirit who carried him along.

> For prophecy never had its origin in the will of man, but men spoke from God as they were carried along by the Holy Spirit. (2 Pet. 1:21, NIV)

Having said all this, there are some people who talk about walking in the Spirit as if it is just a natural application of moral principles to our lives. This is not the case. To walk by the Spirit is to be guided and empowered supernaturally. The point I am making is that the supernatural is not always necessarily the sensational. Sometimes it is anointed thinking that the Spirit uses to guides us.

The Holy Spirit can communicate to us and lead us in varied and exciting ways. I think he takes pleasure in surprising us. In the Bible we see the Holy Spirit speaking and directing people through Scripture, prophecy, angels, trances, visions, creation (even using animals, such as donkeys), circumstances, unbelievers, dreams, his audible voice, riddles and songs. In fact, God can speak to us through just about anything and anyone. The key for us is to be sensitive and open, ready to discern whether God is using something around us to guide and speak to us.

The Lord has spoken directly and led me not only through the regular gifts of the Spirit, but through such means as pop music, TV and magazine adverts, movies and plays, incidents that take place around me, off-the-cuff remarks by both unwitting believers and unbelievers alike, art, nature and sport. The key is to perceive what God is in, and what he is using to direct your walk with him – it could be anything. This isn't some frenzied looking for spiritual meaning in absolutely everything (I have known some people act like that), but it is walking in an effortless environment of openness to the Spirit who will often surprise us with the amazing, creative ways in which he can lead us. It is literally walking *in* the Holy Spirit. And in all God's personal direction, none of it will ever contradict his Word. Rather, it will point us to it.

17.

Flesh or Fruit

(Gal. 5:19–24)

(19) And the works of the flesh are plain, which are unlawful sexual intercourse, impurity, debauchery, (20) idolatry, sorcery, hostile feelings and actions, strife, jealousy, displays of anger, selfish ambitions, dissensions, fractions, (21) envying, drunkenness, excessive feasting, and such things as these. I tell you in advance, as I told you before, that those who behave in such ways shall not inherit the kingdom of God. (22) But the fruit of the Spirit is love, joy, peace, patience, kindness, goodness, faith, (23) gentleness, self-control. Against such as these there is no law. (24) And those who belong to Christ Jesus have crucified the flesh with its passions and desires.

Walking by the Spirit not only empowers and directs us to love others, it also neutralizes and renders inert the flesh or body of sin. Imagine a community that lived according to the works of the flesh. Look at the examples of the flesh that Paul lists, and picture what sort of society that would be. Now spend a few moments imagining a community that only exhibited the fruit of the Spirit. Walking in the Spirit is a shared journey – one of the greatest witnesses to the world regarding the power of Christ is the church walking in the Spirit

By this all men will know that you are my disciples, if you love one another. (John 13:35, NIV)

Works or fruit

The flesh is works, but walking by the Spirit is bearing fruit. Fruitfulness has always been God's way of producing things; work has always been part of the fall. The mandate that God gave to us at the beginning was to be fruitful and multiply

> Then God blessed them and said, 'Be fruitful and multiply . . .'
> (Gen. 1:28, NLT)

This is a very significant insight into both the workings of the flesh and the ministry of the Spirit in our lives. I like what James D.G. Dunn says in his commentary on Galatians, 'The flesh *demands*, but the Spirit *produces*. Where the one list breathes an air of anxious self – assertiveness and frenetic self-indulgence, the other speaks more of concern for others, serenity, resilience, reliability. The one features human manipulation, the other divine enabling . . .'[1]

These 'lists' that Paul gave to the Galatians are not meant to be exhaustive, but rather illustrative of the characteristics of both the Spirit-filled Christian and the carnal believer. Paul wrote a similar list to illustrate the nature of love in 1 Corinthians 13:4–7

> Love is patient, love is kind and is not jealous; love does not brag and is not arrogant, does not act unbecomingly; it does not seek its own, is not provoked, does not take into account a wrong suffered, does not rejoice in unrighteousness, but rejoices with the truth; bears all things, believes all things, hopes all things, endures all things. (NASB)

These lists are meant to give us a feel and sense of the Spirit-filled lifestyle so that we can begin to live in it. It is important to underline that the fruit of the Spirit is exactly that – fruit. It is the Holy Spirit germinating the seed of God's Word, planted in our softened hearts. It is a supernatural process of organic fruit-bearing. Some have said that because the word 'spirit' is not capitalized in the original New Testament Greek that Paul here could be referring to fruit of the born again spirit of the believer, but the whole context of the passage is walking by and in the Spirit, and living life charismatically. Our 'new man' will obviously be united with the desires of the Holy Spirit, but the focus here is on God's Spirit, not ours.

We have already looked at what it means to walk by the Spirit through the principle of love. The key to bearing the fruit of the Holy Spirit is to get to know him and to spend time with him in his presence and his Word. Remember, exhibiting the fruit of the Spirit is essentially an organic process – the more we experience the Holy Spirit and his love for us, the more we will become like him. The presence of God can be experienced in so many different and delightful ways. How he manifests his presence at any given time is up to him, but we must consciously open ourselves to him.

One may ask, how do we experience the presence of the Spirit? His presence is always here in one way or another; we just need to recognize and respond to it. The presence of the Spirit constantly dwells in the believer, but we are also called to dwell *in* the Spirit. This is why we are told not only to be led by the Spirit internally, but to live *in the Spirit* (Gal. 5:16,25). Our focus should not be so much on the various fruit, but on seeking the presence and knowledge of Christ that will produce them. One of my favourite passages from Scripture describes the environment of the Spirit that produces heart transformation

> Now the Lord is the Spirit, and where the Spirit of the Lord is, there is liberty. But we all, with unveiled face, beholding as in a mirror the glory of the Lord, are being transformed into the same image from glory to glory, just as from the Lord, the Spirit. (2 Cor. 3:17,18, NASB)

The word 'beholding' can also mean reflecting. Paul, in Corinthians, has just been comparing the glory of the gospel with that of the Law. He illustrated the glory of the Law by recalling how Moses would come out of God's presence with his face shining and so reflecting the Lord that the Israelites asked him to veil it – such was the brightness of his countenance. The importance of this passage is that it shows us that it is the Holy Spirit who transforms us into the image of Christ, and he does this in an environment of freedom as we experience the glory and presence of God.

We are literally to spend time *basking* in the presence. Son-bathing, we take off the veil of unbelieving carnality and allow the Lord to work transformation through his visitations and his guidance. Transforming love is radiated into our lives through direct encounter and relationship with the Spirit of the Lord.

The works of the flesh

It may be profitable to briefly explain the works of the flesh for the purpose of clarity. The majority of the vices of the flesh are social in nature, and the first three deal specifically with sexual immorality. The next two deal with 'religious' sins; the next eight reflect breakdowns in personal relationships (which was pertinent to the Galatian situation, where they were biting and devouring one another), and the final two refer to sins of excess.

Paul writes that the works of the flesh are obvious, and this list is thus only a sample of such sins, written to speak right into the past and present lives of the Galatian church in particular. One can imagine how the list would vary, depending on the situation Paul was speaking into. We could look at our own churches and their culture and make a list specifically reflecting the works of the flesh there. In some churches, drunkenness and excessive partying would never be a problem, but judgementalism and legalism would; these are just as much works of the flesh as the former.

1. Sexual sins

The first three sins of the flesh refer to immoral sexual activity. Sexual desire in the right context is good, healthy, normal, pleasurable and godly. However, when the sexual appetite gets out of control and begins to deviate and dominate, it can take on an almost god-like status in people's lives.

i) Porneia

We get our English word porn/pornography from this Greek word. *Porneia* refers to immoral sexual relationships, and is often translated as 'sexual immorality'. To Paul, this referred to any type of sexual activity outside the marriage covenant between a man and a woman. William Barclay makes the important point that

> It is significant that it is with this sin that Paul begins. The sexual life of the Greco-Roman world in New Testament times was a lawless chaos. Paul lived in a world in which such sin was rampant, and in that world Christianity brought men an almost miraculous power to live in purity.[2]

Immorality was often a part of pagan cultish religion. For instance, in Corinth priestesses were also sacred prostitutes. Many Gentiles were coming out of an institutionalized pagan immorality, and this is partly why a strict adherence to the Law seemed so attractive to the Jews – it seemed so fresh and clean compared to the sex-charged religion that the Gentiles were immersed in.

ii) Akatharsia

This word is used widely to refer to dirt or dirtiness in a physical sense, impurities or festering pus in a medical sense, and a lack of purity in sexual morality, or ritual uncleanliness. It is used to describe the opposite of holiness in 1 Thessalonians 4:7

> For God did not call us to uncleanliness [*akatharsia*], but in holiness. (NKJV)

Paul is being extremely broad in his reference to sexual impurity, and with this word he is also indicating the effects of sexual immorality – how it stains the soul, festers in the heart and takes the place of intimate devotion to the Lord.

iii) Aselgeia

This word is best translated 'debauchery'. Aselgeia speaks of overindulgence in unashamed sexual deviation and indecency. Peter used the word to describe Sodom and Gomorrah

> and if He rescued righteous Lot, oppressed by the sensual conduct [*aselgeia*] of unprincipled men (for by what he saw and heard that

righteous man, while living among them, felt his righteous soul tormented day after day by their lawless deeds) (2 Pet. 2:7,8, NASB)

In New Testament times, sexual impurity and immorality was one of the major works of the flesh in Gentile culture. G.S. Duncan, in his book, *The Epistle of Paul to the Galatians* is often quoted by scholars when he concludes that 'In nothing did early Christianity so thoroughly revolutionise the ethical standards of the pagan world as in regard to sexual relationships.'[3]

The sexualization of the modern generation, fuelled by internet porn and the rejection of the traditional Christian family, is spiralling out of control. But just as in Paul's days, as the church rediscovers walking by the Spirit we can once again revolutionize society and provide a community that the world can flee to and find healing, forgiveness and deliverance from sexual addiction. We can offer a context that dignifies sexuality in the sanctity of marriage.

2. Religious sins

i) Eidololatria

Idolatry was not only the worshipping of false images or gods, but also a pathway to demonic oppression (1 Cor. 10:9–21). It was also an honouring of the created, rather than the Creator (Rom. 1: 19–23,25). Idolatry is replacing God with anything or anyone as an object of devotion. Such was the popularity of idols that Paul had to give specific advice on how to deal with the food that was dedicated to them. Idolatry in the West today often appears in the form of materialism or hedonism. In other parts of the world, pagan idolatry is as prolific as it was in the days of Paul.

ii) Pharmakeia

This refers to sorcery and witchcraft, including drug-induced hallucinations. The use of the occult to attempt to manipulate people and circumstances was a lucrative business in the Roman world. Occult practitioners were both sought after and feared because of the powers they were perceived to possess. The early church often clashed with sorcery in the book of Acts

Now there was a man named Simon, who formerly was practicing magic in the city and astonishing the people of Samaria, claiming to be someone great; and they all, from smallest to greatest, were giving attention to him, saying, 'This man is what is called the Great Power of God.' And they were giving him attention because he had for a long time astonished them with his magic arts. (Acts 8:9–11, NASB)

But Elymas the magician (for so his name is translated) was opposing them, seeking to turn the proconsul away from the faith. But Saul, who was also known as Paul, filled with the Holy Spirit, fixed his gaze on him, and said, 'You who are full of all deceit and fraud, you son of the devil, you enemy of all righteousness, will you not cease to make crooked the straight ways of the Lord?' (Acts 13:8–10, NASB)

And many of those who practiced magic brought their books together and began burning them in the sight of everyone; and they counted up the price of them and found it fifty thousand pieces of silver. So the word of the Lord was growing mightily and prevailing. (Acts 19:19, NASB)

3. Sins of relationship

There is no need to go through each of the works of the flesh, since they speak for themselves. As Paul says, they are 'evident'. (If you wanted to do an in-depth study on each of the works of the flesh, I recommend William Barclay's book, *Flesh and Spirit*, which is unsurpassed in this area.) All these works of the flesh speak of selfishness and the resulting abuse of fellow human beings for one's own ends. Not all of these sins of relationship are overtly evident in people's lives. The carnal mind can be an expert in disguising its true motivation and justifying its actions to the very people it seeks to abuse for self-gain. Interestingly, the church has often been extremely condemnatory regarding anyone caught in immorality, but there is no evidence that Paul considered these sins of relationship any less a work of the flesh than, say, fornication. These sins devour and destroy lives, and ruin churches.

4. Sins of excess

The final two works of the flesh listed here are *methai* and *komoi*. *Methai* is the Greek word meaning 'drunkenness'. The consumption of alcohol is not a sin, but getting drunk is. *Komoi* describes excessive partying and riotous behaviour. Lager louts, binge drinkers and party animals – I think we in the Western world today understand what Paul is talking about.

Again, this list is not meant to be viewed as a fully comprehensive one. As Paul wrote it he was personalizing it to the situation in Galatia. When he speaks about those who will not inherit the kingdom of God, he is referring to those who practice *such things*, showing that the list is open to additions.

Forfeiting the kingdom of God

> (21) . . . I tell you in advance, as I told you before, that those who behave in such ways shall not inherit the kingdom of God.

Not only do the works of the flesh bring destruction to ourselves and to others, they also prevent us inheriting the kingdom of God. Paul also makes this point forcefully in two other letters, 1 Corinthians 6 and Ephesians 5. Firstly,

> Or do you not know that the unrighteous will not inherit the kingdom of God? Do not be deceived; neither fornicators, nor idolaters, nor adulterers, nor effeminate, nor homosexuals, nor thieves, nor the covetous, nor drunkards, nor revilers, nor swindlers, will inherit the kingdom of God. Such were some of you; but you were washed, but you were sanctified, but you were justified in the name of the Lord Jesus Christ and in the Spirit of our God. All things are lawful for me, but not all things are profitable. All things are lawful for me, but I will not be mastered by anything. (1 Cor. 6:9–12, NASB)

In the above passage we can see that some of the works of the flesh mentioned in Galatians are reiterated and expanded on here. The obvious question that this passage poses for us is, what does it mean to inherit or forfeit the kingdom of God?

If the kingdom of God simply means 'heaven', then to be involved with any of these works of the flesh means that we either lose our salvation or that we were never saved in the first place. Some actually teach that if we are involved with such works of the flesh, we lose our justification. To such teachers, the list of sins in these passages become *mortal sins* – that is, sins that destroy the grace of justification in your life. According to this view, to partake of these sins is to bring the born again spirit of a believer into a state of spiritual death once more. Some think that an occasional lapse into the works of the flesh will not condemn you, but that consistent engagement in any of these sins certainly will.

If it is true that to forfeit the kingdom of God through works of the flesh causes us to lose our saving grace, then we find ourselves in a miserable condition and all the teaching we have received from the preceding chapters is in vain. These passages on losing inheritance give us only samples of the works of the flesh, not a definitive list – we know there are many more. Also, some of these works are so general and all-encompassing that it would give even the best of believers cause for eternal concern.

The sins described in the passage in Ephesians 5 we will come to in a moment speak of such things as silly talk, coarse jesting and having *any kind* of impurity. To teach that the kingdom of God here means 'heaven' would radically change the nature of Christian grace and freedom – for then the overriding motivation not to engage in the works of flesh would be grounded in the context of fear of eternal condemnation.

But we have been taught by Paul that our faith counts for righteousness. The works of the flesh are not now to become the Law revisited! If we look carefully at these passages we can see that Paul is not teaching that to forfeit the kingdom of God by the works of the flesh is to lose our salvation.

The passage taken from 1 Corinthians 6 comes out of Paul's criticism of the way in which members of the church were in such a fleshly conflict that they had to turn to the law courts to sort out their internal issues. Out of this, he warns them of the kind of Christian who will not inherit the kingdom of God, using a list of examples.

Paul here clearly distinguishes their new life from their old. In the past they were, by nature, the types of sinners on the list – but not now! They had been washed, sanctified and justified in Christ (imputed righteousness). Paul was calling the Corinthians to become in their lifestyle who they already were in Christ – to cultivate imparted righteousness. Why on earth would they wish to continually engage in these things now that they were born again? Paul warns them of losing their inheritance, yet immediately after this he confirms and assures them of their justified position in Christ. Losing one's inheritance is not losing one's justification, because we have no righteousness of our own to lose. Christ is our righteousness.

Even more amazing is the fact that after confirming that their justification had already taken place in Christ, Paul then declares such a far-reaching statement of liberty that hardly any commentators seem to have the boldness to simply admit what it actually teaches. Just as Paul proclaims that it was for freedom that Christ has set us free in Galatians, so here in Corinthians he repeats twice that *all things* are permissible for the believer.

There is no textual evidence here that Paul is actually quoting back to the Corinthians their own slogan that they used to excuse their carnality. Nor do I accept that Paul meant all things were permissible for him, but only those things that were Christlike. This view instantly tames his roar of radical freedom. Straight after this statement, Paul continues to speak about works of the flesh, especially sexual immorality with prostitutes, which was a very real issue in the city of Corinth, with its temple's sacred prostitutes. So Paul is speaking about the freedom to choose to live in sin, and yet still remain in Christ.

The context demonstrates that Paul is affirming his freedom from the Law, and that as a believer he could actually abuse that freedom by doing whatever he wanted – that's how secure salvation is. Like he taught in Galatians, one could, if they wanted, turn their freedom in Christ into an opportunity for the flesh and yet remain saved. This interpretation of the passage could give one the same knee-jerk reaction as when we considered whether Paul was teaching the Corinthians that they may continue in sin that grace may abound. Remember how Paul answered his critics (Rom. 6:2) by saying, 'May it never be! How shall we who died to sin still live in it?' (NASB) We must be mad, deluded and deceived as a Christian, Paul contended, to genuinely want to subject ourselves to the very sin that Christ came to set us free from.

Paul explains that all things may be permissible, but not all things are profitable. We know that if we sow to the flesh we will reap corruption, and Paul has just said that an abuse of liberty will forfeit us the kingdom of God. Paul comprehends that although all things are permissible, if the believer chooses carnality he will actually be brought under the bondage and power of the flesh. How many believers have abused their freedom for the flesh, and found themselves sucked into something deeply oppressive that can be extremely hard and painful to come out of? The very things that Paul says he is free to do are absolutely of no benefit to him and will actually overpower and dominate him. Surely he is speaking about the liberty to sin, and its subsequent consequences in the carnal believer's life.

> Therefore be imitators of God, as beloved children; and walk in love, just as Christ also loved you and gave Himself up for us, an offering and a sacrifice to God as a fragrant aroma. But immorality or any impurity or greed must not even be named among you, as is proper among saints; and there must be no filthiness and silly talk, or coarse jesting, which are not fitting, but rather giving of thanks. For this you know with certainty, that no immoral or impure person or covetous man, who is an idolater, has an inheritance in the kingdom of Christ and God. Let no one deceive you with empty words, for because of these things the wrath of God comes upon the sons of disobedience. Therefore do not be partakers with them; for you were formerly darkness, but now you are Light in the Lord; walk as children of Light (Eph. 5:1–8, NASB)

As in the Corinthian passage, so here in Ephesians Paul lists a number of works of the flesh that will disqualify the believer from an inheritance in the kingdom of God. He exhorts the Ephesians to imitate God as his beloved children. Again he writes that the works of the flesh are the very nature of unbelievers – the sons of disobedience. He tells them that although they were once sinners, now they are children of the light. It doesn't make sense for children of the light to partake in the sins of darkness, for it is contrary to their new nature. They are to become what they already are in Christ. He confirms their justification and position in Christ – Ephesians has much to say about this – but warns them of forfeiting their inheritance.

Inheriting the kingdom

The kingdom of God is one of the main themes of the New Testament. The kingdom of God or kingdom of heaven is really a description of God's manifest reign and activity on earth. Wherever God is seen to be active, there is his kingdom. It is also demonstrated by the obedience and love of his subjects. When Jesus launched his ministry, it was in many ways a spiritual D-Day invasion of a world cloaked in spiritual darkness. From that day, the kingdom of God has been advancing. The kingdom of God is often described as 'now, but not yet' because although we experience the kingdom of heaven now, its fullness will only come at Christ's return.

The kingdom of God is demonstrated by the work and presence of the Spirit. His anointing and blessing, miracles, spiritual gifts, supernatural interventions and the work of God in human lives – these and much more are all manifestations of the kingdom. Inheriting the kingdom is linked to our experience of such things just described. Just as the kingdom is both present and future, so is inheriting the kingdom.

Inheriting the kingdom of God in the present is all about experiencing and enjoying the presence and power of the Spirit in our lives. The works of the flesh grieve the Holy Spirit, and actually obstruct God's kingdom power in our lives. They will block our reception of our present inheritance. The active work of the Spirit and his presence in our lives can be so seriously curtailed by the flesh that we actually begin missing out on our inheritance. The works of the flesh will leave us poverty-stricken, but walking in the Spirit will allow us a present experience of the riches of God's kingdom that is our inheritance.

Paul will later tell the Galatians that if we sow to the flesh we will reap corruption, and if we sow into the Spirit we will reap everlasting life (Gal. 6:8). Everlasting life here is simply another term meaning 'inheriting the kingdom'. I often think we have such low expectations of what we can experience from God in this life. We have read how much Paul emphasizes sonship and inheritance in earlier parts of this epistle. We were saved to enjoy our inheritance in this life and the life to come.

Each one of us has a promised land that we can conquer, a spiritual inheritance flowing with milk and honey. If we rise on the wind of God's Spirit there is so much to be enjoyed, but often we just survive on bread and water. The generation of Moses found that their unbelief and works of the flesh kept them from entering their land of inheritance. God cared for them for forty years with manna, water from the rock, the cloud and fire, but there was such a better life they had been promised. They squandered their inheritance.

Do you want bread and water, or flowing milk and honey? Do you want a parched desert experience, or a land watered by the dew of heaven? Eye has not seen nor ear heard the things which God has prepared for those who love him. God has so much of his kingdom for us to enter into and experience in this life – so much kingdom blessing and so much kingdom power promised to us. All God's promises are yes and amen, but we have to inherit them by faith. The 'Moses generation' did not inherit the promise because of their unbelief, but the 'Joshua generation' did. The letters to the Hebrews and James primarily address the role of inheriting the kingdom, and contain further rich teaching on this whole topic.

Our present experience of our inheritance also actively stores up for us a future inheritance or what we can also call a reward. One of the clearest passages regarding future reward is found in 1 Corinthians 3:11–16

> For no man can lay a foundation other than the one which is laid, which is Jesus Christ. Now if any man builds on the foundation with gold, silver, precious stones, wood, hay, straw, each man's work will become evident; for the day will show it because it is to be revealed with fire, and the fire itself will test the quality of each man's work. If any man's work which he has built on it remains, he will receive a reward. If any man's work is burned up, he will suffer loss; but he himself will be saved, yet so as through fire. Do you not know that you are a temple of God and that the Spirit of God dwells in you? (NASB)

The above passage hardly needs an explanation. The picture is someone saved by grace, but living their life in the flesh. Their carnality lost them their future reward, yet they themselves are saved by grace, yet as through fire. They forfeited their future reward because they disdained their inheritance whilst on earth.

The fruit of the Spirit

If we are truly Spirit-filled, his fruit will be evident in our lives. The list of the fruit of the Spirit is the nature and character of God. We should not see this as some sort of checklist of attitudes that we should try to do better at. We are to manifest the fruit of the Holy Spirit, and this is not the fruit of human labour.

The more we live in the Spirit the more we should also open up and allow his divine nature to be diffused through our lives. If you want to see someone who exhibits the fruit of the Spirit perfectly in every way, then look to Jesus. We are not producing the fruit of the Spirit without a wonderful example and model to behold. The closer we are to Jesus, the more the Spirit can flow through us in fruit and gifts. It is really all about Jesus flowing through our lives through the river of his Spirit. We just have to keep the channels of our hearts and minds open wide to this current of eternal life.

The picture of being in the vine of Christ is very similar to the fruit-bearing analogy, and portrays the life of Jesus flowing through our lives:

> I am the true vine, and My Father is the vinedresser. Every branch in Me that does not bear fruit, He takes away; and every branch that bears fruit, He prunes it so that it may bear more fruit. You are already clean because of the word which I have spoken to you. Abide in Me, and I in you. As the branch cannot bear fruit of itself unless it abides in the vine, so neither can you unless you abide in Me. I am the vine, you are the branches; he who abides in Me and I in him, he bears much fruit, for apart from Me you can do nothing. (John 15:1–5, NASB)

There is mention in the above passage of the external pruning of the Father which takes place through such things as trials. Trials should refine our faith and deepen our relationship with God. The Father will also prune us with loving chastening where necessary. But this passage is also a powerful picture of bearing the fruit of the Spirit in our lives. The branch has no life in itself – it can't bear fruit on its own. The key to the branch bearing fruit is abiding. The Greek word used for 'abide' means 'to remain, to tarry, to continue to be present, to wait for, to dwell'. This is another way of describing being led by the Spirit and living in the Spirit.

We need to abide in the presence of Christ through a mystical union. Earlier on in this book I spoke about the doctrine of union with Christ which focused on our position in him. But this union with Christ is not just meant to be a position, it is also meant to be an experience. Christian mysticism is a much forgotten and misunderstood strand of revival history, but its resurgence in mainstream Christianity helps us understand how to abide in the Vine, which is Christ. The following is a good description of Christian mysticism: 'Mysticism, according to its historical and psychological definitions, is the direct intuition or experience of God; and a mystic is a person who has, to greater or lesser degree, such a direct experience – one whose religion and life are centred, not merely on an accepted belief or practice, but on that which he regards as first-hand personal knowledge.'[4]

We really must confront our Protestant distrust of the pursuit of experience. Abiding in the vine is not just a theological notion.

Carl McColman, in *The Big Book of Christian Mysticism*, writes

> The Protestant Reformation forever changed the landscape of Western Christianity. A culture of suspicion developed among both Catholics and Protestants against the idea of personal experience of God. In the Catholic world, obedience to the church became the standard by which faithfulness was measured; in the Protestant world, obedience to the Bible played a similar role. In other words, both sides of the Reformation conflict began to promote a behavioural rather than experiential approach to spirituality. Instead of fostering a spirituality based on encountering the presence of God, Christianity (at least in the West) became increasingly focused on behaviour markers like obedience to authority and moral rectitude as the benchmarks of a 'good' Christian life.[5]

Union with Christ the Vine is an astonishing and amazing concept, and the mystics from church history sought to experience this truth as the beginning of living a life in the Spirit.

As a drop of water seems to disappear completely in a big quantity of wine, even assuming the wine's taste and colour; just as red, molten iron becomes so much like fire it seems to lose its primary state; just as the air on a sunny day seems transformed into sunshine instead of being lit up; so it is necessary for the saints that all human feelings melt in a mysterious way and flow into the will of God.[6]

As we explore the different aspects of the fruit of the Spirit, let us always remember that they are produced out of the love that comes from knowing Jesus intimately.

Love

I have already written about love as *agape* – the God-kind of love. There are four types of love in the Greek language.

Eros

This is the word used to describe love between the sexes. It emphasizes the physical, sexual side of desire. This word can't be found in the New Testament, and it soon became strongly associated with sexual lust. Eros is self-centred and self-gratifying in and of itself. There is nothing wrong in sexual attraction, of course, but a life based on erotic love is a recipe for disaster. The fruit of the Spirit is definitely not erotic.

Storge

Storge refers to familial love. It is the love shared between parents and children, brothers and sisters, cousins etc.

Philia

This is the highest form of love in the secular Greek language. It is the best love that humans can produce by themselves. It is a tender, intimate, warm and affectionate love. It forms the basis of secular marriage and provides a framework in which eros love finds its rightful place. It can also be the love of close, same-sex friendships that carry a deep sense of kinship. But although it is the highest form of human love, it also carries with it a sense of the frailty and fragility of human love, which can all too often fade away.

Agape

The noun *agape* hardly occurs in secular Greek at all. The scholar R.C. Trench (on the study of words) said, 'Agape is a word born within the bosom of revealed religion.'[7] And William Barclay said, 'Agape is a new word to describe a new quality, a word to describe a new attitude to others, an attitude born within Christian fellowship, and impossible without the Christian dynamic.'[8]

This is the God-kind of love, and it comes from him alone. Many Christians mistake *philia* for *agape*. Some Christians are kind, friendly and caring by personality, even exhibiting such qualities before coming to faith. *Philia* at its best is a marvellous thing. Non-Christians can demonstrate incredible acts of kindness, sacrifice and *philia*-inspired love that would shame most Christians. But *philia* is the best that humans can produce. *Agape* is a different kind of love altogether. Maybe you are trying to replicate the highest form of human love and mistaking it for *agape*? Observing the present body of Christ in the Western world, the probability is that you are.

Peter thought that he loved the Lord, but we all know that he betrayed him three times. When Christ restored Peter to the ministry, the question he asked him was: what kind of love would this ministry be based on – *philia* or *agape*?

> So when they had finished breakfast, Jesus said to Simon Peter, 'Simon, son of John, do you [*agape*] me more than these?' He said to Him, 'Yes, Lord; you know that I [*phileo*] you.' He said to him, 'Tend my lambs.' He said to him again a second time, 'Simon, son of John, do you [*agape*] Me?' He said to him, 'Yes, Lord; you know that I [*phileo*] you.' He said to him, 'Shepherd my sheep.' He said to him the third time, 'Simon, son of John, do you [*phileo*] Me?' Peter was grieved because he said to him the third time, 'Do you [*phileo*] me?' And he said to Him, 'Lord, you know all things; you know that I [*phileo*] You.' Jesus said to him, 'Tend My sheep. Truly, truly, I say to you, when you were younger, you used to gird yourself and walk wherever you wished; but when you grow old, you

will stretch out your hands and someone else will gird you, and bring you where you do not wish to go.' Now this He said, signifying by what kind of death he would glorify God. And when He had spoken this, He said to him, 'Follow Me!' (John 21:15–19, NASB)

I may, perhaps, be overemphasizing the difference between the New Testament use of these two words for love, but the reality that there is a love that is the fruit of the Spirit which human beings cannot produce is absolutely clear. In the passage above, the Lord is looking and calling for the fruit of the Spirit in Peter's life. Our love for Jesus is the basis for our ministry to others, but without the Holy Spirit we can't love Jesus with the God-kind of love. I don't mean to be rude, but I think that many of us, like Peter here, love Jesus with human love – with *philia*. But he wants and calls us to be caught up in the love of the Spirit that is agape.

Peter understood that he was not moving in *agape* love for the Lord but, wonderfully, Jesus, after restoring him to the ministry, prophesied how one day Peter would indeed lay down his life for him in *agape* love.

God is *agape*, and as we soak in the love of God it will eventually permeate our being and produce attitudes, reactions, actions and words that will both surprise and delight us. We won't take any credit for this love, but it will amaze others and take us to the place of the next characteristic of the Spirit – joy.

Joy

Chara is the Greek word for joy. Some stoical preachers have called joy an attitude. In their mind, people need to 'press in' to receive a 'deep joy' – so deep, in fact, that it hardly ever surfaces! But joy is not a frame of mind. Joy is emotional.

> As with 'love', so with joy, the emotive dimension is prominent – 'joy' as the felt experience of being joyful . . . Such experiences were evidently a feature of the earliest Christian movement (e.g. Acts 8:8; 2 Corinthians 7:4, 13; 8:2; Philippians 1:4; 2:29; Philemon 7; 1 Peter 1:8). Here again the contrast with 'works of the flesh' is

noteworthy: joy by its nature is something uncontrived, often with an unexpected element in it; in this case a consequence of the believers openness and responsiveness to the leadings of the Spirit . . .'[9]

Think about earthly joys for a moment. They are different for each person – the joy of a scored goal that wins the cup final in extra time, the joy of a wedding, the joy of a child being born, the joy of listening to our favourite piece of music, the joy of a birthday surprise, the joy of something so funny that it brings tears of laughter to our eyes, the joy of bringing a soul to Christ . . .

The kingdom of God is defined as righteousness, peace and *joy* in the Holy Spirit (Rom. 14:17). Joy is part of our kingdom inheritance.

These earthly joys are nothing compared to the joy available from the Holy Spirit. The world runs after earthly joys because human beings were created for joy. But earthly joys, although often not wrong in themselves, aren't the answer. We were born to experience delight, and the Bible is full of references to bliss and exhortations to partake in the joy of the Lord.

> These things I have spoken to you, that My joy may remain in you, and that your joy may be full. (John 15:11, NKJV)

What do you think it must be like to have 'fullness of joy'? Surely it is possible to experience fullness of joy on earth, or at least experience something near to it? We cannot manufacture it, but the closer we are to Jesus the more his joy will permeate our lives.

> . . . the ransomed of the LORD will return. They will enter Zion with singing; everlasting joy will crown their heads. Gladness and joy will overtake them, and sorrow and sighing will flee away. (Isa. 35:10, NIV)

Joy is the characteristic of a Spirit-filled life. We are commanded not to get drunk: 'And do not be drunk with wine' (Eph. 5:18, NKJV). Usually the above is quoted by legalistic Christians with a full stop at the end, but actually there is a comma. Legalistic believers usually attempt to forbid others experiencing 'earthly joys', but they don't have anything to offer in its place. Paul says don't get drunk on wine for your joy, because there is a better alternative – an 'inebriation' that comes from drinking the new wine of the gospel.

> . . . but be filled with the Spirit, speaking to one another in psalms and hymns and spiritual songs, singing and making melody in your heart to the Lord. (Eph. 5:19, NKJV)

The alternative to a pub karaoke, alcohol-fuelled laughter and a drunken chorus of 'Roll Out the Barrel' is instead to be filled with the Spirit, revelling in holy glory, just like on the day of Pentecost. On that day, the disciples weren't drunk as the world supposed, they were filled with the Holy Ghost. Now, that's joy.

> God is calling us not to a mere mediocre joy. The psalmist wrote, 'I will go to the altar of God, to God my exceeding joy' (Psalm 43:4). We are permitted – even commanded – to a joy without limit. How can we have such excess of emotion, without it becoming idolatry? The answer is simple. God does not just give us joy as a gift. God himself is my exceeding joy. He is both the Minister of the Drink and the Drink itself.[10]

Joy is therapeutic and God will turn our mourning into dancing. It is true that Jesus was also a 'man of sorrows'; the Spirit-filled life does mourn over sin, sickness, pain and death – absolutely. But mourning, misery and sadness are not the fruit of the Spirit. In the Spirit-filled life there is an amazing mystery of finding joy even in suffering. It is a strange but true fact that joy and hardship often walk hand in hand.

> Blessed are you when people insult you and persecute you, and falsely say all kinds of evil against you because of Me. *Rejoice and be glad*, for your reward in heaven is great; for in the same way they persecuted the prophets who were before you. (Matt. 5:11,12, NASB, emphasis added)

Maybe the best example of this is how the martyrs through the ages have faced persecution and death and yet, at the same time, exhibited extremely high levels of joy. Many of the Christians who have the most material comforts in life can also be the most miserable in the kingdom. Some of the most joyful people I have ever met have been some of the poorest Christians in the world, facing incredible hardship. But as James said, so often it is the poor of this world who are rich in faith and heirs of the kingdom (Jas. 2:5). All they have is the Lord, yet he is more than enough to produce true joy in their lives.

Peace

Eirene, the Greek word for peace, is found in every single New Testament book. Jesus came to earth to bring peace, and he is the Prince of peace. Peace is a beautiful concept emphasized throughout the Bible. We are familiar with the Hebrew greeting meaning 'peace' – *shalom*. Peace is such an amazing aspect of the fruit of the Spirit because with the *shalom* of God in our hearts we will be able to respond and deal with the turmoil of this fallen world. The word *shalom* in the Old Testament can refer to health in our body (Ps. 38.3), fairing well in all things (Gen. 43:27,28) and to prosperity (Job 15:21). Peace is more *that* the absence of trouble, strife and sickness – it has a positive quality. As Barclay said, 'In Hebrew thought though peace is something much more positive; peace is everything which makes for man's highest good. The greeting Shalom does not simply express the negative wish that a man's life may be free from trouble; it expresses the positive hope and prayer that he may enjoy all good gifts and blessings from the hand of God.'[11]

Eirene is often used in the LXX (the ancient Greek translation of the Old Testament) and the New Testament to refer to an inner assurance, confidence, contentment and security. A life that knows that God is totally sovereign in all things, and that he can use our failures as much as our successes, is a life at peace. The Holy Spirit brings assurance into our hearts – that is one of his main roles – and that assurance brings forth both faith and peace. God does not want us to be anxious for anything, and fear is so often the enemy of faith.

> There is no fear in love. But perfect love drives out fear, because
> fear has to do with punishment. The one who fears is not made
> perfect in love. (1 John 4:18, NIV)

Eirene is not just about inner peace or being in a personal place
of prosperity, it also impacts on our relationships. We are at
peace with God through Christ. 'Blessed are the peacemakers,
for they will be called sons of God' (Matt. 5:9, NIV). We can't be
at peace on the inside if we are not walking in peace towards
those around us. Our relationships should demonstrate all the
aspects of peace that we have already explored. This doesn't
mean that our peace is determined by the response of others, but
we are being transformed by the Holy Spirit into men and
women who bring the presence of peace into the various situations of our lives.

Do you have a tendency to start arguments or to resolve them?
When it comes to forging wholesome relationships, are you part
of the answer or part of the problem? Even when it is necessary
to confront or dissent, do you do it with a spirit of peace? Our
presence should bring wholeness, assurance, affirmation and reconciliation. This is the peace of the Spirit-filled believer.

Patience

I have already mentioned the book *Flesh and Spirit* by William
Barclay, which has been out of print for a number of years. One
of his best chapters is on 'patience' and I make no apologies in
relying on much of it here for your benefit.

Makrothumia is usually translated 'patience' in most of our
Bibles, but a more literal translation would be 'long-tempered'.
We all know of short-tempered people, but how about being
known as long-tempered? Instead of having a short fuse, we have
a long fuse! *Makrothumia* is speaking about patience, but also
endurance. Here are some quotes from New Testament scholars
that Barclay uses in his book in regard to this word

> A long holding out of the mind, before it gives room to action or
> to passion. – *Trench*

The self-restraint which does not hastily retaliate a wrong. – *Abbott*

The forbearance which endures injuries and evil deeds, without being provoked to anger or revenge. – *Plummer*

The tenacity with which faith holds out. – *Moffatt*

The rise of the Roman Empire was attributed to its *makrothumia*. This 'patience' was not a simple passive 'waiting to see' type of policy; it was active and aggressive. The Romans made the decision never to make peace under defeat. Whether they lost a battle or even a campaign, they would never admit defeat in a war. This *makrothumia* is a gritty, determined resolve that refuses to throw in the towel. It is a patient endurance that holds out until the tide against us turns in our favour. *Makrothumia* is essential for us to be able to deal with the circumstances that a Spirit-filled disciple will find themselves in. The word is used by Paul as he prays that the Colossians will have endurance and patience with joy. *The Message* version of Colossians 1:11 gives the feel of the type of patience we are talking about very vividly

> Be assured that from the first day we heard of you, we haven't stopped praying for you, asking God to give you wise minds and spirits attuned to his will, and so acquire a thorough understanding of the ways in which God works. We pray that you'll live well for the Master, making him proud of you as you work hard in his orchard. As you learn more and more how God works, you will learn how to do your work. *We pray that you'll have the strength to stick it out over the long haul – not the grim strength of gritting your teeth but the glory-strength God gives. It is strength that endures the unendurable and spills over into joy, thanking the Father who makes us strong enough to take part in everything bright and beautiful that he has for us.* (Col. 1:9–11, emphasis added)

In times of trial and opposition, the Holy Spirit can bring forth a tenacity, persistence and supernatural resilience that is beyond human capabilities. In tough times, let the fruit of his patience rise to the surface of your life.

Patience and endurance are an absolute part of victorious Christian faith

> Consider it all joy, my brethren, when you encounter various trials, knowing that the testing of your faith produces endurance. And let endurance have its perfect result, so that you may be perfect and complete, lacking in nothing. (Jas. 1:1–6, NASB)

The word *makrothumia* is translated 'patience' in James 5:7–11 in a passage which illustrates the fruit of patience wonderfully:

> Therefore be patient, brethren, until the coming of the Lord. The farmer waits for the precious produce of the soil, being patient about it, until it gets the early and late rains. You too be patient; strengthen your hearts, for the coming of the Lord is near. Do not complain, brethren, against one another, so that you yourselves may not be judged; behold, the Judge is standing right at the door. As an example, brethren, of suffering and patience, take the prophets who spoke in the name of the Lord. We count those blessed who endured. You have heard of the endurance of Job and have seen the outcome of the Lord's dealings, that the Lord is full of compassion and is merciful.

Patience is also very important when it comes to the way in which we treat and love others.

> A hot-tempered man stirs up dissension, but a patient man calms a quarrel. (Prov. 15:18, NIV)

> A patient man has great understanding, but a quick-tempered man displays folly. (Prov. 14:29, NIV)

To be in a place where we never lose patience with people, where we never give up on someone – that is a great thing to be desired. And we can grow in this fruit – not by gritting our teeth and counting to ten when someone annoys us – but by learning the art of responding not to the person provoking us, but to the Spirit who leads us. When someone is doing something that is causing us to lose patience, we normally fail by reacting immediately and directly towards them and what they are doing. But instead, before we do that, we should turn to the Spirit and let his response transform ours. In order to bear the fruit of patience, we must give the Sprit room to intervene, speak and minister to us before we act.

Jesus is such a model of patience and endurance, with the abuse he took on the cross and the hatred he still experiences from the ungodly today; with the patience he shows to a church that lets him down, misrepresents him and blights his reputation. And when we look at our lives we must thank God for his patient attitude towards us. He never gives up on us, never fails us. I want to be like that towards others. I have a long way to go in the fruit of the Spirit, but I find that as it increasingly manifests, the benefits to my life and relationships are remarkable. I love this fruit so much!

William Barclay sums up *makrothumia* like this

> In some ways *makrothumia* is the greatest virtue of all. It is not clad with romance and glamour; it has not the excitement of sudden adventurous action; but it is the very virtue of God himself. God in his *makrothumia* bears with the sins, the refusals and the rebellions of men. God in his *makrothumia* refuses to abandon hope of the world which he created and which so often turns its back on its Creator. And man in his life on earth must reproduce God's undefeatable patience with people and God's undiscourageable patience with events.[12]

Kindness

Kindness is the fifth virtue of the Holy Spirit, and one of the least understood. It really is quite surprising to me how little teaching there is on the fruit of the Spirit – especially when one compares the mass of literature on the gifts of the Spirit. The fruit of the Spirit is as supernatural as the working of miracles and, in my opinion, just as astounding. When you see the fruit of the Spirit coming out of your life it will shock and stun you – you will say to yourself, 'How did I do that . . . say that . . . respond like that?' The answer is, Christ is being formed in us and we are living in the Spirit.

Chrestotes is the Greek word used by the Bible for kindness. Many have looked at this word and totally missed its power and glory. We must beware mistaking natural human behaviour as the same as the fruit of the Spirit. Some people who have a naturally kind disposition may suppose that they are exhibiting the fruit. They aren't. *Chrestotes* kindness can't be counterfeited. It is one of the most powerful characteristics of God himself.

The ancient Greek version of the Old Testament (LXX) uses the word *chrestotes* in a rich and revealing way. Interestingly, it is used not only to mean kindness, but also goodness. Most often, when we read the words 'good' or 'goodness' in the Old Testament, the Greek words used are *chrestos* and *chrestotes*.

> Give thanks to the LORD, for he is good [kind], for his steadfast love lasts forever. (Ps. 106:1, ESV)

Time and time again in the psalms we see amazement at God's goodness and kindness. We aren't really talking about God's goodness in the sense that he is morally good, upright and holy. Rather this is the unqualified and unlimited kindness of God towards his people. This is his gracious, merciful, generous kindness to us. It is goodness on legs, kindness in action. The psalmist knows that his only hope in life is the knowledge and experience of the overflowing goodness and kindness of God.

> Answer me, O LORD, out of the goodness of your love; in your great mercy turn to me. (Ps. 69:16, NIV)

> For the LORD is good and his love endures forever; his faithfulness continues through all generations. (Ps. 100:5, NIV)

> But you, O Sovereign LORD, deal well with me for your name's sake; out of the goodness of your love, deliver me. (Ps. 109:21, NIV)

> Do not remember the sins of my youth or my transgressions; according to Your lovingkindness remember me, For Your goodness' sake, O LORD. (Ps. 25:7, NIV)

God's kindness and goodness is active, it is seen, experienced and steadfast. God gives his kindness

> You give to them, they gather it up; You open Your hand, they are satisfied with good. (Ps. 104:28, NASB)

If God was not kind and overflowing in goodness, we would be left in hopelessness and anguish

> I would have despaired unless I had believed that I would see the goodness of the LORD In the land of the living. (Ps. 27:13, NASB)

We are invited to hope and trust in God, and partake of his goodness and kindness

> O taste and see that the LORD is good; How blessed is the man who takes refuge in Him! (Ps. 34:8, NASB)

It is this kindness and goodness that God looks for in those who are righteous. He expects that his kindness to humankind will also, in turn, be reflected in the way that we treat one another.

In the New Testament, the kindness of God continues to be a major theme. It is the *chrestotes* of God that is meant to lead us to repentance and change (Rom. 2:4). God's kindness towards us melts our hard hearts and causes us to desire to be like him. Peter sees the *chrestotes* of God as a major factor in turning Christians away from the works of the flesh to embrace the new life in the Spirit

> Therefore, putting aside all malice and all deceit and hypocrisy and envy and all slander, like newborn babies, long for the pure milk of the word, so that by it you may grow in respect to salvation, if you have tasted the kindness of the Lord. (1 Pet. 2:1–3, NASB)

As I have said, we can misread the word 'goodness', translated from *chrestotes*, as merely some sort of moral standard of living. But we have seen that it is far more dynamic than that – it is an exuberant outflow of kindness that floods those around us. So when we read the famous verse in Romans 3:12, we understand that without the Spirit of God no one is moving in the God-kind of goodness or kindness:

> All have turned away, they have together become worthless; there is no one who does good [*chrestotes*], not even one. (NIV)

Christ is the model of active goodness and loving kindness. His death was the greatest act of kindness that ever took place, showing the power and strength of the God-type of kindness. Interestingly, when Jesus tells us that his yoke is easy, the word he uses for 'easy' is, in fact, *chrestotes*. Think about that for a minute. His yoke is a yoke of 'kindness and goodness'. When people come into contact with us, wouldn't it be great to lavish such kindness on them? Kindness is powerful, graceful and supernatural. The man or woman who walks in the kindness and goodness of the Lord is a phenomenon to behold.

Generosity

The word often translated 'goodness' here is *agathosune* and doesn't have very much background for us to explore. It can't be understood as clearly as the others words used to express the fruit of the Spirit. Within this word is found *agathos* which means 'good, beneficial, prosperous, and upright'. *Agathosune* seems to me to be best understood in terms of generosity – it is big-heartedness. *Agathosune* is used in the LXX to represent generosity

> They captured fortified cities and fertile land; they took possession of houses filled with all kinds of good things, wells already dug, vineyards, olive groves and fruit trees in abundance. They ate to the full and were well-nourished; they revelled in your great goodness [*agathosune*]. (Neh. 9:25, NIV)

Later on in Nehemiah 9:35 the people are criticized for not appreciating God's generosity

> Even while they were in their kingdom, enjoying your great goodness [*agathosune*] to them in the spacious and fertile land

you gave them, they did not serve you or turn from their evil ways. (NIV)

Agathosune is only found in three other places than Galatians in the New Testament

> . . . encourage your hearts and strengthen you in every good deed and word. (2 Thess. 2:17, NIV)

> I myself am convinced, my brothers, that you yourselves are full of goodness, complete in knowledge and competent to instruct one another. (Rom. 15:14, NIV)

> . . . for the fruit of the light consists in all goodness, righteousness and truth. (Eph. 5:9, NIV)

Generosity of spirit is such an important part of a successful Spirit-filled lifestyle. Meanness of spirit, word and action is the opposite to the nature of God's love. This generosity of Spirit is illustrated in the sayings of Jesus, when he tells us that if anyone wants our tunic we should also give them our cloak, or if anyone compels us to go one mile with them, we should go two, and also that we should give to him who asks (Matt. 5:40,41). The generous goodness of the Father is evident throughout the New Testament

> If you then, being evil, know how to give good gifts to your children, how much more will your Father who is in heaven give what is good to those who ask Him! (Matt. 7:11, NASB)

> Every good thing given and every perfect gift is from above, coming down from the Father of lights, with whom there is no variation or shifting shadow. (Jas. 1:17, NASB)

> He who did not spare His own Son, but delivered Him over for us all, how will He not also with Him freely give us all things? (Rom. 8:31, NASB)

Generosity flows from a person who understands the generosity of God towards them. When we think of his mercy to us, it produces mercifulness in us towards others. When we think of his gracious dealings with our lives, it causes us to be gracious in our dealings with others. Freely we have received and so freely we give.

How generous a person are you in your relationships, your marriage, with your children, with your colleagues, with other believers, with people who fail you? Imagine yourself in partnership with the Spirit becoming that generous-spirited person you always wanted to be. Imagine bringing the spirit of generous good works and attitudes right into the circumstances that you face now. I guarantee that if you go to the Lord about bearing this fruit of *agathosune*, there may well be a revolution in the way you live your life that will bless many, including yourself.

Faithfulness

The word used here, *pistis*, can simply mean faith. We have already seen how the faith of Christ works in our lives, and the Holy Spirit can produce powerful overcoming faith within us. But here in the midst of the fruit of the Spirit we can also translate *pistis* as 'faithfulness'. It carries with it a high sense of both trust and trustworthiness. Paul often describes his helpers in the ministry as 'faithful' in the Lord. Timothy, Tychicus, Onesimus and Epaphras are all described using this word, highlighting their faithfulness, trustworthiness and loyalty. Reliability and dependability express themselves through faithfulness. This faithfulness is both towards God and humanity.

> Let a man regard us in this manner, as servants of Christ and stewards of the mysteries of God. In this case, moreover, it is required of stewards that one be found *trustworthy*. (1 Cor. 4:1,2, NASB, emphasis added)

The Parables of the Talents use the word when referring to good and faithful servants. The teaching that Paul gave was to be committed to 'faithful' men able to teach others (2 Tim. 2:2). Our faithfulness, both to God and people, finds its source of strength in God's unconditional and unshakeable faithfulness to us.

If we are faithless, He remains faithful, for He cannot deny Himself. (2 Tim. 2:13, NASB)

God is faithful, through whom you were called into fellowship with His Son, Jesus Christ our Lord. (1 Cor. 1:9, NASB)

Faithful is He who calls you, and He also will bring it to pass. (1 Thess. 5:24, NASB)

High levels of trust produce great fruitfulness in relationships. Christ's absolute faithfulness to us, even when we are unfaithful to him, is priceless in giving us confidence to be both faithful in our following him, but also in our commitment to others. Mother Teresa of Calcutta famously said, 'I do not pray for success, I ask for faithfulness.'

If you have ever been betrayed you will have an acute awareness of the value of faithfulness and loyalty. I remember my mentor, Colin Dye, telling me that one of the highest qualities he had learnt to value in people was loyalty. In a world of situational ethics, loyalties shift and change, depending on circumstances. Some say that the divorce rate in Christian marriages is similar to those in the world. If that is so, it indicates that the cultivation of this fruit of the Spirit is greatly needed. Loyalty always costs, but it will always be rewarded – by God, if not by human beings.

Disloyalty and unfaithfulness destroy relationships, communities and churches. But faithfulness is the cement that causes the living stones of the church to bond together in unity.

Strength and gentleness

Mention the word 'gentleness' and you may think of a person who is very placid and mild-mannered in nature. The characteristic of gentleness can often be presented as something undesirable. In this dog-eat-dog world, don't the gentle get crushed by the bold and the brash? But gentleness as a fruit of the Spirit does not reflect a 'doormat' philosophy of living – quite the contrary. The Greek word Paul uses is *prautes*, and it is a word that brings strength and gentleness together.

In the secular ancient Greek language, *prautes* was used to describe such things as ointments for a painful sore. It also described the soothing effect that some people have on others, or the kind of words someone might use to calm an angry person, or comfort someone. This soothing, calming, healing aspect of gentleness is very important.

Prautes also describes how people in authority treat kindly those who they have power over. Cyrus of Persia was described as 'gentle and forgiving of human errors' when he showed mercy to a servant who failed to carry out his command. Agesilaus of Sparta was known as cheerful in fear and gentle in success. Often those in authority (including the church) can forget the principles of servant leadership and, driven by their own sense of spiritual importance, may show little *prautes*. Gentleness in strength is one of the signs of a great leader. The question to ask ourselves in regard to this fruit is, how do we treat those we are in authority over at work, in the church, or in the family?

Prautes also speaks of a strength of character that is not easily moved to anger or a frustrated reaction. The word gives the picture of harnessed power, and has been used to describe the calm but firm way an expert disciplines and trains a feisty horse. It is a wild animal, tamed; strength brought under control.

The word 'gentleness' can also be used in the context of taking things lightly and letting go of things that might otherwise anger or offend us. A very good illustration of *prautes* is found when Plato uses the word to describe a guard dog that is brave and hostile to strangers, yet gentle and friendly to those he knows.

The men that impressed me most as a young boy were the ones who had tremendous strength and vigour, and yet at the same time exhibited a gentle, even tender attitude towards others. I think of my grandfather, Jacob, who fought in World War One and farmed the land all his life. The gentleness of this powerful and well-respected man made him all the more a hero to a young boy. I recall my football manager as a teenager, a strong, tough builder – a 'real man' – and yet tender and caring too. Gentleness and strength are partners.

Self-control

The last fruit that Paul lists here is self-control – *egkrateia* in the Greek. Titus 1:8 uses this word when explaining that elders should be sober, just, holy and self-controlled. Paul also uses this word in 1 Corinthians 7:9 when speaking of permitting marriage if a couple can't exercise self-control. In the LXX, when Joseph was overcome with emotion when he saw his brothers, he went into a private room, washed his tears away and 'restrained' his emotion before returning to them (Gen. 43:31).

The word *egkrateia* itself comes from the root verb *kratein*, which means to take hold of, to grip or to grasp. In English we have the phrase 'get a grip of yourself', and this really illustrates what Paul means when he talks about self-control. *Egkrateia* is taking hold of your life and being in the driving seat of your actions and words. Plato uses the word to mean mastering and controlling pleasures and desires. Self-restraint, self-control and self-discipline – this is what Paul is talking about here.

The opposite of self-control is losing your grip. Have you ever felt that you're losing your hold on your life? That desires and emotions are spiralling out of control, and it seems there is very little you can do about it? It is a tragedy when lives are being dominated by impulse and passion.

Self-control is not simply us trying harder to get a grip of things. Remember, this fruit is as supernatural as the gifts of the Spirit. We are talking about the self-control that flows from the Spirit himself. Neither is it simply a negative matter, where we deny ourselves inappropriate appetites and feelings. Psychologically, we are motivated to turn away from negatives only when we see the incredible benefits of the positive alternatives. Our desire to exercise self-control should not just be because it is the right thing to do, but because we desire the benefits that self-control will bring. I understand the importance of Christian counselling in these areas, and as well as counsel we should also realize that the pursuit of the Spirit-filled life is to come increasingly under the influence of the divine character and passions of the Holy Spirit. A passion for righteousness that brings self-discipline is only imparted through an intimate relationship with Jesus through the Spirit.

As we come to the end of this section on the fruit of the Spirit,
I am acutely aware that I have only scratched the surface, not
only of what it means to be led by the Spirit, but also how to bear
the fruit of God in our lives. It really does concern me that there
are hundreds of books on the gifts of the Spirit and very few on
the fruit; bearing the fruit of the Spirit is the alternative to living
by the Law, yet many of us have hardly even learnt the list that
Paul gives us, let alone studied, meditated and taught on how the
fruit of the Spirit is produced in our lives. When was the last time
there was a sermon series in your church on the fruit? And when,
and if, the subject was taught, was it merely presented as a bunch
of attitudes we should try harder to have, or pray harder to
exhibit, or was it taught in its proper supernatural and spiritual
context – that is, the supernatural environment of cultivating the
fruit through an intimate relationship with the Spirit, with our
eyes fixed on Jesus?

Cultivating the fruit of the Spirit is the only hope to fix broken
Britain. It is the basis of a new spiritual social order. It is the salt
and light the world is looking for; the city on the hill. But a new
emphasis on cultivating the fruit is needed to fix the broken
church before we can properly fix our broken society – for the
fruit of the Spirit will not only bring healing into our lives, but
also into the lives of those around us.

> By this all men will know that you are my disciples, if you love
> one another. (John 13:35, NIV)

No more Law

> (22) But the fruit of the Spirit is love, joy, peace, patience, kindness,
> goodness, faith, (23) gentleness, self-control. Against such as these
> there is no law. (24) And those who belong to Christ Jesus have
> crucified the flesh with its passions and desires. (25) If we live by
> the Spirit, let us also follow the Spirit.

Paul is answering the question, how does a Christian live without the Law? He writes that just as we can't be justified by works
of the Law, neither can we be sanctified by it. It is not until we

have come to the place where we proclaim over your lives, *No More Law!* that we can even begin to live the dynamic, Spirit-filled life that God has planned for us.

In verse 23, Paul confirms that the fruit of the Spirit is produced totally independently from the Law. There is no relationship between them whatsoever. There is no law against the fruit of the Spirit. The Law could never produce this fruit; only the Holy Spirit can. Life in the Spirit is a far higher righteousness than that of obedience to the Law. For the Christian, the Law is utterly and totally abolished, there is literally *no more law.*

Not only are we free from the Law, but we also have power over the flesh with its passions and desires. One might think that we should walk in the Spirit and ignore the flesh, but Paul speaks in terms of an executing or mortifying of the flesh. Paul uses the past aorist tense, *we have crucified* the flesh, but this doesn't mean that we no longer have any present issues with it in our Christian lives. In chapter 5, Paul is teaching the Galatians how to actually identify and oppose the works of the flesh. It was a present concern.

Using the past tense, *we have crucified the flesh*, is a bold, confident declaration. It means that we need not be intimidated by the power or pull of the flesh in our lives any longer. We are dealing with the flesh from a position of victory. The flesh and the Spirit are not two equal and opposite forces at war in our lives. The flesh has already been nailed to the cross, but the Spirit is alive and working powerfully in us. This is essential for us to grasp, because in our experience it can feel at times that the flesh is overpowering us, and we feel so weak in resisting it. But this is a deception. In reality the flesh has been crucified, and guess who did the crucifying – we did!

We have crucified the flesh with its passions and desires. What was done to Christ on the cross, we have done to the flesh. The past tense here emphasises that this is a done deal. The flesh has been crucified, and any time it seeks to come down from the cross we bang the nails in harder! The responsibility is ours – we have both the authority and power to see the crucifixion of the flesh right through to the end. We are like the Roman soldiers who used to stand guard at the foot of the cross to ensure that any criminal that *was crucified, stayed crucified* and nailed to the tree until it was all over.

With a fresh sense of brutality, we should nail the flesh whenever it rises up. Pet sins need to be murdered, enticing thoughts exterminated, and evil impulses strangled. This is the brutal picture of crucifixion that Paul uses, and we are the executioners.

Michael Eaton, in his *Walk by the Spirit* Bible notes on Galatians, has an excellent observation regarding verse 24: 'The emphasis may be on the people who "belong". In other words, those who are close to Jesus are the ones who have crucified the flesh. They've resisted unholy passions and desires and are living blamelessly before God. As a direct result of this, he draws very near to them and blesses them in a special way.'[13]

Here, this connection between the crucified life and belonging to the Lord is very powerfully put; after all, Paul told the Galatians that they had become estranged from Christ (Gal. 5:4) and the reason they had become estranged was that they were trying to be justified in the flesh through the Law. It is true that the closer we become to the Lord the more we will experience the flesh having been crucified.

Of course, as we grow in the fruit of the Spirit, the works of the flesh will concurrently be being dealt with. That is why Paul concludes his list of the fruit with the assertion that those who are in Christ have crucified the flesh and its passions. The passions of the flesh have been replaced by the passions of the Spirit. Although putting to death the flesh is important, the major focus is not dealing with the body of sin, but rather walking in the Spirit. We are to be Christ-centred, not preoccupied with the flesh.

18.

In Step with the Spirit

(Gal. 5:25 – 6:6)

(25) If we live by the Spirit, let us also follow the Spirit. (26) Let us not become conceited, provoking one another, envying one another. (6:1) Brothers, if however a person is detected in some transgression, let you who are spiritual restore that person in a spirit of gentleness, keeping an eye on yourself lest you also be tempted. (2) Bear one another's burdens and thus you shall fulfil the law of Christ. (3) For if anyone thinks he is someone important, when he is not, he deceives himself. (4) Let each evaluate his own work, and then he will have reason for boasting with reference to himself alone and not with reference to the other person. (5) For each will have to bear his own load.

Living and walking (v. 25)

Having received the Holy Spirit, our whole lives are now meant to be lived in the Spirit. We are abiding in his supernatural environment. If the Holy Spirit is to bear fruit in our lives and use us for the glory of Christ, it is reasonable for Paul to ask us to keep in step with the Spirit. Paul uses a different word for 'walk' in this verse than the word he used in verse 16. The word he uses here was originally a term used to refer to soldiers standing in rows and marching in step together. There is an element of discipline required for the Spirit-filled believer to march to the Spirit's command. This phrase is calling us to come into alignment with the will of the Spirit in our life.

I remember discussing this verse in my men's cell group, and we began to chat about different situations that we had faced that very week. In each incident the men had tried to respond to the promptings of the Spirit and to keep in step and alignment with what they thought he desired. What struck us was that in each circumstance there was a number of legitimate ways to respond, all of which would have upheld the Golden Rule and law of Christ. The responses were extremely different in their approaches and the question raised was, *which one should have been chosen?* We each gave our opinions on what we thought we would have done in each scenario.

But then it dawned on me: as valuable as our contributions were, the chief fact was this – we were not in the actual shoes of that person in that situation at that moment in time. Not only that, but due to our different personalities and experiences, we had a prejudiced view on what we ourselves thought we might have done, had we been there.

What really mattered was that the Holy Spirit had engineered each scenario for each individual to deal with at that particular time. He knew all about the person involved, and he therefore knew the perfect way to handle the situation for the best kingdom result. Each of the men in our group, therefore, was the right man in the right place at the right time to be led by the Spirit in his particular scenario – and the rest of us weren't.

So often we think about what others would do in our place, but they aren't in our place. God can speak to us through the example of others, but we have to trust God that whatever we face in life, we are the right person in the right place at the right time. It is you and me that the Spirit is leading, and as long as we do not violate the law of love, he will show us the steps to take and we will increasingly learn to keep in step with the Spirit – as long as we remain teachable and humble, that is.

The higher you rise . . .

The swiftest way to step out of line with the Spirit and mishear his directions is pride.

I prefer to take verse 25 as the beginning of the new train of thought Paul is introducing into Galatians – and not place that marker in Galatians 6:1 as some commentators do. In chapter 6, Paul is continuing to expand on the theme of keeping in step with the Spirit through humility that he has started here. Just because he addresses his readers as 'brethren' in 6:1 is not enough to establish that it is here that Paul is changing theme. If we do think of chapter 6 as a 'new' section in Paul's teaching, the material becomes disjointed and its purpose unclear. If, however, you see chapter 6 as an expansion of 5:25,26, his message makes much more sense.

> (26) Let us not become conceited, provoking one another, envying one another.

We know that Paul has already warned the Galatians not to use their freedom for the flesh and to beware of biting and devouring one another (v. 15). Here he warns against pride, provocation and envy. I think Paul is referring to spiritual elitism.

In my life I have had a great deal of experience of the inner workings of a number of major Christian traditions, each with its strengths and weaknesses. Now, as a charismatic, I would say one of the major dangers we can fall into in our particular stream of ministry is conceit, provocation and envy. It seems to me that there is an inherent danger that accompanies those who claim to be 'of the Spirit' of falling into elitism. Paul is highlighting the peril here, but he will have to deal with this problem head on with the Corinthian church in the very near future.

The Corinthian church had backslidden in the opposite way to that of the Galatians. Many of them were using their freedom as an opportunity for the flesh and that is why Paul had to re-establish the principle of love among them in 1 Corinthians 13. They lacked no spiritual gift and they vied for popularity and position, but they didn't really think too much about the fruit of the Spirit or the law of Christ. They were more concerned with the who's who in the charismatic zoo. They had turned the subjective element of walking in the Spirit into an opportunity for excusing their behaviour, with the pretence that they were hearing from the Spirit. They had lost their anchor and were drifting all over the place spiritually.

To truly wield the sword of the Spirit effectively it takes a great deal of humility before God and humanity. The more spiritual authority we carry, the more open we are to the subtleties of pride. Provocation will always follow pride. Envy is the fear of someone else eclipsing us, or the desire to eclipse another. All this is a long way from 'love your neighbour as yourself'.

Remembering the context of Galatians, Paul may also be confronting the pride and provocation that the Judaizers had brought into the church – the superiority complex of those who were circumcised over those who weren't. Paul knows that those who think they are walking by the Law successfully through their own efforts are indeed conceited. Legalistic cultures always produce the 'righteous' who lord it over the 'sinners'. Law always produces finger-pointing, accusation and self-righteous boasting – the perennial 'plank in the eye' syndrome.

Paul will now show us examples in chapter 6 of what walking humbly in the Spirit really means.

Healing the broken

The first example that Paul gives illustrating walking in the Spirit is how to respond to a fellow Christian caught in sin. This is a fascinating subject for Paul to address here. We have learnt the difference between those living in the Spirit and those operating in the flesh. How do those walking in the Spirit and manifesting the fruit of the Spirit deal with someone who falls in to sin?

There is a well-known saying that the church is the only organization that shoots its own wounded. When dealing with people who fall into sin, unfortunately most churches identify the situation as a *matter of discipline*. But when someone gets caught in sin, it is not about discipline or punishment at all – it is only about restoration. Many feel very strongly that if someone falls into sin they must be made an example of in order to reinforce codes of righteousness. In other words, the rejection of such actions by the fellowship must be demonstrated to all, and the punishment must serve as a warning to others.

At the other extreme, some churches talk about forgiveness rather than restoration. The usual line is that if God has totally forgiven, for example, a fallen minister, then who are we to continue punishing them? I recall one situation where a leader had an inappropriate friendship with a lady other than his wife. When it was found out, he went through a divorce and then married the other lady. Within a few months he was back on television with his new wife, both asking for forgiveness for their mistakes. Yet, at the same time, they were back in full-time ministry. This is confusing the issue of forgiveness with what Paul calls 'restoration'.

The word for restoration in Galatians 6:1 is *katartizo* which means 'to restore or put back in order'. The word was used in secular Greek to refer to the setting of broken bones. In Matthew 4:21 *katartizo* is used for the mending of broken nets. When someone falls into sin, and Paul is purposely vague about the nature of the sin, it hinders their ability to keep in step with the Spirit, just as a broken leg or ankle would hinder someone's natural walking ability.

Restoration is about mending and setting what is broken back into position, so that healing and full restoration can take place. In each particular situation there needs to be both a healing prognosis and a personalized restoration programme. Restoration always comes with hope, and sometimes reset broken bones can become even stronger than they were to begin with. The place of forgiveness is very much in the hands of the body of Christ, who should receive the restored Christian back into fellowship as if they had never fallen in the first place. For this to happen, the restoration has to be transparent and effective for all involved.

I hope you can see that restoration is very different than the two extremes I have just mentioned. In the first scenario, any mention of restoration is usually placated with a cursory offer of counselling, but the main focus and energy is expended on the disciplinary aspect. In the second extreme, hardly any healing happens at all and the person is thrust back into life like someone with a broken leg wearing a simple band aid, declared fit for service. Of course, sometimes the spiritual patient himself refuses to undergo restoration and limps off into life broken and unhealed.

Thinking about these issues, even in a brief, introductory way, leads us to think of the tremendous responsibility that falls upon those handling the restoration. No wonder Paul said, 'you who are spiritual'. The last thing we would want is a conceited, self-righteous legalist trying to handle our healing when we are broken. Such people would probably break even more of our spiritual bones. The spiritual people referred to are the ones best suited to bring healing into a situation. Not everything is a matter for church boards. These people could be some loving friends who help, or a cell group leader. Sometimes people don't 'break' their spiritual bones, but they sprain them or bruise them with their wrong actions. We don't need to dial 999 and have people admitted to casualty in such circumstances – they just need some loving care from the first-aid kit to get them back on track.

Notice how Paul applies one of the fruits of the Spirit that he has just listed to the issue of restoration. The restoration is to be done in a spirit and environment of *prautes* – gentleness with strength. Such situations are a real test of the humility and spirituality of those who are walking in the Spirit. This is why Paul is bringing this issue up – to apply walking in the Spirit to a concrete circumstance we are likely to encounter.

But for the grace of God . . .

The humility that Paul promotes is one that identifies with others and treats them in the way we would like to be treated if we were them. Paul tells us that the misfortunes of those caught in sin should be a cause for self-reflection rather than self-righteousness. All of us can backslide; all of us can buckle under pressure. If we remain standing, it is simply by the grace of God. Paul wants us to remember that. Verses 3 and 4 will continue this warning against self-exaltation and pride in regard to one another.

The main principle of Christ

I would like to add a little to what I have already said regarding the law of Christ. As we have already seen, the law of Christ is another way of saying 'love your neighbour as yourself' or 'carry one another's burdens' or 'do unto others as you would have them do to you'. The law of Christ is simply the principle of love. This is not a reference to a new Torah or a new set of regulations.

The word 'law' (*nomos* in the Greek) does not always refer to the law in the sense of a codified book of rules. It can also mean a principle. Some have tried to replace the Mosaic Law with a new 'Christian law' based on such things as the Sermon on the Mount, but as we have seen, the Sermon on the Mount is illustrative of the Spirit-filled life, not a new form of Christian regulations.

The law of Christ is the pattern set by Christ's example, especially his carrying of the burden of the world on the cross. Restoring someone who has been caught in sin is to carry their burden while they can't. The Son of Man came not to be served, but to serve.

Paul continues to press home the danger of being self-deluded about one's spiritual status. The Judaizers certainly felt themselves to be something very special, but instead of carrying the burdens of the Galatians, they were actually adding to them.

The Judaizers believed that circumcision and the works of the Law made a person something superior. It is striking that much teaching on spirituality today in the church still majors on an individual's personal walk with the Lord – how much Bible study they do, how much they pray, the frequency of their church attendance and the quality of their personal devotional times. These things are extremely important, but the fruit of true spirituality is always the love of other people. The Judaizers had new laws, rituals and rites for the Gentiles to give their attention to, and obedience to these would give them an appearance of religious spirituality. But the Galatians were examining their own spirituality using the wrong criteria – the Law of Moses instead of the law of Christ.

When Paul writes that the Galatians should 'examine' their own work, he is asking them to test and appraise their lives by the principle of loving others. True sanctification is measured by how we treat others and how we carry their burdens, not by religious acts or duties. This self-critique is a positive exercise, it is not an occasion for those with low self-esteem to castigate themselves for not being 'good enough' as a Christian. It is about being realistic and clear-headed in regard to how well we are walking as a disciple of Jesus Christ.

This spiritual appraisal is not even a comparison with those around us

(4) Let each evaluate his own work, and then he will have reason for boasting with reference to himself alone and not with reference to the other person.

In English, the word 'boasting' always seems to have negative connotations. But in the Greek language it can be very positive and not related to the putting down of others. Scholars often use indirect translations of this word to help us understand this. I particularly like the New Living Translation

> Pay careful attention to your own work, for then you will get the satisfaction of a job well done, and you won't need to compare yourself to anyone else.

We should enjoy walking in the Spirit and blessing other people. Each one of us has a specific load to bear in the kingdom of God, and that load is related to other people's burdens. Our burden is the responsibility to bear other's burdens. One of these burdens that Paul will now emphasize is that we take responsibility for the financial support of those who teach and lead us in the church.

19.

Reaping the Reward

(Gal. 6:6–10)

(6) But let the one who is taught the word share in all good things with the one who teaches. (7) Be not deceived: God is not mocked! For whatever a person sows, that is what he or she shall also reap. (8) For those who sow to their own flesh shall from the flesh reap corruption; but those who sow to the Spirit shall from the Spirit reap eternal life. (9) Let us not become weary in well-doing, for in due time we will reap, if we do not lose heart. (10) So then, as we have opportunity, let us work for the good of all, especially the members of the household of faith.

Many people find Galatians 6 disjointed, and see Paul jumping from one thought to another almost haphazardly. I have already stated, I believe that this particular section starts at 5:25 and finishes at 6:10 and that it does indeed display a unified theme. Why would Paul write such a skilful letter up to this point and then, in chapter 6, start jumping around in a disorderly way? In chapter 6 he continues to illustrate the practicalities of living in the Spirit.

The theme of Galatians 6:6–10 is the giving of financial provision for full-time teachers in the church. Some have thought that verse 6 has no real relationship with the four verses after it, but then why did Paul say it – was it just a moment of distraction? I do believe that we can apply the principles of sowing and reaping to the Christian life in general (*whatever* a person sows, they shall reap), for Paul is giving us examples of walking in the Spirit that can be applied elsewhere in our lives. But first and foremost

Paul is speaking about the sowing of financial provision into the Christian ministry.

It may be possible that when Paul talks about each one bearing his own load in verse 5, he means that each of us should bear our own *financial* load for the ministry, and that verse 6 follows on from that thought. The bearing of the financial burdens of others was always a theme of Paul's ministry and we know he raised offerings for the poorer believers in Jerusalem. But here he specifically refers to the support of those in the teaching ministry and thus who are leading the churches. Paul says that a teacher who sows spiritually into lives should also benefit materially from those being taught. This is a generous giving that is being referred to, because the teacher is to share in 'all good things'.

Jesus had much to say about our use of money as an indication of our spirituality, and Paul believes that the Spirit-led life will transform the way we utilize our finances

> Do not store up for yourselves treasures on earth, where moth and rust destroy, and where thieves break in and steal. But store up for yourselves treasures in heaven, where moth and rust do not destroy, and where thieves do not break in and steal. For where your treasure is, there your heart will be also. (Matt. 6:19–21, NIV)

Jesus also believed in the support of teachers

> Stay in that house, eating and drinking what they give you; for the labourer is worthy of his wages. Do not keep moving from house to house. (Luke 10:7, NIV)

We can imagine what someone walking by the Spirit according to the law of Christ would be like in regard to giving. That person would be a very open-handed and generous person, especially towards the building up of the body of Christ.

Whenever Paul speaks about 'sowing and reaping', it is in the context of financial giving. Take 1 Corinthians 9:3–14 for example

> My defence to those who examine me is this: Do we not have a right to eat and drink? Do we not have a right to take along a believing wife, even as the rest of the apostles and the brothers of

the Lord and Cephas? Or do only Barnabas and I not have a right to refrain from working? Who at any time serves as a soldier at his own expense? Who plants a vineyard and does not eat the fruit of it? Or who tends a flock and does not use the milk of the flock? I am not speaking these things according to human judgment, am I? Or does not the Law also say these things? For it is written in the Law of Moses, 'YOU SHALL NOT MUZZLE THE OX WHILE HE IS THRESHING.' God is not concerned about oxen, is He? Or is He speaking altogether for our sake? Yes, for our sake it was written, because the ploughman ought to plough in hope, and the thresher to thresh in hope of sharing the crops. If we sowed spiritual things in you, is it too much if we reap material things from you? If others share the right over you, do we not more? Nevertheless, we did not use this right, but we endure all things so that we will cause no hindrance to the gospel of Christ. Do you not know that those who perform sacred services eat the food of the temple, and those who attend regularly to the altar have their share from the altar? So also the Lord directed those who proclaim the gospel to get their living from the gospel. (NASB)

The above passage speaks for itself – spiritual things are sown through ministry and material things ought to be reaped in return. Paul did not always insist on his own right to be supported in full-time ministry and at times provided for himself, especially when he felt the believers were too immature to receive this teaching.

In 2 Corinthians 9:5–15 we also see sowing and reaping used in terms of financial giving

So I thought it necessary to urge the brethren that they would go on ahead to you and arrange beforehand your previously promised bountiful gift, so that the same would be ready as a bountiful gift and not affected by covetousness. Now this I say, he who sows sparingly will also reap sparingly, and he who sows bountifully will also reap bountifully. Each one must do just as he has purposed in his heart, not grudgingly or under compulsion, for God loves a cheerful giver. And God is able to make all grace abound to you, so that always having all sufficiency in everything, you may have an abundance for every good deed; as it is written, 'HE

SCATTERED ABROAD, HE GAVE TO THE POOR, HIS RIGHT-
EOUSNESS ENDURES FOREVER.' Now He who supplies seed to
the sower and bread for food will supply and multiply your seed
for sowing and increase the harvest of your righteousness; you
will be enriched in everything for all liberality, which through us
is producing thanksgiving to God. For the ministry of this service
is not only fully supplying the needs of the saints, but is also overflowing through many thanksgivings to God. Because of the proof
given by this ministry, they will glorify God for your obedience to
your confession of the gospel of Christ and for the liberality of
your contribution to them and to all, while they also, by prayer on
your behalf, yearn for you because of the surpassing grace of God
in you. Thanks be to God for His indescribable gift! (NASB)

It would be very strange indeed, especially having looked at the
two passages above, for Paul to speak about financial support for
teachers in Galatians 5:6 and then completely change the subject
when writing about sowing and reaping in verses 7 and 8. Paul
warns the Galatians not to be deceived for God is not mocked.
The word for 'mocked' in the Greek language means literally
turning up one's nose in contempt. This is a warning about treating God and his kingdom with disdain.

One of the greatest ways we mock God is by not esteeming
that which he values. We usually spend our money on what we
value. Good intentions and fine-sounding words are cheap, but
representing what we value by financial giving is one of the most
powerful demonstrations of our earnestness we can make. Paul is
using the illustration of giving as an example of walking in the
Spirit. When Jesus saw the widow give her tiny mite, it told him
all he needed to know about what that lady valued and honoured
most in her life. When the woman poured perfume over Jesus
and was criticized for not selling it to help the poor, Jesus praised
her for expressing how greatly she valued him in such a costly
way.

In Paul's mind, the sowing to the flesh and the sowing to the
Spirit is primarily about giving to Christian ministry. Sowing to
the flesh is selfishly spending and using wealth on one's own
fleshly pleasures. The drunkenness, revelries and sexual impurities (such as prostitution) in Paul's list of the works of the flesh all

needed to be financed. Hedonism has its price! Greed and materialism are all works of the flesh.

If, for example, you spend all your money on alcohol, it is obvious the type of corruption you will end up reaping in your health, career and family. If you spend your money on prostitution (and this was a huge problem among the Gentiles of the time), you are probably going to reap some sexually transmitted disease that will corrupt your body. Where you choose to sow your finances will produce a corresponding harvest in your life.

Sowing your finances into the propagation of the gospel is sowing to the Spirit. When Paul speaks about this sowing elsewhere, he explains that this type of giving will sooner or later produce a harvest of blessing back to the giver. The phrase 'everlasting life' does not, in this instance, mean justification. Sowing to the Spirit does not reap justification – that would make a nonsense of everything we have learnt so far in Galatians. R.T. Kendall comments on this verse in his book *Once Saved, Always Saved*

> What Paul calls inheriting the kingdom of God he also calls 'life everlasting' (Galatians 6:8). Is Paul contradicting John 3:16? Of course not. But as Jesus described eternal life as knowing the true God and his Son (John 17:3), so Paul could warn Timothy to 'lay hold on eternal life' (1 Timothy 6:12) . . . One is not justified or saved by 'not being weary in well doing' (Galatians 6:9). But the reaping 'if we faint not', is surely what Jesus called being given the 'kingdom' by the Father's 'good pleasure' (Luke 12:31).[1]

It makes sense that Paul, when he uses the phrase 'everlasting life', is referring to the inheriting of the kingdom God mentioned back in 5:21. The example of walking by the Spirit in our giving is part of inheriting the kingdom of God. But this is equally true in every other aspect of walking in the Spirit. That is why we can take this verse on sowing and reaping and use it to refer to every aspect of discipleship.

It is interesting that Paul has spoken on bearing the fruit of the Spirit, and now he speaks about sowing seed to the Spirit. Only by sowing seed can you eventually bear fruit. Right at the heart of creation God placed the principle of sowing and reaping, seedtime and harvest. Multiplication and fruitfulness all come out of the sowing of seed. Whether it is an apple seed sown for an apple tree or a sperm seed sown to produce offspring – all fruit begins with sowing a seed.

Everything we do is either sowing to the Spirit or to the flesh, and it is important to use this teaching to apply to the whole of Christian living. However, it is still amazing to me that Paul decides to use one of the most down to earth and practical examples one could find to illustrate walking in the Spirit – our giving.

Verse 9 continues this theme and encourages the believer not to grow weary in working hard and giving of their substance, because in due time they will be rewarded. This encouragement to not weary in supplying the needs of the ministry is very similar to what Paul said in 2 Thessalonians 3:7–13

> For you yourselves know how you ought to follow our example, because we did not act in an undisciplined manner among you, nor did we eat anyone's bread without paying for it, but with labour and hardship we kept working night and day so that we would not be a burden to any of you; not because we do not have the right to this, but in order to offer ourselves as a model for you, so that you would follow our example. For even when we were with you, we used to give you this order: if anyone is not willing to work, then he is not to eat, either. For we hear that some among you are leading an undisciplined life, doing no work at all, but acting like busybodies. Now such persons we command and exhort in the Lord Jesus Christ to work in quiet fashion and eat their own bread. *But as for you, brethren, do not grow weary of doing good.* (emphasis added)

Doing good is connected to earning and giving. This parallel further supports my position that Paul is indeed speaking about financial giving in Galatians 6:6–10.

Verse 10 concludes this section with an encouragement to do good to all, especially those who are of the household of faith. This verse brings us to the end of Paul's arguments to the Galatians regarding the defence of the gospel. Paul has explained how we live without the Law and by the Spirit, and he has given practical examples of what this means in different areas of life.

We are to restore the fallen, bear each other's burdens, financially support the ministry and do good to all, especially in the church. We must be humble, not boastful or puffed up, and realistically appraise our own spirituality.

20.

Conclusion: Glory Only in the Cross

(Gal. 6:11–18)

(11) See with what large letters I have written to you in my own hand. (12) It is those that want to make a fair showing in the flesh, they are trying to compel you to be circumcised, but only to avoid being persecuted for the cross of Christ. (13) For even those who have themselves circumcised do not themselves keep the law, but want you to be circumcised in order that they might boast in your flesh. (14) But as for me, God forbid that I should boast except in the cross of our Lord Jesus Christ, through whom the world has been crucified to me and I to the world. (15) For neither circumcision counts for anything, nor uncircumcision, but a new creation. (16) And as many as will follow this rule, peace be on them and mercy, as also on the Israel of God. (17) From now on let no one cause me trouble. For I bear the marks of Jesus on my body. (18) The grace of our Lord Jesus Christ be with your spirit, my brothers. Amen.

In the concluding paragraph of the epistle to the Galatians, Paul highlights how he is writing to them in such large letters and by his own hand. People have wondered why Paul would do this. Some think that Paul had a physical eye problem and that the large letters were due to this infirmity. This is quite a popular view, but really doesn't have any strong evidence to back it up. It was common for writers to have an *amanuensis* (a highly skilled secretary) to take down dictation for such things as letters.

The *amanuensis* would write down the words of the author, but often the author himself would complete the letter in his own handwriting. This is similar to signing a letter today. The author's own handwriting would authenticate the letter and personalize it. The change in handwriting would also offer the author a device with which he could emphasize anything with his own hand. We see Paul 'signing off' in other letters

> The greeting is in my own hand – Paul. If anyone does not love the Lord, he is to be accursed. Maranatha. The grace of the Lord Jesus be with you. (1 Cor. 16:21–23, NASB)

> I, Paul, write this greeting with my own hand, and this is a distinguishing mark in every letter; this is the way I write. (2 Thess. 3:17, NASB)

> I, Paul, write this greeting with my own hand. Remember my imprisonment. Grace be with you. (Col. 4:18, NASB)

It seems that Paul wanted to emphasize to the Galatians that this really was an authentic communication from him. He writes in big letters to highlight this. In the ancient world, big letters were the capitalization of modern times. We use uppercase letters when we want to make a section of text more prominent. By writing this concluding paragraph with his own hand, Paul was automatically increasing the impact these last words would have on the Galatian readers. It is as if he has taken a highlighter pen and coloured over the last seven verses.

So although this is the concluding paragraph, we should take it very seriously because it shows us the last things that Paul wanted to call attention to and leave in the minds of the Galatians.

Circumcision symbolized the whole issue that was at stake, and this is the subject that Paul ends with. We know that for Paul, circumcision is shorthand for the whole Law and everything it stands for. The Judaizers put their trust in the outward act of circumcision and we have seen the importance of this act to the Jews earlier on in Paul's letter. This was a show of Jewish identity. Paul exposes the motivation behind the Judaizers' actions, and accuses them of cowardice. He believes they are capitulating to the threat of persecution from Jewish zealots. We know that the letter to the Hebrews warned persecuted Jewish Christians not to succumb to the pressure of persecution, and return to life under the Law.

But there is a deeper issue here, other than simply preaching circumcision as a covenant necessity to placate their compatriots – a charge the Judaizers would have no doubt refuted. The persecution and suffering that the Judaizers are avoiding is that which is associated with the very cross of Christ. In concluding his letter, Paul goes right to the central issue of the gospel – the cross of Christ. Faith in the death of Christ on the cross has replaced circumcision (and thus the Law) as the ground of covenant inclusion. Ben Witherington III, in his book *Grace in Galatia*, puts it like this: 'It must be stressed that the most fundamental thing that Paul wants his audience to understand and embrace is not the experience of the Spirit, or even justification, but rather the cross. Justification is only possible, and the Spirit can only be experienced, because of the prior reality of the cross.'[1]

The cross alone is our plea before God – it was the sacrifice for the sins of the whole world. To preach circumcision is to directly assault the power of the cross of Christ. Any stance which teaches that faith in the cross is not the sole right of entry into God's covenant people is another gospel. Faith in the cross gets you saved and it alone keeps you saved. It is the only thing Paul believes is worth being persecuted for.

The cross was and is a huge offence to the Jews, because Paul preached that circumcision and the Law of Moses have been replaced by a bloodied and bruised naked man hanging on a tree! We must never forget the reaction of repulsion and disgust that crucifixion caused across the ancient world. Cursed is the man who hangs on a tree as we have already read in Paul's letter. Whilst the Judaizers wanted to make a good, outward, religious showing, Paul had been beaten to within an inch of his life in the past for proclaiming Christ crucified.

In verse 13 Paul further attacks the Judaizers. He asserts the hypocrisy of those circumcised because even though they preach the Law they can't keep it. The Law no longer had sacrifices to cover sins. Christ crucified had become the Passover Lamb and none of the sacrifices of the Law were of any use at all. In order to be justified by the Law one had to walk according to it in every

single way and there was no second chance – no blood of bulls or
goats could cover even the smallest sin any longer (Heb. 10:4). All
the sins that had been covered by the Levitical sacrificial system
before Christ came had now been uncovered and placed upon
him on the cross. It was now impossible for anyone to keep the
Law. These Judaizers were in fact judged guilty by being circumcised. Circumcision put them under the very Law that condemned them for not being able to obey it.

The Galatians were nothing but a 'scalp' for the Judaizers
– they wanted to boast about converting Gentiles into Jews. This
boasting was that circumcision separated the Jew from the
Gentile sinner, that circumcision was the difference between
being in the covenant community of God and being left out of it.
The boast was in the flesh. We know that the flesh represents
everything that is opposed to faith and the Holy Spirit. By contrast, Paul refuses to boast in anything except the cross. Both were
boasting about what they believed justified them. It was a head-
to-head confrontation between circumcision and the cross. This is
what the letter of Galatians is all about.

The power of the cross of Christ crucified Paul to the world
and the world to Paul. Right at the start of this epistle Paul said
that Christ gave himself for our sins that he might deliver us
from this present evil age (1:4). The cross has taken us out of the
realm of sin and into the realm of grace. The *stoicheia* (4:3),
including the Law, no longer rule over us. We are now inheritors
of the kingdom of God. In this realm of God's kingdom, being
circumcised or not being circumcised is totally meaningless.
What really matters is being a new creation, being regenerated
by the Spirit. The gospel transforms your nature as well as placing you in a new world that works by the totally new principles
of the Spirit and the Word.

Paul is closing the letter by boasting in the cross and its
power. He ends by blessing those who walk according to this
principle. The phrase 'Israel of God' most probably refers to all
believers, both Jew and Gentile, circumcised and uncircumcised
– those who through faith in Christ have become the true
descendants of Abraham. They are the Israel of God, the community that God has been working towards creating since the
beginning of time.

Lastly, Paul gives a warning that no one troubles him because he bears in his body the marks of the Lord Jesus. Paul is referring here to the scars that he carried on his body from being persecuted. He has proven his mettle for the truth of the gospel through his beatings. The Galatians would be left with a picture of the battered Paul who first visited them – a powerful reminder of the price he paid to bring them the gospel in the first place.

Finally, Paul blesses the Galatians with the greatest blessing he could possibly hope for them to enjoy. Indeed, it was for them to have this blessing that he had written to them in the first place, that the grace of the Lord Jesus Christ would be with their spirits.

And may it also be with yours.

BIBLIOGRAPHY

I have chosen to limit the bibliography to a few books that I found especially helpful.

Barclay, William, *Flesh and Spirit: An Examination of Galatians 5:19–23* (Norwich: SCM Press, 1962).

Barrett, C.K., *Freedom and Obligation: A Study of the Epistle to the Galatians* (London: SPCK Publishing, 1985).

Bruce, F.F., *The Epistle to the Galatians* (The New International Greek Testament Commentary) (Grand Rapids, MI: William B. Eerdmans Publishing Company, 1996).

Dunn, James D.G., *The Epistle to the Galatians* (Black's New Testament Commentaries) (London: Continuum International Publishing Group, 1993).

Fung, Ronald Y.K., *The Epistle to the Galatians* (New International Commentary on the New Testament) (Grand Rapids, MI: William B. Eerdmans Publishing Company, 1995).

Jervis, L. Ann, *Galatians* (New International Biblical Commentary) (Milton Keynes, UK: Paternoster Press, 2000).

Luther, Martin, *Commentary on Galatians* (Kregel Classic Reprint Library) (Grand Rapids, MI: Kregel Publications, 2006).

Longenecker, Richard N., *Galatians* (Word Biblical Commentary No. 41) (Nashville, TN: Thomas Nelson, 2010).

MacArthur, John, *Liberated for Life: A Bible Commentary for Laymen – Galatians* (Ventura, CA: Regal Books, 1984).

Stott, John R.W., *The Message of Galatians* (Bible Speaks Today) (Nottingham: InterVarsity Press, 1988).

Witherington III, Ben, *Grace in Galatia: A Commentary on Paul's Letter to the Galatians* (Grand Rapids, MI: William B. Eerdmans Publishing Company, 1998).

Endnotes

Introduction

[1] F.F. Bruce, *The Epistle to the Galatians* (The New International Greek Testament Commentary) (Grand Rapids, MI: William B. Eerdmans Publishing Company, 1996).

1. The Supernatural Gospel

[1] Martin Luther, *Commentary on Galatians* (Kregel Classic Reprint Library) (Grand Rapids, MI: Kregel Publications, 2006).

[2] James D.G. Dunn, *The Epistle to the Galatians* (Black's New Testament Commentaries) (London: Continuum International Publishing Group, 1993).

[3] Dr Martyn Lloyd-Jones, *Romans: The New Man: An Exposition of Chapter 6* (Edinburgh: The Banner of Truth Trust, 1972).

2. Shocked to Cursing

[1] John R.W Stott, *The Message of Galatians* (Bible Speaks Today) (Nottingham: InterVarsity Press, 1988).

3. Paul's Testimony

[1] John Calvin, *Calvin's New Testament Commentaries: The Epistles of Paul the Apostle to the Galatians, Ephesians, Philippians and Colossians*

(Grand Rapids, MI: William B. Eerdmans Publishing Company, 1996).

6. Trusting in the Faith of Christ

[1] Dr Martyn Lloyd-Jones, *Romans: The New Man*.

7. Receiving the Spirit with Power

[1] James D.G. Dunn, *Baptism in the Holy Spirit* (Louisville, KY: Westminster John Knox Press, 1977).
[2] William Barclay, *Flesh and Spirit: An Examination of Galatians 5:19–23* (Norwich: SCM Press, 1962).

10. The Purpose of the Law

[1] F.F. Bruce, *The Epistle to the Galatians*.

15. Love Your Neighbour

[1] Ben Witherington III, *Grace in Galatia: A Commentary on Paul's Letter to the Galatians* (Grand Rapids, MI: William B. Eerdmans Publishing Company, 1998).

16. How to Be Led by the Spirit

[1] In its footnote explaining verse 13 the 2011 edition of the NIV still perpetuates the understanding that the flesh is the sinful nature or sinful state of human beings: 'In contexts like this, the Greek word for flesh (*sarx*) refers to the sinful state of human beings, often presented as a power in opposition to the spirit; also in verses 16, 17, 19 and 24: and in 6:8.
[2] Dr Martyn Lloyd-Jones, *Romans: The New Man*.
[3] John MacArthur, Jr., *Liberated for Life: A Bible Commentary for Laymen – Galatians* (Ventura: Regal Books, 1984).

17. Flesh or Fruit

1 James D.G. Dunn, *The Epistle to the Galatians*.
2 William Barclay, *Flesh and Spirit*.
3 G.S. Duncan, *The Epistle of Paul to the Galatians* (London: Hodder & Stoughton, 1948).
4 Evelyn Underhill, *The Mystics of the Church* (Cambridge: James Clarke & Co Ltd., 1975).
5 Carl McColman, *The Big Book of Christian Mysticism* (Newburyport, MA: Hampton Roads Publishing Company, 2010).
6 Bernard of Clairvaux, *Treatises V.2* (Collegeville, MN: Cistercian Publications Inc., 1981).
7 Source unfound.
8 William Barclay, *Flesh and Spirit*.
9 James D.G. Dunn, *The Epistle to the Galatians*.
10 John Crowder, *The Ecstasy of Loving God* (Shippensburg, PA: Destiny Image, 2008).
11 William Barclay, *Flesh and Spirit*.
12 William Barclay, *Flesh and Spirit*.
13 Michael Eaton, *Walk by the Spirit* (Milton Keynes: Paternoster Press, 1993).

19. Reaping the Reward

1 Dr R.T. Kendall, *Once Saved, Always Saved* (Milton Keynes: Authentic Media, 2005).

20. Conclusion: Glory Only in the Cross

1 Ben Witherington III, *Grace in Galatia*.

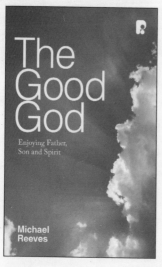

The Good God

Enjoying Father, Son and Spirit

Michael Reeves

In this lively and refreshing book, Michael Reeves unfurls the profound beauty of the Trinity, and shows how the triune God of the Bible brightens everything in a way that is happily life-changing. Prepare to enjoy the Father, Son and Spirit!

'At the heart of the universe is the passionate love between the members of the Trinity. Mike Reeves not only helps us grapple with a difficult doctrine but draws us to the magnetically attractive centre of all things. His light touch and theological wisdom combine to provide a truly helpful book which both clears your mind and warms your heart' – **Terry Virgo, Newfrontiers, UK**

'*The Good God* is a wonderful read. Reading it feels like you're eating candy floss – sweet, fun, easy. But in fact you're getting a nourishing, nutritious meal of real substance. This book will enlarge your view of God and increase love for God. You'll be blown away by the lavish love between the Father, Son and the Spirit that overflows to the world. If you want to enjoy God more then read this book – **Tim Chester, Crowded House, Sheffield, UK**

Michael Reeves is the Head of Theology for UCCF

978-1-84227-744-7

Sharing God's Passion

Prophetic Spirituality

Paul Hedley Jones

This book seeks to illuminate the critical role the prophets played in God's overarching purposes for his creation, and how we in the 21st century may also learn to collaborate with God. *Sharing God's Passion* provides a comprehensive overview of the various dimensions of a prophetic spirituality through a series of fifteen studies, each based on events in the life of the prophets, starting with Moses through to John of Patmos, including two chapters on Jesus, himself. The studies offer in-depth analyses of biblical texts, suggestions for life application, and questions for personal reflection or group discussion.

> 'Paul Jones has written a persuasive walk through the prophets. His interpretations are reliable, with an eye on the contemporaneity of these old texts. An interesting feature that commends the book is Jones's continuation of the prophetic trajectory into the New Testament' – **Walter Brueggemann, Columbia Theological Seminary**

Paul Hedley Jones is a doctoral student, working under Professor R.W.L. Moberley, at Durham University, UK.

978-1-84227-745-4

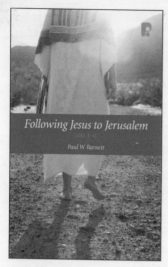

Following Jesus to Jerusalem

Luke 9–19

Paul Barnett

Taking the metaphor of life as a journey, Paul Barnett follows the journey of Jesus to Jerusalem and suggests that we journey with him. Barnett stresses the important place of kingdom in this and the ethics of Christian living which naturally follow from being in the presence of a humble saviour. More than a commentary, then, this important book challenges the way we live in the light of Jesus' last days and self-sacrifice. Paul Barnett expounds Luke, chapters 9–19, with the intention of provoking faith and faithfulness in the lives of Jesus' followers today.

Paul Barnett is the former Bishop of North Sydney and lec-turer in New Testament, Moore College, Sydney, Australia

978-1-84227-767-6

Light on Prophecy

Retrieving Word and Prophecy in Today's Church

Jennifer Campbell

The author correlates the vision and thinking of two powerful prophetic leaders: Hildegard of Bingen, a twelfth-century enclosed nun/mystic, and Dietrich Bonhoeffer, the twentieth-century German pastor/theologian executed by the Nazis. With a view to recovering a balanced and rounded theology of prophecy for the church today, she discusses the closely rel-ated workings of both the Word of God (viewed as Christ and the Scriptures) and the Holy Spirit in the works and lives of these famous Christians.

'Rarely do we encounter maturity, depth and wisdom when the subject at hand is the prophetic gift. Jenny Campbell's book is the exception. With rare insight she offers us a workable and thorough theology of Prophecy' – **Mike Breen, 3DM Global Leader.**

Jennifer Campbell is a lecturer in Christian Doctrine at Westminster Theological Centre, Cheltenham, UK. She is also the leader of Eaglesinflight.

978-1-84227-768-3

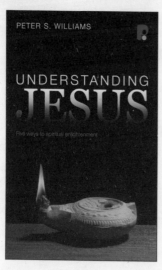

Understanding Jesus

Five Ways to Spiritual Enlightenment

Peter Williams

Peter Williams examines the Gospel accounts of Jesus' life from an apologetic perspective clearing the ground from pre-conceived ideas and prejudices and opening up five ways to consider the claims of Jesus' life and ministry. Williams encourages readers to take Jesus seriously and gives serious reasons why we should. Understanding Jesus helps readers to make their own informed response to the historical Jesus.

'Aquinas offered five ways to God; Peter Williams gives five powerful reasons for thinking that God revealed Himself in Jesus Christ. While the new atheists recycle nineteenth century doubts about the historicity and divinity of Jesus, Williams appeals to the most recent work of qualified scholars, including secularists and Jewish scholars as well as Christian authorities. He shows the evidence is stronger than ever for the New Testament account of Jesus' life and works, and that Jesus continues to transform lives today – **Angus J. L. Menuge Ph.D., Professor of Philosophy, Concordia University Wisconsin, USA.**

Peter S. Williams is a Christian philosopher and apologist. He is an Assistant Professor in Communication & Worldviews, Gimlekollen School of Journalism and Communication, Kristiansand, Norway.

978-1-84227-739-3

Primitive Piety

A Journey from Suburban Mediocrity to Passionate Christianity

Ian Stackhouse

In *Primitive Piety* Ian Stackhouse takes us on a journey away from the safety and pleasantries of suburban piety and into a faith that is able to embrace the messiness as well as the paradoxes of the Christian faith.

In a culture in which there is every danger that we all look the same and speak the same, Stackhouse argues for a more gritty kind of faith – one that celebrates the oddity of the gospel, the eccentricity of the saints, and the utter uniqueness of each and every church.

Ian Stackhouse is the Pastoral Leader of Millmead, Guildford Baptist Church.

978-18-4227-786-7

Paternoster:
thinking faith

We trust you enjoyed reading this book from Paternoster. If you want to be informed of any new titles from this author and other releases you can sign up to the Paternoster newsletter by contacting us:

Contact us
By Post: Paternoster
52 Presley Way
Crownhill
Milton Keynes
MK8 0ES

E-mail:paternoster@authenticmedia.co.uk

Follow us: